No.9

HOPES DIM FOR 78 TRAPPED MEN

The Long Mine Vigil in Silhouette

The West Virginian

...cue Workers Wait...Trying to Ease Their Minds

SUPPORT STATE WORKMAN'S COMPENSATION BILL

No.9

THE 1968 FARMINGTON MINE DISASTER

BONNIE E. STEWART

MORGANTOWN 2011

West Virginia University Press, Morgantown 26506

Copyright 2011 by West Virginia University Press

All rights reserved

First edition published 2011 by West Virginia University Press

Printed in the United States of America

19 18 17 16 15 14 13 12 11   9 8 7 6 5 4 3 2 1

Cloth: 978-1-933202-78-5

Paper: 978-1-933202-77-8

E-book: 978-1-935978-22-0

Library of Congress Cataloging-in-Publication Data

Stewart, Bonnie E. (Bonnie Elaine), 1952–

No.9 : the 1968 Farmington Mine Disaster / by Bonnie E. Stewart.

p.   cm.

Includes bibliographical references and index.

ISBN 978-1-933202-78-5 (cloth : alk. paper)

ISBN 978-1-933202-77-8 (pbk. : alk. paper)

1. Mine explosions—West Virginia—Farmington. 2. Coal mine accidents—West Virginia—Farmington. 3. Mine fires—West Virginia—Farmington.

4. Farmington (W. Va.) I. Title.

TN313.S724 2011

622'.3340975454—dc22

Library of Congress Control Number: 2011011054

WEST VIRGINIA HUMANITIES COUNCIL

This project is being presented with financial assistance from the West Virginia Humanities Council, a state affiliate of the National Endowment for the Humanities. Any views, findings, conclusions or recommendations do not necessarily represent those of the West Virginia Humanities Council or the National Endowment for the Humanities.

Jacket photos by Bob Campione. Book design by Than Saffel.

For the 78 men who died in the No.9 mine

and for all their families and loved ones.

"It is infuriating that in this day and age, and in this country, that such a disaster could still happen. I am sick. I am saddened and I am angry. We have the laws. We have the resources. These tragedies, on this scale, should no longer be happening."

—*Senator Robert C. Byrd, following the deaths of 29 men in Massey Energy's Upper Big Branch mine in Montcoal, West Virginia, on April 5, 2010*

Contents

....

Appendices

Photographs

Maps

Introduction

....

When I came to West Virginia University in 2005, I knew nothing about coal mining. I had never seen a coal mine, and I did not know anyone who labored underground so that I could turn on my lights and run my beloved central air conditioner.

Then one evening, I was in a downtown Morgantown restaurant having appetizers with Associated Press reporter Vicki Smith. We were talking about journalism, going over stories we had written or wished we could write. I told her I was looking for a good story that needed to be told.

She said, had she the time, she would write about the Farmington coal mine disaster. Then she told me what happened on November 20, 1968, in a coal mine less than 30 miles from where we were sitting. That cold November morning, Consolidation Coal Company's No.9 mine blew up, trapping 78 men underground. It continued to explode until the company sealed the mine with the men inside 10 days later. I was horrified. In 1968, I was still in high school, leading an insulated life on a rural Indiana farm. I did not remember hearing about the disaster or even seeing it on the news. I felt as though I had missed an important piece of history.

I asked Vicki if I could steal her idea. She said, "Sure." And that is how this book began.

I do not pretend to be a coal mine expert, but I have learned a lot about mining over the past four years, and I can say with confidence that rarely, if ever, are coal mine disasters accidents. Historically, at least during the past century, most mine disasters have been the result of poor management, inadequate regulation and enforcement, greed, negligence, carelessness, foolishness, selfishness, complacency, indifference—add your own descriptor. All too often, the drive to produce coal—to make money, to meet contracts, to satisfy stockholders—has trumped safety. When that happens, miners pay a steep price. Usually, they are killed or disabled one by one, and few people outside their own communities notice. However, every few years, a mine explodes or a roof falls and crushes or traps an entire crew, and everyone is surprised. After examining inspection records from the No.9 mine and from mines that more recently have claimed lives, I am amazed that mines do not explode more often.

At this writing, the mine disaster at Massey Energy's Upper Big Branch (UBB) has filled newscasts. The April 5, 2010, deaths of 29 men in Montcoal, West Virginia, were predictable. Nonunion miners who worked there have testified that the mine was dangerous. Both state and federal inspectors knew the dangers, too, judging from the hundreds of violations and fines they issued to the UBB before the disaster. Similarly, many of the miners in the Consolidation No.9 coal mine predicted their own demise long before November 20, 1968.

At the Upper Big Branch, federal inspectors were in the mine at least 10 times in March 2010. They cited the company for coal dust, ventilation and roof control violations, any one of which could cause a disaster. They levied fines in the tens of thousands of dollars.[1]

State inspectors, too, spent at least seven days in the mine in March. They found electrical, coal dust and ventilation violations. On the morning the mine exploded, a state inspector was in the mine and cited the company for an unsupported roof and lack of ventilation in one of the working sections. He was unable, however, to complete his inspection. He came out for a break, and the mine blew up before he could go back inside.[2]

Immediately, the media swooped in, as they did after the No.9 exploded. Politicians began promising new laws and tougher enforcement. Government officials launched investigations. The full story of Massey Energy's mismanagement of the Upper Big Branch disaster has yet to unfold, but already flagrant violations have come to light. National Public Radio reported that UBB managers ordered an electrician to disable methane monitors on mining machines, devices that shut a machine down if gas is building up, which a spark could explode.

Safety devices routinely were disabled at the No.9 mine, too. There was too much gas and not enough air, too much coal dust and not enough rock dust, too much money to be made and not enough safety to be had. This book attempts to piece together what can be learned from the No.9 disaster not only because it ruined many lives but also because it saved so many lives later by forcing Congress to adopt the landmark 1969 Federal Coal Mine Health and Safety Act.

The law required federal officials to inspect underground mines four times each year, instead of once. For the first time, federal officials could levy fines, and they could even file criminal charges if companies willfully violated the new and stricter rules. The new law also provided health benefits for miners with pneumoconiosis or black lung disease. By their deaths, the 78 coal miners prevented thousands of underground miners from a similar fate. (See appendix A.)

This book is a true accounting of the 78 dead, based on a three-year investigation. What you will read comes from sworn testimonies taken after the disaster; state and federal inspection records and correspondence; confidential Consolidation Coal Company records produced during two lawsuits; analysis of coal mine practices and laws; and media accounts of the tragedy. This account also includes information gathered during personal interviews with coal miners who survived the disaster; men who worked in the mine prior to the disaster; and others who worked on recovery teams, bringing out what was left of the bodies of their co-workers that had lain in the mine for years. Other parts of the book are based on interviews with families of the dead, federal inspectors and mining technology experts.

The record shows that the No.9 mine disaster easily could have been prevented. The company men responsible for the mine's day-to-day operations knew the mine was dangerous, but did not slow or stop production to make it safe. Everyone in the mine was under intense pressure to produce coal. The union had limited influence. State and federal inspectors ignored the mine's glaring and egregious ventilation violations.

This investigation reveals that Consolidation Coal's managers routinely took illegal shortcuts, as did some of the men who worked for them. Before the mine exploded, a coal company employee disabled a ventilation fan's safety alarm that could have saved the men who were working underground when the mine exploded. Court documents and interviews with the relatives of the dead reveal the widows' struggle for justice and Consolidation Coal's efforts to conceal evidence that could have been used to determine the cause of the disaster. This book also explores the failure of federal and state government officials to investigate the disaster properly and their failure to hold anyone responsible for the deaths of more than six dozen men.

Twenty-one No.9 miners escaped the inferno that morning. But the mine would not give up the others.

For 10 long days, television cameras rolled in Farmington, West Virginia, and the nation watched as the horror streamed into their living rooms. All the major networks carried the story. Walter Cronkite of CBS and other news anchors gave nightly updates. They told Americans about the relentless fires and the safety violations federal inspectors had found in the mine just three months before explosions ripped it apart. Commentators lamented the lack of regulations to keep the country's miners safe.

About a year after the mine was sealed with the 78 men inside, the company reopened No.9 and began clearing away the rubble. Federal and state officials monitored the recovery effort for nine years. Teams of coal miners, many who had worked side-by-side with the men who died, found 59 bodies and brought them to the surface for burial. Then the mine was sealed again, becoming the permanent grave for 19 men.

Emilio Megna was one of those 19 men. He went to work on the eve of his retirement, but he never came home. His son Joe, who became a coal miner, has never recovered from the trauma and the lack of resolution. He is haunted by his memories of the day the mine exploded and by the words of Gary Martin, one of his father's buddies who escaped the inferno. Before he died, Martin told Joe the disaster was no accident. In fact, Joe said, Martin called it murder: "Murder One, 78 times."

Good Night, Dad

....

Emilio Megna had one more shift to work in the Consolidation Coal Company No.9 mine before he would retire and open his own service station in Worthington, West Virginia. Just eight more hours, 600 feet underground inside the cold and dark tunnels, then he would no longer have to breathe coal dust or scrub it from his face and clothes each day. No longer would he have to worry about methane gas explosions or roof falls that could bury him alive. Instead, he would wake with the morning sun and work in the midday light, pumping gas and fixing his neighbors' cars and trucks. Best of all, he could pass the business on to his son. Emilio would become the last person in his family who had to mine coal. He was still young, only 48, with a lot of life left to live.[1]

As a young boy, Emilio had followed his father into the coal mines of West Virginia, picking up chunks of coal and doing odd jobs. He had come to America from Italy in 1923, when he was a three-year-old, wearing a skirt and an earring. His family was one of thousands who crossed the Atlantic Ocean hoping to earn a good living in the coalfields. When he turned 16, Emilio took a permanent job underground, earning 50 cents a day. More than 30 years later, he was ready to come out of the mines.

The day before the No.9 exploded, Emilio's 16-year-old son, Joe, tried to convince his father to play hooky and go trout fishing. But Emilio would not do it, said he owed it to the company to work his last shift. That evening, Emilio took Joe to his best friend's house for a sleepover. The two boys planned to go to school and then spruce up the gas station for the grand opening that Saturday.

Joe tried again to convince his father to stay home.

"No, I love you. You be careful. Don't get in trouble," Emilio said. He then drove away in their Dodge Dart station wagon. It was the first time Joe could remember hearing his father say he loved him.

Emilio Megna went home, gathered his lunch box and reported for work with 98 other men who went underground at midnight. Unlike third-shift workers in other industries, No.9 miners did not call it the "graveyard shift." They dubbed it the "cateye" shift.

On November 20, 1968, as he had done hundreds of times, Emilio entered the mine through the Llewellyn Run portal, located in the hollow for which it was named. He rode a large elevator to the floor of the mine, where he boarded a passenger rail car, called a "jeep." The electrically-powered vehicle carried him more than a mile to section 9North on the far west side of the mine.

A section foreman, Emilio likely checked his work area for methane gas and any other dangerous conditions. Earlier that week, he had found gas in his section, but his written reports indicate it had not accumulated to hazardous levels. Some of the machinery in the section was not working properly that morning. At some point, the dispatcher sent Emilio and his crew to another part of the mine.

As Emilio worked, his son Joe slept, until the phone call came, the call that no mining family wants to answer. The first words are as devastating as the sight of a black sedan pulling into a military family's driveway: "The No.9 blew up."

"Joe, which mine does your father work in?" his friend's mother called upstairs.

"The No.9," he answered.

Joe jumped out of bed, put on his pants and shoes and ran bare-chested two miles through the wintery woods to get home. One of his sisters was fixing her hair for work. He told her the news. His mother came in, and they turned on the television. It was true. The TV screen was filled with images of smoke pouring from the mouth of the mine.

Emilio Megna (first row) with his wife, two daughters and son, Joe (back row).
Courtesy of Joe Megna.

They climbed into their car and drove toward the mine. At a roadblock, they were rerouted to the mine's company store, where people already had begun to gather. They waited and waited and waited, participants in a morbid ritual that had come to define coal mining in America.

Emilio had talked about the dangers in the mine in the weeks before it exploded. "It's so hot. It's bad," he told his wife, referring to the methane gas. "Somebody is gonna get killed over there. Somebody is gonna get killed," he said.

Joe sensed something strange in his father's words. "My dad was not scared of anything, but he was scared of No.9 mine," Joe said years later.[2]

Emilio Megna was not the only miner who was worried about the working conditions in the No.9. In the days before the explosion, Pete Kaznoski told his wife, Sara, that the mine was going to blow. It was too gassy. She asked him to quit.[3] He would not.

Frank and Mary Matish with their son, James. Courtesy of James Matish.

Frank Matish was not happy with the conditions in the mine, either. He had been injured in the mine a few weeks earlier, just before Election Day. Hot oil from a mining machine had sprayed him in the face, which put him into the hospital. However, his accident did not stop him from voting. His wife, Mary, tried to convince him to stay in the hospital while she drove people to the polls.

"Dad, one vote's not going to matter," said his 14-year-old son, James.

"You never know," his father replied. "Besides, we don't want Richard Nixon in the White House." Frank Matish, who was 57, cast his last vote in 1968 and then went back to work.

The weekend before the mine exploded, James overheard his parents talking about the mine. Frank, who had been working in coal mines since he was 11 years old, told Mary that the mine was in the worst shape he had ever seen. Coal dust was knee-deep.

"Maybe I should quit," he said.

"Well, why don't you just call, why don't you just quit and not go?" she asked.

"Well, we've got a son that we need to worry about educating," he said.

"Don't worry about that. I'm cleaning houses. I'm cleaning the church. We're making money and we can get by, and we'll get you a job doing something," she said.

"Well, we'll think about it," he said.

A few days later, Frank Matish kissed his son goodbye as he always did before he went to work at the No.9.

"So long, Dad. Don't work too hard and be careful," said James, who already was drifting off to sleep.

A few hours later, the boy had a bad dream. He was in a coal mine, and one miner called out, "Fire in the hole, fire in the hole, fire in the hole."

"At that time, my whole body shook, and I woke up and looked at the clock and it was 5:20 a.m.," he said later.[4]

Government documents show that the first of many violent explosions that rocked the No.9 hit sometime between 5:15 a.m. and 5:30 a.m., when Frank Matish, Emilio Megna and Pete Kaznoski were laboring somewhere deep inside the mountain. No one knows exactly how the three men died. Their bodies were never found.

Dangerous History

No one should have died in 1968 in the No.9 mine. When Emilio Megna and his buddies went underground for the last time, the coal industry and its regulators knew well what causes mine disasters and how to prevent them. They had learned the hard lessons over and over again during prior decades.

In the 1800s and early 1900s, injuries and deaths in the mines were common, and most people simply accepted that fact.[1] The coal industry was a mighty political force, which had completely blocked federal regulation and had kept state laws and enforcement at a minimum. West Virginia was one of the first states to regulate the industry, hiring its first mine inspector in 1883 and adopting its first significant coal mining law in 1887, a year after the state's first recorded major disaster in the Mt. Brook Mine in Newburg.[2] The open flames on the cap lights the men wore had ignited a pocket of methane gas, blowing the inside of the mine apart. "When the work of exploration began it was found that the whole force of the mine, 39 men and boys, were stark and cold in death."[3]

The laws, however, did not stop the carnage. Men and boys continued to die in the mines, a dozen here, two or three dozen there. Large numbers of miners were killed by roof falls, as the ceilings of the tunnels gave way and covered them with coal and slate. No woman knew if her man or sons would come home from work from one day to the next. In coal country, miners were expendable, more so than the horses, oxen, mules and goats that worked underground with them. As many coal miners have noted, coal companies had to buy another mule, but a man, well, they could easily find another one.

What happened in 1907, however, could not be ignored. That year, an estimated 3,232 of the country's 680,000 coal miners died on the job.[4] The worst coal mine disaster in U.S. history occurred on December 6, 1907, in Monongah, West Virginia. Government records show that the Monongah explosion killed at least 358 miners.[5] Some experts, however, believe the number was much higher because mining companies kept poor records of the people working underground. In his book *Monongah*, Davitt McAteer, a former federal coal mine official, estimates that as many as 578 men and boys may have perished that day.[6]

That same December, 239 men died in a horrific explosion in the dusty,

In the 1800s and early 1900s, mining companies often used animals, such as goats, to pull coal cars in and out of the mines. Courtesy of John Brock.

gaseous Darr Mine in Jacobs Creek, Pennsylvania; 34 miners died in another Pennsylvania mine disaster; 11 died in a New Mexico pit; and 57 miners died in an Alabama mine explosion. The December death toll that year was so high that the month was dubbed "Bloody December."[7]

At that time, coal mining was one of the most dangerous and disabling industrial occupations in the country. Following Bloody December, federal officials began a serious study of coal mine explosions. They already knew that coal naturally emits methane gas. They knew that a spark or the open flame from a coal miner's cap could ignite the gas and set off an explosion. They also knew that an ignition source could cause coal dust to explode. They knew that even a small explosion could become a major disaster: It could stir up and ignite loose coal dust, which would explode and stir up more coal dust. As long as there was loose dust or certain concentrations of methane in its path, one explosion could set an entire mine ablaze.

What most people in the coal industry may not have known then, but would soon learn, was that under the right conditions, coal dust thrown into suspension can self-ignite and set off a powerful explosion. In 1910, the newly formed U.S. Bureau of Mines announced that finding.[8] It was clear then, as it is now, that to keep miners safe, coal companies had to control both coal dust and methane gas.

Over the years, the industry also learned that winter months are particularly dangerous. When cold fronts move into the mountains and the temperature and humidity drop, underground tunnels dry out. The drier the mine, the dustier it gets and coal dust is everywhere: on the roof of the tunnels, the rib or walls of the tunnels and the floor. It is produced at the working face, where men and machines dig coal out of the mountain. It builds up around the machinery and in the loading areas and unloading areas. It blows off the coal cars as they move through the mine, and it settles along the haulage tracks. To keep coal dust from exploding, miners have to wet the dust, haul it out of the mine or neutralize it by mixing it with a pulverized inert material, usually limestone, called rock dust.

Barometric Pressure

That so many disasters happened in the winter is no coincidence. When cold fronts move into an area, the barometric pressure drops, which allows more methane to seep out of the coal seam. The pressure change also can weaken seals that close off mined-out tunnels. When the integrity of the structures fails, the methane that builds up behind the structures leaks into the mine. A drop in pressure also can force methane from unsealed mined-out areas, known as gobs, which contain coal and slate. If the gobs are improperly ventilated, as often has been the case, the methane moves into the working sections. The outcome can be disastrous.

Obviously, managing methane and coal dust is a continuous, hour-by-hour, minute-by-minute activity. Every time miners carve out a load of coal, cut a new tunnel or advance in any other way, they make more dust and expose more coal that can emit methane. It takes time to spread rock dust or wet down the working sections to mitigate the dust. It takes time to stop mining and check the methane levels. It takes time to make adjustments that will bring more air to the working face in order to sweep away the methane. In the coal mining business, time for these tasks is time taken away from mining coal, and coal is money, big money.

A Gassy, Dusty Mine

The No.9 mine, opened by Jamison Coal and Coke Company in 1910, always was plagued by coal dust and methane gas, as were the Jamison No.7 and No.8, its sister mines.[9] All were located in Marion County, West Virginia, in the heart of the Pittsburgh coal bed, which extends more than 5,000 square miles into parts of Pennsylvania, Ohio, Maryland and West Virginia. The bituminous coal, which on average is 96 inches thick, lies between 300 to 800 feet below the surface.[10] It is a soft coal that has a high energy value when it is burned, and it produces methane gas during the mining process. Thousands of miners have died digging it from the Appalachian Mountains, hundreds in Marion County, West Virginia alone.

In October 1916, 11 men died in an underground explosion at the Jamison No.7 mine in Barrackville, West Virginia, and a state inspector died trying to rescue them. Officials believed cigarette smoking or an electrical arc set off methane gas and, as often happens in mine disasters, coal dust carried the explosion and fire through the mine.[11]

In January 1926, a gas explosion killed 19 men in the Jamison No.8 mine in Farmington, West Virginia. Forty-seven men were underground that day. One group survived by hunkering down for 18 hours in the underground stable's feed room. To seal out noxious gases, the men had stuffed hay around the doorway.[12]

No.9's Record

State inspection records show that the Jamison No.9 mine, later known as the Consol No.9, did not have a good record. A 1935 report, the earliest No.9 inspection record in the West Virginia State Archives, describes the mine as "very dusty." The inspector recommended rock dusting.[13]

By January 1936, the inspector was losing patience with No.9's owner. "Very little has been done at this mine for the past 1½ years to put it in shape. The main haulage road is the only way of escape from the faces, except through the old workings. Very little rock dusting is done. The sections are dry & dusty. There are three solid sections that liberate gas very free."[14]

A few months later, the inspector found gas again. He wrote, "There is no improvement of conditions at this mine since my last inspection."[15]

The No.9 had a dismal beginning in 1937 as miners worked with too much dust and gas and not enough air. By summer, a new superintendent was trying to improve the conditions, but by October, the state inspector found chaos.

"So many changes has [sic] been made at this mine during the past 3 months I am afraid that no one knows just what they are doing," he wrote. He decided to give the men a few more weeks before he began "working on them."[16]

Throughout the 1930s and 1940s, state inspectors found inadequate ventilation, high levels of methane gas and too much coal dust in the No.9. One of the worst years was 1942. A state inspector found 64 violations in February and 64 violations in June. However, the number dropped to 45 violations in September and to 32 in December.[17]

One of the most damning inspections took place in 1943. During World War II, coal was so important that President Franklin D. Roosevelt issued an executive order, commanding the U.S. Bureau of Mines to conduct coal mine security inspections "to insure uninterrupted production of essential war minerals."[18]

Federal inspectors visited the No.9 that April. They found little danger from "pro-Axis sympathies" or sabotage, even though the management did not investigate its "key men" or other employees to make sure they were patriotic.[19]

The worst threats to the No.9's war production capabilities came from extremely dangerous mining practices. The once confidential report lists numerous major hazards, including:

- dust explosion hazard where coal was unloaded outside the mine
- explosives magazine stored near the ventilating fan in illegal housing
- electric wires not in conduits in numerous areas
- inadequate fire protection above and below ground, including inoperable fire extinguishers and no water hoses underground to fight a fire
- no plan for control of a fire
- kerosene used for cleaning purposes
- no mine rescue equipment
- very little rock dust[20]

The report also noted that many of the company's miners lived in 124 company-owned houses. "Observed living conditions are poor, and accommodations are not adequate," the inspector wrote.[21]

Despite the No.9's condition, the government still considered the mine an important source of coal for the war effort, noting that in 1942, the 301 men who worked at the mine had produced 619,449 tons of coal.[22] The company, however, reported problems that were hindering production: absenteeism of 8 percent each week and a labor turnover that had hit 40 percent annually.[23]

Federal Law

Even though coal production for the war effort had become a high priority, the federal government did little to keep miners safe. In 1941, the U.S. Congress passed the Federal Coal Mine Inspection and Investigation Act that allowed federal inspectors to inspect mines, but gave them no enforcement powers. The law did require the government to notify the public about its inspections. The press releases became sanitized summaries that lauded the coal companies for fixing hazards in their mines after an inspector had pointed them out.

For instance, in May 1951, a federal inspector found 24 violations in the No.9, including two "serious hazards:"

- The elevator shaft used to carry the men underground had loose and defective boards supporting it. The inspector had noted the problem on four earlier inspections, but the company still had not replaced the boards.
- Men were drilling rocks and coal without wetting the area, which could produce sparks and ignite methane or coal dust. Also they were not using dust collectors on the drills to keep the coal dust from flying into suspension and self-igniting.[24]

After this inspection, a federal press release commended No.9's owner for making more than a dozen improvements since the mine's last inspection. It noted the problems, but did not indicate their seriousness or the number of times the mine had been cited for the same hazardous conditions.[25]

The press release praised the company for installing a new ventilating fan that increased the quantity of air in the mine. The release, however, did not tell the public that the inspector cited the company for failing to equip the new fan with an alarm system that would alert the miners if the fan stopped or stalled.

Eight months later, in January 1952, T. J. Ward, a federal inspector, noted that the fan still had no alarm. He also discovered that there had been an explosion in the No.9 on October 11, 1951.

Ward's frustration with the state is evident in his report: "Information obtained during this inspection indicates that the ignition was investigated by the West Virginia Department of Mines; however, the [U.S.] Bureau of Mines did not make an investigation because the fact that an ignition occurred became known to the Bureau only after an elapse of several months."[26]

The federal report notes that no one died in the explosion and explains what happened. A No.9 miner had set off explosive shots in loose roof material. This practice was dangerous and, in most cases, illegal. Miners were supposed to use "confined shots," which meant drilling holes in the coal, inserting government-approved or "permissible" explosives, and topping off the hole with incombustible material, such as clay.[27]

Shooting Stumps

Even when No.9 miners used confined shots, they did not always detonate them legally, particularly when they were shooting stumps, which were columns of coal left to support the mine's roof in room-and-pillar mining. This mining method required that miners drive several long tunnels, or entries, parallel to each other. Then they connected the tunnels with shorter entries, called crosscuts, creating a checkerboard pattern. Each long tunnel in the No.9 was named for its location in relationship to the mine's main passageway, which was being driven to the west. For instance, 4Left-2North referred to the fourth entry off the second section north of the main passageway.

Once the miners finished taking all the coal they could from the pillars, leaving only stumps, they began to retreat from the section. As they backed out of the area, they blew up the stumps. At that time, No.9 miners were not recovering the coal from the demolished stumps.[28]

To shoot a stump, a miner was supposed to run a long blasting cable from the explosives to an approved battery that was kept a safe distance away. Then a miner was supposed to activate the cable with the battery, setting off the explosives to bring down the stumps, one at a time. After each stump was shot, the miner was supposed to let the smoke and dust clear and check for gas before setting off the next explosion. This method was the legal way to do the job, but it was not always the most expedient way. Furthermore, it was not the way some No.9 miners were shooting stumps in 1954. Records show miners did not always shoot from a battery, an illegal practice that would cost lives.

How Such Things Happen

....

On November 13, 1954, shortly after Consolidation Coal Company bought the No.9 mine, section foreman George C. Alberts and his crew were shooting stumps in 4Right-2North. He took a dangerous shortcut in his work. As a result, more than a dozen men died after an explosion ripped through the mine and set it on fire.

Later, men who had worked for Alberts testified under oath that he had routinely broken mining laws when he used explosives. Physical evidence unearthed a few months after the disaster supported their claims.[1]

The disaster could have been even worse: The mine blew up on a Saturday, when few men were working. On a weekday, more than 100 men would have been inside the mine during any one of No.9's three daily shifts. Most would have been trapped in the far reaches of the mine, which in 1954 stretched nearly 16 square miles. The only miners who could have escaped would have been those near the slope, a long tunnel used to enter and exit the mine. The rest would not have been able to reach the "man shaft," a vertical tunnel equipped with an elevator that lowered men into and lifted them out of the mine.

Conditions in the mine could not have been much worse. The night before the first explosion, the barometric pressure had begun to drop as a moderately strong cold front had begun to move rapidly into the area from the west. The change likely pulled more methane off the gobs. The month had been dry, too. No rain had fallen that week, and less than half an inch had fallen all month, which meant the mine was dry and possibly dusty.[2]

On November 13, 24 men traveled underground to work. Some checked the ventilation system and came out of the mine. By early afternoon, 17 men were still underground.

Some were working on machinery, and Alberts and his crew were blasting in 4Right-2North.[3]

The Explosion

At about 1:45 p.m., section foreman Harry Floyd Jr. was filling out a report in an office building outside the mine when he heard a ventilation alarm sound. He knew the alarm could mean a fan had slowed or stopped, a sure sign of trouble. He also knew his father, Harry Floyd Sr., was in the mine.[4]

The No.9 depended upon two large ventilation fans, the No.1 fan and the Athas Run fan, to exhaust and circulate about 348,000 cubic feet of air through the mine every minute. In 24 hours, the fans swept more than 3 million cubic feet of methane from the mine. When a fan malfunctioned, the entire ventilation system was compromised.[5]

The warning horn had been wailing only a few seconds when Floyd spotted papers blowing under the door of another office. Then he heard a blast, a short, blunt crack—like a firecracker going off in a barrel. Plaster began cracking off the walls, and the light fixtures shook. Floyd ducked under a metal table as a roar from the blast escaped from a nearby airshaft.[6]

When the blast hit, 38-year-old Howard Jenkins was on duty in the lamphouse, where miners kept battery-operated lights for their caps and numbered metal identification tags. The explosion brought down a steel beam that hit Jenkins. He died instantly.[7]

Underground, mechanics Gilbert Kiger and Paul Barthelow had finished their work. They were waiting at the slope bottom for a ride out of the mine. The electric lights began to flicker. The blast wave hit, and clouds of rock dust and flying boards engulfed them.[8] "It was like someone had thrown a sack of flour in my face," Kriger said.[9]

Someone outside the mine signaled for the two men to board an electric trolley car and ride up the slope. They managed to find the car. However,

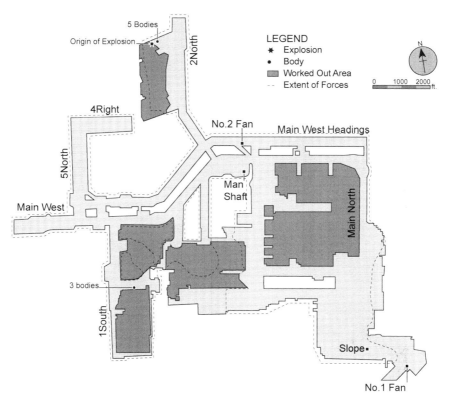

A Map of the No.9 in 1954. Map by Rachel Davis.

they had traveled only about 20 feet before someone cut the power, forcing them to walk out of the mine.

Seventeen air miles away, a West Virginia University seismograph picked up the tremor, which lasted for 17 seconds.[10] Windows in nearby houses shattered, and pictures fell from walls.[11]

Mrs. Charles Duncil heard the noise from her home. "I looked over the hill and I saw big clouds of black smoke. I couldn't figure it out. Then my husband called and said 'No.9 has blown up.'"[12]

The couple operated a taxi service, hauling men to and from the mines. They knew them all, laughed and joked with them. Mrs. Duncil's first thoughts went to one young mother with three small children. She knew the woman's husband worked the afternoon shift and probably was in the mine, and he was. Mrs. Duncil went to the woman and tried to comfort her.

Men, women and children gathered near the mine, warming themselves near bonfires, waiting for words of hope that never came. It was the scene that always plays out when a mine explodes—hoping, waiting, crying, praying. People with loved ones inside the mine did not have to wait long for resolution.[13]

The mine blew up again at 10:30 p.m., shooting flames as high as 100 feet out of the Athas Run fan shaft. Thirty minutes later, smoke and fumes containing carbon monoxide began to roll from the mouth of the slope entrance.[14] Officials knew the mine was burning out of control, and shortly after midnight, they decided to seal the mine to smother the fires.

"I could hear them hauling the dirt," Mrs. Duncil said. "Can you imagine this girl hearing the trucks and knowing her husband was in there, and it was her husband that was being sealed up?"[15]

Company officials and union leaders speculated about the cause of the disaster. "They had the best housekeeping here of almost any mine I know of, and there is just no answer how such a thing can happen when conditions were as favorable as they were here," Cecil J. Urbaniak, the president of the local district of the United Mine Workers of America, told reporters.[16]

Consolidation Coal officials wanted to believe the miners had cut into one of the many abandoned gas wells near the mine. "Something suddenly happened to release a considerable part of methane," concluded James Hyslop, a vice president for the coal company.[17]

Three days after the explosion, officials began looking for possible causes during closed hearings held at the Hannastown Supply Company store near the mine.[18] They called in a few of No.9's miners and the two men who walked out of the mine. It was not much of an investigation.

No one conducted formal hearings until February 1956, more than a year after the explosion. At that time, West Virginia officials appointed a board to hear testimony. It included a federal and a state official, a member of the United Mine Workers of America, and Consolidation Coal's general manager. By then, some men claimed to have trouble remembering details about how the company operated its mine before the explosion. Being questioned by a coal company executive who controlled their jobs possibly contributed to their lack of recall.

Other miners, however, told the board they had been having problems with methane gas long before the mine blew up. Roof falls had clogged some of the airways known as "bleeders" or "bleeder entries" that ventilated the gobs. When the bleeders were blocked, methane seeped off the gobs into the work areas, particularly in 4Left-2North. Paul Gordi told investigators what he had seen in that area about two months before the explosion. Methane-detecting lamps hanging from his two buddies' belts had lit up as the men walked toward the working face. The light meant they were walking in methane gas, and it meant the coal-cutting machine was operating in the gas. Gordi immediately notified his boss, Walter Pickett, who sent him after brattice cloth, a heavy burlap-like material that was hung in the tunnels to direct fresh air where it was needed and bad air out of the mine. Gordi, Pickett and several other men spent 45 minutes hanging up brattice cloth before they were able to clear the gas.[19]

Other miners testified that they had found gas on 4Left-2North in the weeks and days before the explosion. Two months before the explosion, investigators found company records that showed methane was found several times coming off the 2North gob at levels ranging between 1.5 percent and 1.7 percent.

Harry Floyd Jr., whose father died in the disaster, told investigators that when he found 1.7 percent methane in the air that passed by 2North gobs, he recorded the figure in his books. He did not bring his findings to anyone's attention because discovering that much gas was not unusual.[20]

Miners also testified that they had found gas in other sections. John Tracy said he refused to keep working one day when he found gas in 3North. The section foreman, George Alberts, called in the mine superintendent, George Cain, who insisted the area had enough air. Later, Tracy said Cain accused him of interfering with mine management and threatened to fire him.[21]

In the 1950s, everyone in the coal industry knew that gas was explosive when its concentration in the air reached between 5 percent and 15 percent. Miners also knew that when methane reached levels greater than 1 percent, particularly at the working face, it was time to stop and clear the gas.[22]

Coal First, Safety Second

Getting the coal out quickly often superseded safety.

When shuttle cars snagged the brattice cloth and ripped it down, miners rolled up the cloth and wired it to the rib or roof. It saved time, but interfered with ventilation.

Alex Petro testified that No.9 miners rolled up the brattice cloth all the time. "Yes, they're pretty bad about that. I would have to say they're pretty bad. The only time they don't do that is when a federal or state inspector or high official of the coal company are in the mine, but as soon as they leave, why they—in fact we had a lot of arguments over that."[23]

He had become disillusioned with inspections, which he deemed superficial. At one point, Petro took an inspector who was in the mine and showed him a loose roof bolt, a long rod that was driven into the ceiling to stabilize the layers of coal and slate above the tunnels.

"I said, 'Here, now, you twist this. Is this tight? Does this support anything?'"[24] Petro said the inspector noted the problem, but did not do a thorough inspection. When the inspector asked him to sign the report, Petro said he refused.

Other miners, too, felt reporting problems did little good. John Miller said he told his safety committee that he did not have enough water on his cutting machine to keep the coal dust under control. When he came back to his section after lunch break, the dust had settled, and it was so thick that he could write his name on his machine.[25] The safety committee took his complaint to the mine superintendent, George Cain, who told them that nothing could be done about the lack of water.

After Miller contacted a state inspector about the problem, Cain reprimanded him for making the call. "Well, he held me outside until he came out, and I thought gave me a pretty good going over for it," Miller said. "He told me he didn't need that kind of men and had a notion to send me home, and a number of other times he was driving me."[26]

At first, Cain denied chastising any of the miners for reporting safety issues. Later, however, he changed his testimony, admitting that he had taken Miller aside for calling state inspector Bernard Horton. "It was no way to report stuff like that, and I didn't like it a bit, doing a thing that way . . ." said Cain.[27] Cain was upset, in part, because Horton responded to the complaint but found no dust problems.

In the year before the explosion, state inspector Horton uncovered few violations at the mine, but a federal inspector found many serious problems. In December 1953, Horton noted that 3Left did not have enough roof bolts. He cited the company for a couple of other violations, but said the mine had good ventilation, was well rock dusted, and miners stored and used explosives properly.[28]

Thirteen days later in January 1954, federal inspector W.D. Baldwin found dangerous amounts of loose coal and coal dust near a shuttle car, an unsafe roof, and machinery and electric cables that were not spark-proof.[29]

The state inspector came back in March and again found almost everything in good order. The mine, he wrote, was well ventilated and rock dusted, and miners were handling explosives properly.[30]

On the next two federal inspections—one ending in June 1954, the other in late October—Baldwin cited the company for numerous violations in June, including:[31]

- unsafe roofs in two areas
- inadequate rock dusting
- failure to inspect the return airways (passages that carry air away from the working faces)for methane gas for as long as two weeks
- improper use of explosives, including the use of too much powder when blasting coal from the working face
- failure to provide enough shelter holes (small areas carved into the side of a tunnel where men take refuge to avoid vehicles on the railway) along the slope
- obstructed shelter holes
- several electrical violations

Baldwin concluded a 9-day inspection of the mine on October 20, 1954. Among other violations, he found:[32]

- unsafe roofs in three areas
- inadequate rock dusting
- equipment that was not spark-proof
- a shot-firer who used too many explosives
- return airways that had not been examined on a weekly basis
- too few shelter holes on the slope
- shelter holes obstructed with refuse
- unguarded trolley wires and trolley feeder wires (the overhead electrical power sources for vehicles that used the mine's underground railway)

Twenty-four days later, the mine exploded.

Recovery Begins

Four months after the 1954 explosion, officials reopened the mine, and recovery crews began bringing out bodies. They found four victims lying within 400 feet of the man shaft. The men had been rock dusting in the mine, but had completed their duties, parked their equipment, and were walking toward the man shaft when the explosion hit. The fires had burned all the clothing from the men, except for their shoes and socks. Their bodies were badly burned and covered with "red dog," an ash-like byproduct of burning coal.[33]

The crew loaded the men onto a mine car pulled by a team of horses and took them out of the mine. "They couldn't have no power, see," Bill Bunner, who was on the recovery team, said in an interview years later. According to Bunner, they had to use horses because there was too much coal dust, too much damage, and too much danger of running into gas to use electrical power.[34]

"If you were there in '54 when it blew up and you could see what it did— it's because of gas," Bunner said.[35] To detect methane, the miners used hand-held safety lamps. In the presence of methane, a flame inside the lamp would light up. However, a lot of miners never bothered to use them, Bunner said.[36]

"Didn't know what the hell, you know. A lot of times the lights were out and they never even worried about it. That's all we had in those days. We had no protection. No state, no federal, and a safety light and no air," said Bunner, who later became a federal inspector.[37]

Furthermore, they had few ways to escape a mine if it exploded. If the men were not close to an exit, they had to build barricades to shield themselves from fire and noxious fumes. Breathing devices were kept on each section, but they did not last long. Although crews of seven or eight men usually worked on each section, the coal company usually kept only two all-service gas masks there. The rest of the crew had "self rescuers," breathing devices that fit inside a miner's mouth, but, unlike gas masks, did not cover the eyes or nose. The self-rescuers usually lasted about 30 minutes, sometimes up to an hour. They also produced heat, which often blistered the miners' mouths. At that time, self-rescuers cost about $9 each; gas masks, $65.[38]

The federal government's final report on the disaster reveals what was happening in the mine before the explosion and months later when the men's bodies were recovered.[39]

When the No.9 exploded, some of the miners had managed to find the safety equipment caches. Two mechanics, who had been repairing electrical equipment in 2Left-1South, and a foreman from another section were found near their dinner hole, a small area carved out of the wall where miners ate. The three men were lying close together on a piece of canvas, partly covered by a blanket. Three spent self-rescuers were found nearby, and each man had a self-rescuer on his body. One man had a gas mask around his neck, but he was not wearing the face piece, nor had he broken the canister seal, which would have activated the device. Seven unused self-rescuers and an unopened gas mask were found near the men.

Before the explosion, they had been on their way to the man shaft; two had been riding in a locomotive, another in a smaller vehicle called a "jeep," both energized by rods attached to an electrically charged line that ran along the roof of the mine. Judging by the distance the men had walked to the dinner hole, investigators speculated the three may have lived about 90 minutes after the explosion. None suffered injuries or was burned. They were badly decomposed, and their faces and heads covered with a greenish-grey mold. However, they were fully clothed, which was a sign that the explosive forces did not kill them. Instead, they died from breathing afterdamp—a deadly combination of gases created by the explosion.

Origin of the 1954 Explosion. Map: Mine Safety and Health Administration. National Mine Health and Safety Academy. Historical Summary of Mine Disasters in the United States. Vol. 1, Coal Mines, 1959-1998. 1998. Reprinted 2001.

Investigators concluded that the three men were doomed the minute the mine exploded. They had no chance of reaching safety or being rescued: the man shaft was destroyed, the slope was four miles away, and the mine

quickly filled with fire, smoke and noxious gases. Perhaps they realized their fate when they stretched out on the canvas and tried to cover themselves with the blanket.

Three other men died on their way to the man shaft. Two mechanics had finished repairing electrical equipment in 4Left-CFace. They were thrown from their locomotive as they neared the underground workshop. Their bodies were found 70 feet apart under a huge roof fall.

Harry Floyd Sr. was driving a jeep along the railway when he died. He was about 600 feet from the man shaft when he was covered by a roof fall. Nothing remained of his body except bones.

A recovery crew found the last five bodies and the source of the explosion on 4Left-2North. They uncovered the first miner near the mouth of the section. He appeared to be on his way out of the section. He was badly decomposed and partly covered by a roof fall. The crew spent four days hand-loading the coal and slate and hauling it away in wheelbarrows. Every 10 to 15 feet, they found another body. All of the men had died instantly.

The last man on the section—most likely George Alberts—was lying about three feet from the materials he had been using illegally to set off explosives.

Explosives had been set in a stump, and a blasting cable had been attached, not to a blasting battery but to a 275-volt cable used to deliver power to a large piece of machinery. Alberts had driven two nails into the cable so that one nail touched a positively charged conductor and the other nail touched a negatively charged conductor. Then he touched the untwisted ends of the blasting cable to the nails. Likely, the other end of the cable was connected to explosives in multiple stumps. The explosions were strong enough to bring down the stumps and set off the methane gas that permeated the 2North gob. The first violent explosion killed Alberts and his crew where they stood.

Along side the recovery crews, federal officials investigated the disaster. They found what state and federal inspectors and company officials either had ignored or had failed to see. They reported that the 2North gob "was filled with methane in concentrations ranging from below, through, and above the explosive limits, since this area could not possibly have been ventilated with the system of ventilation" used in the mine.[40]

The officials found that many tunnels were in dire need of rock dust. Loose coal and coal dust were eight inches deep in many places, even deeper in others. Lacking the neutralizing effect of rock dust, the coal dust had propagated a second explosion and set the mine on fire. The violent forces tossed about heavy machinery, ripped tracks from the floors, and tumbled timbers. The forces blew out 600 cement stoppings—the block walls built in crosscuts to direct the flow of air. The stoppings separated the incoming fresh air from the return air, which had moved past the working face and the gobs, sweeping away methane.

The testimony of No.9 miners also revealed shocking practices.

Afraid to Complain

Men needed their jobs at the No.9. If they wanted to keep them, they knew they had to play the game by company rules. At the No.9, company men had been given bonuses based on productivity. At one time, a point system was used, but managers testified such a system had not been used for a while. Men who had complained about their working conditions told investigators that they were given the worst and sometimes the most dangerous jobs in the mine.

The high-production culture of the mine led No.9 managers routinely to shoot stumps by connecting the blasting cables to the live overhead trolley wires. Everyone in the coal industry knew the practice could be deadly. In 1916, the U.S. Department of Mines published a booklet, "The Use and Misuse of Explosives in Coal Mining" that described the practice. It warned that arcing would occur, which would ignite any gas or coal dust present.[41]

During the official hearings, several miners said that George Alberts and at least two other foremen shot stumps and coal using this dangerous method. Upper management feigned ignorance. Section foreman Lloyd N. Fleming and Roosevelt Stevenson, who ran a cutting machine, both testified they had seen Alberts shoot stumps from the trolley cable. Section foreman Harry Pickett admitted he saw his own crew shoot four stumps with ten powder sticks by touching the blasting cable to a main power line. At first, Pickett insisted he had never done the shooting. When pressed, he said he saw the shooting. When pressed harder, he admitted he was the supervisor

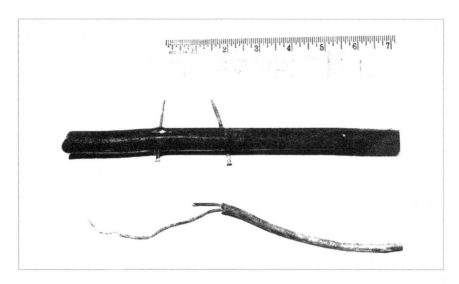

Federal investigators discovered No.9 miners had been violating the law by driving nails through high-voltage trailing cables and using that electricity to set off explosives in the mine. Source: Final Report on Major Explosion and Fire Disaster No.9 Mine, U.S. Department of the Interior, Bureau of Mines.

on the section. He explained that his crew had once used the power line to blast a difficult area.[42]

Motorman Paris Joseph Bryant, who drove locomotives that pulled the coal cars, testified that Harry Pickett's crew shot stumps off power lines two and three times each week on 4Left-2North and 3Left-2North. Bryant said he knew the shooting was dangerous, but he did not report it. He had gotten in trouble before for discussing safety issues.

"At the time before the explosion, any time you brought up anything you would always get in trouble. I figured I needed a job and it was best to keep my mouth shut; whether it would be from the boss or the guy you spoke to, you got mixed up," said Bryant.[43] He said he wanted to quit, but he needed his job.

Shot fireman Stanley Bazan said he had set up the blasting on Harry Pickett's section. He loaded several stumps with powder sticks and strung several blasting cables together until they were long enough to reach the main power line. Someone else set them off. Bazan knew the shooting was a violation of the law, but he did not report it to anyone either. "Well, I don't know no one else ever reported anything like that. I thought there wasn't any use sticking my neck out either," Bazan said.[44]

Section foreman Mike Verbonic said that on the day shift, just 24 hours before the disaster, he tried to use his battery to set off seven shots on 2Left-1South, but the battery did not have sufficient power. So, instead of shooting one stump at a time, which was the legal way to work, he decided to use the power from a nearby mining machine. He drove two nails into the cable and shot off the wire.

On that same shift, the crew on 4Left-2North found gas and had to stop production and hang up brattice cloth. They loaded only five coal cars. Joe Butcher, who ran the coal-cutting machine, said that almost every time he worked in that section, he found gas.

The cateye shift on 4Left-2North had problems, too.

Paul James Sabo, who ran a coal-loading machine, said a stump fell while he and other men were setting posts to hold up the roof. One of the men found gas near the fall. After Sabo had loaded a couple of cars of coal, he found gas, too, next to the gob. Sabo and Arthur Anderson Jr. stopped their work and put up more brattice cloth.

Hartis McIntire was one of the last men to come out of 4Left-2North alive. After he made his last cut in the coal, he stabilized the roof, set some posts, and checked the brattice cloth. As he was leaving his section, he met his foreman, David Mainella Sr.

"Did you get your posts set?" Mainella asked.[45]

"Yes, we got our posts set, the canvas all been set and the place is in good shape," McIntire said.[46]

"Just a minute, I want to see it," Mainella said.[47]

Mainella checked the area himself before the crew left the section. On their way out of the mine, they met George Alberts, who was making his morning check for methane gas. It was the last time they saw him.

David Mainella and his crew walked out of the No.9 less than seven hours before it exploded. Neither he nor Arthur Anderson Jr. would be so lucky in 1968.

Rules of Survival

....

N o.9's management failed to learn an important lesson from the 1954 explosion: always keep bleeder entries open and gobs well ventilated. At 9 a.m. on Friday, January 3, 1958, the mine's ventilation problems had grown so critical that the union miners filed a complaint with the United Mine Workers of America Safety Department in Washington D.C. By 1 p.m., the mine was swarming with union officials and state and federal inspectors. They stayed for three days.[1]

What the inspectors found easily could have caused a massive explosion. Methane measured from 1.8 percent to 3 percent in some of the bleeders. Highly explosive levels of methane between 8 percent and 10 percent were found in six crosscuts, extending from the bleeders to the gobs. One spark could have killed everyone in the mine.

The federal report indicates that the company had planned to clear the methane on Saturday, but had to repair the fans that day. The records do not show whether the mine's fans were broken or how long ventilation had been compromised. A fan problem, however, would explain the methane buildup and the men's refusal to work underground.

The report shows that the company began clearing the gas on Sunday and that by Monday federal inspectors closed their inspection even though methane measuring 2.25 percent and 3.5 percent still lingered in two crosscuts. The federal inspectors left this recommendation: "Precautions should be taken to keep the accessible edges of caved and pillared areas in and adjacent to bleeder entries reasonably free of gas."

The federal law required the company to ventilate or seal its gobs, but federal inspectors had little power to enforce that law. They could make recommendations, or they could declare miners were in imminent danger and order them out of the mine. To do that, however, they had to be prepared to face the wrath of high-ranking coal company officials.

State inspectors had more power, but available records show they visited the No.9 only once in 1956. At that time, an inspector noted that the mine's 4North ventilation was not up to standard. No records could be found that indicated the state had inspected the mine in 1957, and only one inspection is on file for 1958.

More Ways to Die

Ventilation always has been a key component of safe mining. That fact did not change when mechanization made coal mining faster and more efficient. By the 1950s, fewer men were needed underground, but they faced new dangers from new technologies.

Open-flame cap lamps became obsolete, and miners wore sealed electric cap lamps powered by batteries. Black blasting powder was replaced with stick explosives that had been tested by the federal government. Smoking was outlawed underground, but in practice not totally eliminated.

New equipment allowed coal companies to boost their production, but the mechanical mining machines and the electricity that powered them introduced hundreds of hazards. Openings on electric machinery had to be in "permissible" condition, which meant air-tight and dust-tight. For instance, a loose headlight or a missing bolt from an engine casing could leave just enough room for an electrical arc or a spark to escape and ignite a pocket of methane or coal dust. At the working faces, the big metal teeth on mining machines created extra dust. They also caused sparks when they hit veins of sulfur or sandstone, which could set off a methane or a coal dust explosion.

Frictional sparking could come from drills used to bore into stumps being prepared for explosives. Sparking also could come from the moving parts on conveyor belts. Sparks could jump from the electric trolley lines

A coal miner operates a continuous mining machine manufactured by the Joy Mining Machinery Company in an unidentified Consolidation Coal Company underground mine. Source: West Virginia and Regional History Collection, West Virginia University Libraries.

that powered the locomotives—also called motors—that moved the coal trains through the mine.

Dangerous, too, were the long trailing cables that carried high-voltage electricity to the machinery. These cables often took a beating as miners hauled them by hand from place to place or as the cables fell beneath the wheels of the machinery. Bare cable wires sometimes went unnoticed. Even when miners saw them, they did not always splice them together properly. Sometimes, cables were spliced so many times they were no longer safe.

In 1964, federal inspectors cited the No.9 for numerous electrical violations, including trailing cables with six and seven temporary splices.[2] In the summer of 1965, a federal inspector found at least five splices in trailing cables on five different pieces of equipment.[3] In December the same year, an inspector found five shuttle cars and five loading machines with numerous problems, including six to nine temporary splices on five trailing cables.[4]

Electrical violations were serious. They could cause injury and death by electrocution and, of course, ignite coal dust or methane. Between 1959 and 1967, electrical arcs caused ignitions that killed 157 U.S. miners and injured another 83.[5]

A 1965 Explosion

A frayed wire or a spark from a dropped tool was blamed for a No.9 blast that killed four people in 1965.[6] It was the last day of April. The company was completing work on the 577-foot-deep Llewellyn airshaft to better ventilate the west side of the mine. Employees from the R.G. Johnson Company from Pennsylvania were standing on a scaffold 230-feet inside the shaft, painting the steel inserts in concrete walls. A spark hit a pocket of methane gas and set off a violent explosion.

Chester Hildreth, Glenn Curfman, Robert Digman and Donald Mickel might as well have been in the barrel of a shotgun. The blast propelled them up and out of the shaft. Their mangled bodies were scattered like buckshot. One man and parts of the scaffold were found 75 feet from the shaft, lying in the waters of Llewellyn Run.

Mercifully, all four men died instantly.

Curfman had survived World War II and the Korean War. He was 42 and had a wife and four boys. Digman and Mickel, who were in their 30s, also had survived the Korean War. Mickel left behind a son. Hildreth, 30, was supporting a wife and three children.[7]

Two other men escaped the blast that day by climbing through a small doorway that led to a water ring, an area that trapped water as it leaked into the shaft. The men were working about 50 feet below the four who died. After the explosion, workers outside the mine hoisted the two miners out in a bucket, which was attached to a derrick on the surface. One man was hospitalized; the other was not injured.[8]

Records do not indicate how the shaft was ventilated.

A Beautiful Mine

Consol invested a lot of money in the No.9. Its underground rails were straight and easy to travel and its equipment modern. Some miners thought it was the most beautiful mine in the state. Bill Bunner was one of them. "They had the biggest motors in West Virginia. Westinghouse, big Westinghouse motors, but they lacked air," he said.[1]

Bunner worked in the No.9 mine twice. In the 1950s, he was assigned to the cateye shift. He was lucky he was not at the mine the Saturday it exploded in 1954. However, that disaster left him and hundreds of other miners without jobs. "The federal government would give out butter and flour, and I don't know what all for Christmas," Bunner said. But there was no money coming in, so he took a job in Cleveland making car axles.[2]

When the mine reopened in 1955, the company asked him to come back. He knew he was facing a three-month layoff in Cleveland, so he returned to West Virginia and helped bring the bodies out of the mine. He stayed on and completed the training to be a foreman and a fireboss. The promotion meant leaving the UMW but earning more money as a salaried employee. The new position also gave him additional responsibility over conditions in the mine.

As a fireboss, Bunner was trained to examine the mine for methane using a flame safety lamp instead of the legendary canary. If he ran into methane, the flame would climb, and he would adjust the ventilation to clear the gas.

A coal miner uses a flame safety lamp to check for methane in an underground mine. A flame grows in the lamp in the presence of methane. Courtesy of John Brock.

In the 1950s and 1960s, West Virginia and federal laws required coal companies to thoroughly check their mines for methane and other dangers each day at least four hours before sending their first shift of miners underground. Firebosses and section foremen were supposed to check all active working areas, examining the face, the rib and the roof. They were supposed to check for methane on every active roadway and travelway, around roof falls, sealed areas and gobs. They also had to make sure enough air was reaching the right places and the mine was free of other dangers.

When Bill Bunner firebossed, he said he often found gas in the No.9. When that happened, he let the dispatcher know mining would have to be delayed until he adjusted the ventilation. Sometimes, however, before he could clear the gas, his bosses would arrive and the push to produce would begin.

"Well, they were getting pressure from headquarters because we weren't mining coal," Bunner said. "They always wanted you to get started. If you started at least you had a little bit of coal you could mine."[3]

But keeping ahead of the gas took time. When miners moved forward, they had to stop and check for gas. Often they had to hang brattice cloth and make other adjustments in the ventilation, which slowed production.

"You know if you get five cars, you get five cars. If you got ten, you're lucky. You're talking about 20-ton mine cars at that time," he said. "It was hard to mine coal because of the methane and the bleeders. . . . [Miners] really didn't check their bleeders very good."[4]

Bunner had little faith in federal inspectors who had almost no enforcement powers or in the state inspectors who rarely used their power. "We had no state, no federal, and we had the boss telling us we need more coal. So what do you do? You do what you can do," Bunner said.[5] You mine coal.

The pressure to produce and the deteriorating conditions in the mine began taking a toll on Bunner. His arms were breaking out in hives, and he had developed ulcers. His doctor told him he had to quit worrying or he would have to have surgery. "How do you keep from worrying when you're in that condition?" he asked.

Then one Saturday, while firebossing the mine, he found gas on two sections. It made him think about his life and his work. "If I'm finding gas and something happens, it's gonna catch me," he told himself. "I've had enough of it."[6]

In 1965, he told his boss he wanted out of the No.9. The company transferred Bunner to its Williams Mine and made him a shift foreman, which gave him more control over safety.

New Owners

The No.9 changed ownership again in 1966, when Continental Oil purchased Consolidation Coal during an era of mergers between oil and coal companies. Continental Oil did not change the company's name, and most people referred to it simply as "Consol."

Continental Oil executives wanted greater production. Demands from the top moved down the line through Consol's executives, who increasingly pressured the managers at Consol's Mountaineer Coal Division. They, in turn, leaned on the managers at No.9 and several other mines in northern West Virginia.

In 1967 and 1968, the management team behind the No.9 had the following tiers:[7]

Consol's corporate managers in Pittsburgh included:
- John Corcoran, president
- William N. Poundstone, executive vice president, Consolidation Coal Company
- C. R. Nailler, vice president of operations, Consolidation Coal Company
- C. William Parisi, chief inspector

Located near the No.9 mine in Marion County, Consol's Mountaineer Coal Division managers included:
- D. H. Davis, president
- Kenneth K. Kincell, manager of mines
- Eugene Lieving, safety director
- Jess G. Bowers, safety inspector

No.9 mine's onsite managers were:
- Lawrence "Lockie" Riggs, general superintendent
- Foster Turner, superintendent
- Fay Casseday, general mine foreman
- Cecil Selders, chief maintenance supervisor

No.9 also had several company section bosses who oversaw the UMW miners on each section and each shift. The UMW miners had a safety committee, but its power was limited. The committee members could take complaints to No.9's managers, but issues were not always resolved. By law, one safety committee member was allowed to accompany the federal inspectors inside the mine. However, that law was not followed at the No.9. Federal inspection records show that in 1967 and 1968 no safety committee member traveled with federal inspectors on any of their four inspections.

Stanley Plachta, who was on the safety committee, said he was not in the mine long before he realized Consol "didn't push very hard for safety." He soon learned that production was the number one priority. This was evident every day at about 4:15 p.m., when a Mountaineer manager called the mine for the daily coal report. If the report was not good, Foster Turner and Lockie Riggs would argue about who would answer the phone.[8] "I guess if the coal report wasn't too great, they caught a lot of heck," Plachta said.[9]

If the numbers were bad, the company foremen were upbraided. Section foreman Pete Sehewchuk said Foster Turner criticized him one morning for bringing out only 14 cars of coal instead of the 35 or more cars that could be mined if conditions were optimal. Sehewchuk told Turner he and his crew had encountered methane gas that had to be cleared. Then Turner accused him of using gas as a crutch, an excuse for his low production.

"I kind of blowed my stack, and I said, 'Well, if that's the way you feel about it, you can go ahead and fire me,'" Sehewchuk said. Then he threatened to take his complaints to the company's Pittsburgh office, where he believed top management cared about safety. After that incident, Sehewchuk was never criticized again.[10]

"I told my wife at the time, I said, 'That mine is going to blow up.' I just had that feeling that something was going to happen."[11]

Methane Madness

After a long downturn following World War II, coal was back in demand in 1968.[1] Some of the industry's biggest customers were public utilities that were stoking their plants with coal to produce electricity for homes and new businesses. Annual U.S. bituminous coal production reached 542 million tons, with 342 million tons coming from underground mines.[2] Consol was the second largest coal producer in the United States; its mines yielding almost 50 million tons of coal a year. The No.9 accounted for almost 2 million tons of that total.[3]

In Marion County, West Virginia, coal mining and manufacturing created most of the income for some 60,000 people.[4] Mechanization had changed the industry, but Consol's No.9 mine still was sending 320 men underground each day. They were bringing out about 10,000 tons of coal each day, almost twice as much coal as 380 men did in 1954.[5]

The mine was much larger, too. Its tunnels ran beneath the 22 square miles between two small mining communities—Mannington and Farmington. Most No.9 miners lived in and around the two towns or in nearby Fairview, Rachel, Worthington, Barrackville, Owings, Shinnston or Fairmont, the county seat.

Some miners were skilled and semiskilled union men, who grossed between $28 and $33 a day (adjusted for 2009 dollars, up to about $200 a day). Their salaried nonunion bosses earned more.[6] Some union miners, particularly those with large families, struggled to meet their financial obligations. In general, coal miners lived relatively quiet lives in the wooded folds of the Appalachian Mountains. They worked hard, went to church on Sundays, hunted, fished and spent time with their families. The turmoil in the outside world came to them mainly by way of newspaper headlines or television and radio newscasts.

The Civil Rights Movement touched little of the population, which was 96 percent white. However, "placard-carrying Negroes" did picket Hartley's

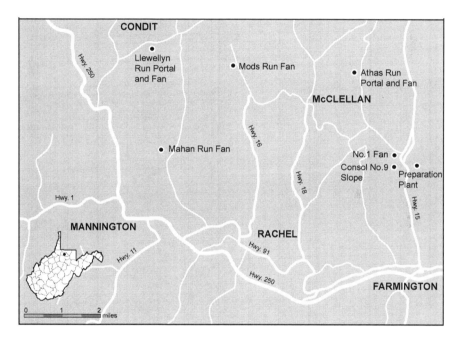

Central Marion County, West Virginia. Map by Rachel Davis.

downtown Fairmont department store one day in 1969. The police gave them one minute to stop the noise or keep moving. The chanting stopped immediately.[7]

The Vietnam War, however, was continuously front-page news. Some 1,400 Marion County residents served in Vietnam, and 28 of them lost their lives fighting the Viet Cong in the jungles of Southeast Asia.[8] Still, the greatest and most constant threat to the rhythm of the Appalachian community was the mountain, should it turn against the men who entered it to take away the coal..

A Gassy Mine

Methane gas was becoming more and more of a problem as No.9 miners pushed deeper into the mountain along the Main West Headings and into 7South. The mine was liberating about 8 million cubic feet of methane every 24 hours, more than double its 1954 rate of 3 million cubic feet.[9] Even when the mine had adequate ventilation, the men had to check for methane frequently. In West Virginia, the law required all men operating continuous mining machines at the working faces to check for methane every 20 minutes. Testimony taken after the 1968 disaster indicated that some No.9 miners were not checking often enough.

Dan Thomas, who ran a mining machine in A-Face, said he stopped to check for gas about seven times during an eight-hour afternoon shift.[10] Joseph Duda, a mining machine operator who had been working in the No.9 for 26 years, said he checked for gas about every 30 minutes—sometimes more often and sometimes less often, depending on how the shuttle cars were running.

"Do you know what the law is on gas examination?" an investigator asked him.

"Well it's about—no I don't really—I don't to be truthful about it," Duda said.[11]

New Monitors

Two of the No.9's mining machines were equipped with methane monitors, which were relatively new at the time. The coal miners liked them, but said they did not rely on them, which was fortunate. The monitors could have been calibrated to detect methane when it reached 1 percent, the point at which West Virginia law required miners to shut off their power and contact a mine foreman. But the company did not calibrate the devices to meet

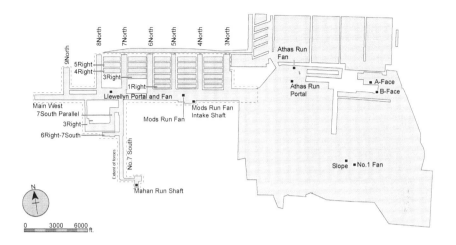

By 1968, Consolidation No. 9 had grown to 22 square miles of tunnels running between Mannington and Farmington with 320 miners bringing out approximately 10,000 tons of coal each day. Map by Rachel Davis.

that sensitivity level. Instead, the monitors were set to detect methane at 2 percent, which allowed miners to continue to produce coal as methane built up in their sections.

Fan Failures

To flush methane from the mine, the No.9 used four large surface fans: the No.1 fan at the slope, the Athas Run fan near 2North, the Mods Run near 4North and the Llewellyn fan near 7South. To better ventilate the ever-expanding mine, the company also had sunk the new 513-foot deep Mahan Run air shaft at the far end of 7South. Although it had no fan, it brought in fresh air.

By law, all of the fans had to run 24 hours a day, seven days a week, unless the state gave the company a permit to shut one down. Each fan had to be visually inspected by a person at least once a day. If a fan stopped and ventilation could not be restored within 15 minutes, all the mine's power had to be shut off, and all the men had to be withdrawn from affected areas and/or from the mine. This practice was the law.

As a safety measure, Consol and many coal companies had fitted their fans with FEMCO brand safety systems. At the No.9, the FEMCO system on each fan was connected to a display board in the lamphouse. If a fan was running, its light on the display board was green; if a fan slowed or stopped, a red light came on and an alarm sounded.[12] The miners in the lamphouse would then contact the men underground. If a fan was down more than 12 minutes, the system was designed to cut off all the power in the mine, which would be another signal to the miners to come to the surface.[13]

Unfortunately, neither safety feature was reliable. Many times a fan would stall or stop, but the power did not shut off automatically, and the men kept working. Often, the men underground were the first to notice that fresh air was not moving in their sections. When that happened, they then had to notify the men on the surface that a fan was down. Sometimes when the system malfunctioned, setting off false alarms, managers deliberately circumvented the safety alarms altogether.[14]

Walter Slovekosky alerted a boss to a ventilation problem in the months prior to the 1968 explosion. A motorman, he was one of two men who drove the locomotives that pulled and pushed the coal cars through the mine. If the cars were full, they were called a "trip of coal." If they were empty, a "trip of empties." One locomotive pulled the trip and the other, attached to the end of the cars, pushed. One day, Slovekosky became concerned as he watched rock-dusters filling their tank cars.

"I noticed that dust was just laying in there and wasn't moving, so I hollered at Lester and asked if the fan was down and he said, 'Don't know, I'll check in a minute.' So he hollered at Albert Tackas [a shift foreman] and Albert immediately went to Llewellyn . . . and that took a considerable amount of time."[15]

The Llewellyn fan was down. The miners on the surface tried but could not get it started, and so someone decided to call the men out of the mine. How long that action took is hard to say, but the power in the mine did not shut down automatically. As the section foremen were notified, they pulled the power on their sections, gathered their men and together they walked

The No.1 fan shaft (large circular figure) sat next to No.9's preparation plant, where the coal was cleaned and loaded for shipping. Courtesy of James Matish.

out of the mine. Nobody, however, had been able to contact the men who were still mining coal in 7South. They were at the working face, far from the communication system. "You can't get them on the telephone. The telephones are down at the dinner hole and the loading point, and there's just no way to notify them that the fans are down," Slovekosky said.[16]

Finally, according to Slovekosky, a shift foreman had to send a mechanic to 7South to tell the men to cut their power and come out. He estimated it took at least another 45 minutes to alert the miners.[17] "It wasn't because the shift foreman wanted them to work, he certainly to God didn't, but he didn't have any way of getting word to them to get out of there," he said.[18]

Coming out of the mine took even more time, because the men on 7South had to walk in darkness to the Llewellyn Run portal, which was about a mile and a half away, and a mine's floor does not make for easy walking.

That was not the first time Slovekosky and other miners had to walk out of the mine. Loading machine operator Layman Hall said a fan was down for 35 minutes before his crew on 5Right-8North was called out of the mine. The power on the section did not shut down automatically, either. The men had to pull the power as they left the section and walk out of the mine.[19]

The company had experienced problems with both the Llewellyn Run fan and the Mods Run fan, Slovekosky and others said. Records show that the Mods Run fan broke down on February 18, 1968, but the FEMCO alarm system did not shut off the power in the mine. In fact, most of the men did not know a fan was down, and they continued to work.[20]

At the time, Dana E. Harris Sr. was operating a shuttle car. When he was finally notified that a fan was down, he did what he was trained to do. He pulled the power on his buggy, gathered his coat and lunch bucket and started to leave his section. "We can't go off and leave that miner in there," his foreman said.

Harris reminded him the fan was down.

"Ain't nobody going to smother to death in here," the foreman said.

"No, I ain't worrying about smothering to death in here," Harris said. He was worried about methane.[21]

Following orders, he put his power back on and worked another hour and a half. He moved two or three more loads of coal, cleaned up the area, and moved all the machinery around. When he and the other miners came out, they contacted their safety committee and refused to go back into the mine until a state inspector deemed it safe.

State inspector Walter Miller, who had been examining the mine that week, noted in his report that the Mods Run fan had been shut down with a "mechanical defect," so the Llewellyn fan was adjusted. Miller approved the ventilation change and the mine resumed production even though the loss of the Mods Run fan left the mine with 22 percent less air.[22]

When Harris reported back for work the next afternoon, he saw that the fan alarm monitoring panel at the Llewellyn portal showed two fans were down. He began to question Foster Turner and Kenny Kincell.

"No, there's just one down," Turner said.

"There is two not a showing on that monitor there," Harris said.

"Oh, that one is just blocked out," Turner said.[23]

Harris retired the next month.

Overload Protection

Other safety devices were deliberately "blocked out" for the sake of increasing coal production. A federal inspector cited the No.9 in April 1968 for using blocks of wood to disable the electrical overload protection reset switch on two shuttle cars.[24] Two months later, state inspectors found the overload protection reset switches disabled on three shuttle cars,[25] and in October, state inspectors again found the reset switches blocked on two shuttle cars.[26] Blocking out the switch allowed the miners to transport larger loads of coal, but it also made it easier for the shuttle cars' motors and their electric cables to overheat. In short, the practice created a fire hazard, which could lead to an explosion if methane or coal dust was present.

Before he retired, Dana E. Harris complained to Foster Turner about a shuttle car, also called a "buggy," that he was supposed to operate one night. It had bad seals on its electrical parts, no fire extinguisher, no lights, no brakes and the overload protection reset switch was blocked out with a piece of wood.

"I come out and I told Foster Turner, I said, 'Foster, I don't mind running a buggy with one violation on it and probably would run it with two, but five is just plum ridiculous.' He (Turner) said, 'It's the buggyman's fault.' He said, 'If he would park it, they would fix it.'"

Harris parked the shuttle car. However, the shuttle car operator on the next shift came in, got on the buggy and ran it. "This machinery at No.9 has got to blow up and it has got to cause fires when it's treated like that," Harris said.[27]

A compressor did catch fire about four months before the mine exploded, and Robert Bland's boss told him to get out of the mine. "We knew something was the matter because the dispatcher at the time was hollering for Albert Tackas," said Bland, who worked on the slope bottom. Tackas was a foreman.

Bland did not go back into the mine on that shift.[28]

Gas on the Gobs

Another fire hazard and a serious source of methane came from the No.9's gobs. Mined out areas often heat up inside, and gobs often set themselves on fire. One study found that between 1952 and 1969, 65 of the 877 underground mine fires were caused by spontaneous combustion of gob areas.[29]

In 1968, the No.9 had massive gobs on both the east and west side of the mine. On the west side, where most of the men were working, gobs had been left from mining out 3North, 4North, 5North, 6North and parts of 7North and 8North. No.9 managers, who chose to ventilate their gobs instead of sealing them, created bleeder tunnels that stretched almost two miles along the top of those sections and 4,000 feet down the side of 8North to the Main West Headings. By law, bleeders had to have enough air coursing through them to dilute the gas and carry it out of the mine through the return air shafts.

In the fall of 1968, No.9's firebosses frequently found gas liberating at the working faces and from the gobs, but the fireboss record books do not indicate any gas accumulations. Sections liberating gas included 9North, 8North bleeder, Main West Headings, 7South, 6Right-7South, 7South Parallel's gob area and the A-Face bleeder. As fall turned to winter, the firebosses found gas most often on the Main West Headings, 9North and 7South.

Crosscuts and Stoppings

Firebosses and section foremen also were finding crosscuts that lacked permanent stoppings. As miners advanced their sections, they left open only the crosscuts necessary to move machinery and ventilate the working face. In the No.9, miners sometimes erected temporary stoppings by hanging brattice cloth, which was usually made of plastic. Sometimes they installed tin stoppings until concrete ones could be built. Temporary stoppings, however, usually allowed fresh intake air needed at the working face to leak into the return airways. Even permanent stoppings could leak, but they were superior to brattice cloth or tin. Having too many temporary stoppings or no stoppings could jeopardize the ventilation patterns in individual sections and could impact the mine's overall ventilation.

In the fall of 1968, the men constructing permanent stoppings could not keep pace with the mining. Day after day, in section after section, fireboss George Glover noted that crosscuts in the working sections needed permanent stoppings. From August 19 through November 19, 1968, in addition to his Sunday fireboss runs, Glover made at least 31 fireboss runs, often examining 9North, one of the newest and gassiest parts of the mine. On 11 days he found 9North's crosscuts needed permanent stoppings. On eight of those days, he detected gas in 9North. During that period, he saw missing stoppings a dozen times in 8North. On 11 runs, he detected gas in that section.[30]

In August 1968, a federal inspector spent 17 days in the No.9. On five of those days, Glover noted missing stoppings seven times in six different sections, but the federal inspector did not make a record of finding the problem or citing the company for a stoppings violation.[31]

Federal inspectors had been missing lots of problems in the No.9 and in other mines. Their own 1967 Coal Mine Inspectors' Manual chided them for shoddy work:

> "There has been some constructive criticism offered to the Bureau of Mines because of the apparent superficiality of coal mine inspection work on the part of our inspectors. There is, in fact, substantial evidence that at least some Federal coal mine inspectors spend a large portion of their time on trivialities and consequently fail to devote sufficient time and attention to the prevention of disasters and other serious accidents."[32]

State inspectors were not catching problems, either. Two state inspectors spent 13 days in the No.9 in October 1968 and did not cite the company for any stoppings violations even though on five of those days, Glover found missing stoppings 12 times in seven different sections.[33]

Despite Glover's reports and perhaps because mine inspectors never cited the company, mine managers apparently did not stop production to allow masonry workers to build stoppings as quickly as the sections advanced. Consequently, the danger in the mine continued to grow.

No.9's preparation plant operated near the No.1 fan and the slope by which some men entered the mine. Photo by Bob Campione.

Brothers Walk Out

In late September 1968, Arthur Eugene Cook took a job in the No.9, where both his brother and his father worked.

From the first night, he did not like what he heard or what he saw. He immediately became uncomfortable when he went to pick up his metal identification tag from Albert Tackas, an assistant mine foreman.

"Albert was in the bosses' quarters where they were all making out their daily reports, and I seen he was busy and started to leave and he said, 'No, Cook, just wait right here.'

"Now he jumped on those bosses and it embarrassed me. I started to leave again, and he stopped me and the exact words that he told them was that: 'Production is down. I don't give a damn how you get it, but you get it or else; I don't want no excuses,'" Cook said.[34]

Cook was a miner operator who worked the cateye shift. He floated from section to section, working wherever he was needed. On one shift, when he was driving deep into the coal seam, advancing his section, Cook found gas. He refused to continue mining until an auxiliary exhaust fan was provided. He was told it was broken, so he refused to mine until someone fixed it and brought it to the working face. He was not being unnecessarily cautious. The company's policy was to use an auxiliary fan when advancing a section because that was the when methane was most likely to leach from the coal.

On the Main West Headings, Cook watched another miner operator advance a section without an auxiliary fan. He said the foreman, Albert Tackas, watched but did not intercede. By then, Arthur Cook had seen enough. He lasted one month at the No.9. When he left, he convinced his brother to leave with him, and they took jobs in another mine. His father, who stayed at the No.9, asked him what he thought about the mine.

His son replied, "I don't see why they haven't blown that place up, driving with no air."[35]

Dry and Dusty

Year round, No.9 miners battled coal dust. It clogged machinery, and the finer dust, called "float dust," settled in the crosscuts and airways. Float dust was particularly dangerous if there was a fire or explosion in the mine. A layer of float dust the thickness of a sheet of paper lying on top of a mix of 80 percent rock dust and 20 percent coal dust can propagate mine explosions for days.[1]

Mining companies were supposed to neutralize their coal dust with rock dust. The mixture had to contain at least 65 percent rock dust, and in areas where methane was present, the percentage of rock dust was supposed to be even higher.[2]

In 1967, state inspectors surveyed the mine three times and each time cited the company for dangerous accumulations of coal and coal dust along the conveyor belts that carried coal through the mine. During a March inspection, federal officials found 500 feet of dangerous accumulations of fine coal and coal dust under a coal conveyor belt line in 5Right-6North. Another 50 feet of coal and dust had built up under the 1Right-5North conveyor belt. Inspectors also found more than a dozen areas in the mine that were not well rock dusted.[3]

In 1968, both state and federal inspectors cited the No.9 for coal dust violations:

- In February, a state inspector found "dangerous accumulations" of coal and coal dust along the belt conveyors in 4Right-7North, 5Right-7North and 2Right-6North.[4]

- In April, a federal inspector found nine areas that needed rock dust.[5]

- During June, July and August visits, a state inspector discovered "dangerous accumulations" of coal and dust along the 1Right-6North and 6Right-8North conveyor belts. Rock dust also was lacking in 5Right-8North and 9North.[6]

- In August, a federal inspector found inadequate rock dusting in four entries along the Main West headings.[7]

- During an October visit that ended just 19 days before the No.9 exploded, a state inspector cited the company for inadequate rock dusting in 6Right-7South and the 7South parallels. He found dangerous accumulations for 800 feet along a conveyor belt in 5Right-8North and found a load of coal piled on the ground in an entryway of 6Right-7South and loose coal along the ribs in 6North. He also cited the company for multiple fire hazards, including excessive accumulations of oil on a mining machine, numerous shuttle cars and other equipment. In his report, the inspector noted: "Cleanliness of equipment was thoroughly discussed at the close of this inspection with mine management."[8]

Sprayers were attached to some of the continuous miners in No.9 to keep the dust down at the working face. However, the water pressure was so poor on 7South that the sprayer on the mining machine could not take care of the dust, said Gary Martin, who worked cateye shift. At times, as Martin was loading coal behind the mining machine, the dust was so thick he could not see Lewis Lake, the man sitting on the mining machine.

Lake said when he first started working on 7South, he could work an entire shift using only one filter on the respirator he wore over his nose and mouth. In the weeks before the explosion, however, he had to change the filter two and three times every shift. Lake also had worked in 7North and 8North on the west side of the mine and on B-Face on the east side. "In my opinion, I don't think there was enough rock dust in any of the sections I

Coal miners used rubber-tired shuttle cars to carry the coal from the working face to rail cars that carried the coal to the slope bottom. Courtesy of John Brock.

worked on," Lake said.[9]

Before he left the No.9 in March 1968, Dana E. Harris had become concerned about many violations in the mine, including coal dust hazards. On one shift, he shut down a coal conveyor belt line because of the dust.

"Them carriers on them rollers and stuff; they were just filled up with dust, just all the dust that could set in them," Harris said. "They wasn't wet down, they wasn't washed down, there wasn't anything. . . . I just picked up the water hose and I turned the water on and I gave it a real good washing down. I wet everything. I washed it all off and you couldn't see. You couldn't see your light for the dust a flying from that water."

When he came out of the mine, he told general mine foreman, Fay Casseday, about the dust. "The first word he said, 'If it was that way down there, them bosses ain't a doing their job.' I wonder what he thought his job was. He was in charge over them bosses," Harris said.[10]

About a week before the No.9 exploded, Ancle B. Morris reported to

6Right-7South on his afternoon shift. He found so much dust on the conveyor belt, he had to shut it down. "There was dust all around the belt and it was piled up between the belt until the roller was just rolling around and grinding it up and it was so bad you couldn't see."[11]

He and three other men had to use their hands to claw the caked dust out from around the roller. It took them about 30 minutes to get the job done.

Keeping the belt area clean and running was only part of his job. As a mechanic, Morris had to repair and maintain the machinery on the section. He had to help the roof bolter who was injecting long metal pins into the roof. He had to help rock dust the section and keep the water sprayers running. "I have went to them at different times and I have told the boss and I have told the mine foreman that there was just more work than I could do, that I couldn't keep up," Morris said.

He said the company had a man who cleaned belt lines in different sections from time to time, but that was not enough to keep the section clean. Morris often lacked rock dust in his section, too, even though state law required the company to keep 500 pounds of rock dust at each active working section and at several other places in the mine, including near each conveyor belt. "I have seen it where there wasn't a sack of rock dust down on the section and I'd get on the jeep and go clear out to the mouth and maybe pick up some rock dust along the main line or somewhere," Morris said. He had worked underground for 30 years and at the No.9 since 1956.

Morris said he reported numerous serious problems to both the safety committee and Foster Turner, but little changed. The week before the mine exploded, he reached his limit. He found a trailing cable on a shuttle car in 6Right-7South riddled with splices. "I counted 24 splices in the cable and I didn't have all the cable pulled off it. I counted 24 splices and I quit."[12]

Warning Signs

No.9 miners were working in extremely dangerous conditions in the weeks and days before the mine exploded. Many of them knew it; some sought help from their managers, from the union and even from state mining officials. Nonetheless, safety issues were not resolved, and everything—even the weather—was working against them. A fairly clear picture of the underground conditions before the mine exploded emerges from the testimony taken during the investigation, interviews with No.9 miners, court documents, three No.9 fireboss record books and U.S. Weather Bureau data collected in Morgantown, which was 17 miles from the mine.

Saturday, November 16

The Saturday before the mine exploded, workers completed the connection between 7South and the new Mahan Run air shaft, which was delivering fresh air to the mine but not exhausting tainted air. The fresh air from all of the mine's shafts was dry because the area had received very little precipitation that month. In short, the winter weather was drying out the mine.

Motorman Walter Slovekosky began worrying about coal dust that Saturday. He and Lester Willard were doing some hauling through the mine and additional work on 9North. Slovekosky, who was a certified fireboss, said some of the crosscuts were black with coal dust. "When you're on that motor, you're always looking and observing or I always do anyhow, because it's my safety I'm looking after, and I'm always looking and observing and usually the first one that does any hollering too . . . some things just absolutely didn't look right to me."[1]

He decided to complain.

Sunday, November 17

Walter Slovekosky spoke up at a local UMW meeting on Sunday. "My main complaint was that every time we go up the hill with a trip of coal there is so much dust blows off that trip and not all of it accumulates on the main line; a lot of it accumulates in the crosscuts and in the other headings," he said.[2]

He felt so strongly about the dust issue that he tried to make a formal motion so a vote would be taken to ensure his complaints reached top management. He was told that a vote would not be necessary. He had complained before, too, about thick clouds of dust that had been stirred up when the motormen pulled a trip of coal cars out of 6North, 7North and 8North. "You couldn't hardly see at all," he said.[3]

The two men who firebossed the mine that evening documented dust problems, too. When they left the mine at 11:45 p.m., they wrote that all the shuttle car roadways needed to be wetted down to eliminate dust.[4]

The dry air was not the only weather issue. The barometric pressure had begun dropping on Thursday, November 14, as a cold front moved toward the area.[5] Because such drops cause methane gas to expand, it is not surprising that the two firebosses found gas liberating in 9North and in the Main West Headings. They also noted 6Right-7South needed four stoppings and 4Right-8North and 9North needed stoppings. Regardless, when the firebosses left the mine, they indicated in their report that the sections they checked were "safe."[6]

Monday, November 18

When the cateye shift entered the No.9 on Monday, the temperature outside was 59 degrees Fahrenheit. The wind, gusting up to 23 miles per hour, was bringing the cold front closer to Farmington.[7] As the cateye

Two coal miners man a locomotive used to pull trips of coal through the No.9 mine. Date unknown. Source: West Virginia and Regional History Collection, West Virginia University Libraries.

shift left and the day shift went underground at 8 a.m., the barometric pressure had dropped significantly, making coal dust and methane even greater problems than usual.[8] Company managers should have been well aware of the weather changes; their offices, which were in nearby Monongah, were equipped with barometers. When the day shift ended at 4 p.m., the temperature had dropped about 15 degrees and continued to drop throughout the shift.[9]

Fireboss George Glover began checking parts of the mine at 4:30 p.m. When he left the mine at 11:45 p.m., he reported finding gas liberating off the gob into the 8North return airway. He also noted crosscuts without permanent stoppings in 9North and 4Right-8North. Furthermore, his report shows that the 7South Parallel's belt drive and coal dumping area needed to be cleaned.[10]

Section foreman Paul Watson began his fireboss run of 6North at 11 p.m. His section needed stoppings.[11] When he left the mine at midnight, the outside temperature had dropped to 35 degrees Fahrenheit, the barometric pressure was still low and the wind was blowing.[12]

Tuesday, November 19

Cateye Shift. The cold front kept outside temperatures in the thirties and the barometric pressure low as the cateye crew went underground.[13] Some miners struggled to keep the gas at bay. The 7South crew mined only a few cars of coal before they were gassed out. When they first found gas, section foreman George Wilson pulled the power, sent his men to the dinner hole and called the shift foreman, Albert Tackas. The section was lacking permanent stoppings on four crosscuts, so Tackas called for concrete blocks. Masonry men began building stoppings as others tightened brattice cloth. Tackas also helped Wilson bring more air into the section by opening a regulator, or large ventilation door, which could have interfered with the functioning of the fans or compromised the airflow in another section. It took the men several hours to clear the gas.[14]

On 9North, section foreman Emilio Megna began a fireboss run at about 6:30 a.m., and he left the mine at 8:06 a.m. He noted 9North was liberating gas, but he had found no accumulations. He also reported that 4Right-8North needed stoppings.[15]

Day Shift. A roof fall covered part of the mining machine on 5Right-8North during the 8 a.m. to 4 p.m. shift, and some of the men began trying to free it. Loading machine operator Laymond Hall, who was on that crew, was sent to work on 4Right-8North, where he began checking the mining machine's trailing cable. He did not like what he found. The first joint of the cable had six splices and bare wires. "We're going to tape those splices before I handle that cable," he told his foreman. Hall was particular about trailing cables because No.9 miners were moving them around while they were energized. Twice, electrical shocks had knocked Hall to the ground when he had handled damaged cables. During the shift, Hall also repaired the auxiliary fan tubing that helped ventilate the working face. "We had about 18 tubes and out of 18 tubes, there was only about six good tubes; the rest of them was full of holes," he said. He and another miner used brattice cloth and rock dust bags to repair the holes.[16]

As the shift ended, the section foremen firebossed their areas and found stoppings were missing on crosscuts in 4Right-8North, 6North, 9North, 6Right-7South and the Main West Headings.[17]

At some point during the day, Stanley Plachta, who was on the mine's safety committee, became so worried about conditions in the No.9 that he decided to call the West Virginia Department of Mines. He was discouraged by the way the company handled the safety committee's complaints. Supervisors would write down safety issues, but do little, if anything, to correct them.[18] A union mechanic, Plachta had firsthand knowledge of the conditions underground because he traveled throughout the mine to fix equipment. He wanted a state inspector to take dust samples on sections he believed did not have enough rock dust. Plachta called Leslie Ryan, the state's top inspector, but Ryan was not in that day. His secretary took the call.[19]

Afternoon Shift. When the 4 p.m. to midnight shift entered the mine, the wind had picked up and was gusting at around 20 miles per hour.[20] There were problems in the mine.

In 6Right-7South, a piece of machinery broke down about midway through the shift, and the crew moved to 6North.

Gas stopped production twice in the far end of the mine, where section foreman Pete Sehewchuk and his crew were breaking off 10North, a new section along the Main West Headings. Sehewchuk called that area the "gas box." He wanted a transfer from the section, but his bosses would not change his assignment.[21]

On the haulage route, at about 9:30 p.m., motorman Robert Cook noticed something strange about the ventilation. The temperature outside was below freezing, but the air around an airshaft was not cold. The airshaft should have been drawing the frigid winter air into the mine.

"Did you notice that there was some kind of change?" he asked his buddy.

"It's either raining outside or else I'm running a fever because I am warm," Cook said.[22]

When an intake shaft stops bringing in fresh air, the change often indicates an interruption in the mine's ventilation pattern. A stalled or stopped fan can cause the air to reverse. The variance also could have resulted from a ventilation change in another part of the mine.

Another factor could have been the unusually high gusting winds, which could have affected the air moving into the mine shafts, altering the ventilation pattern and creating a push-pull effect. That effect, in turn, could have weakened or broken a mined-out area's seal, allowing methane to seep out. Such a change also can pull more methane out of the coal or off the gobs.[23]

As the afternoon shift neared its end, the section foremen began their fireboss runs. Pete Sehewchuk said that 10North was liberating gas, but he had found no dangerous accumulations. He noted that crosscuts needed stoppings.

Other fireboss reports showed that 4Right-8North and 7South crosscuts needed stoppings, and that the 7South crew had found gas and stopped to remove it. Still, the reports showed the section was safe.[24] Contract fireboss, George Glover, covered part of the mine. He found gas liberating in the return airways of 7South and 6Right-7South. Crosscuts stoppings were missing in 6Right-7South and in 1Right-6North. He noted no excess dust and no need for rock dust in the areas he had checked. At 11:15 p.m., he deemed the sections he examined to be "safe." He entered his finding into two fireboss books: the "Sections Only" book and the "Abandoned Areas" book, indicating that he had checked individual sections and gobs and airways.[25]

When the shift ended, the mining machine on 5Right-8North still was caught under rock. Paul Watson, an assistant mine foreman, said his crew had hand-loaded and shoveled two shuttle cars of rock off the miner. Watson said he stayed on his section until two men from the cateye crew arrived.[26]

The section foremen's fireboss book included a strange entry—an incomplete report for 9North.[27] The page shows that section foreman Joseph McNece called out a report. An oncoming section foreman for 7South, George Wilson, took the call. But most of the form was empty, including the lines that asked important questions:

- Did you detect gas?
- Did you remove gas?
- Did you find any crosscuts needing stoppings? Where?
- What parts of the mine are dusty?
- Did you examine any abandoned workings?
- Is line brattice erected up to the face of all gaseous places?

Even though none of these questions was answered, Wilson wrote "Reported Safe" at the bottom of the 9North fireboss page. The law required that McNece sign the written report when he left the mine and that another mine manager countersign it. The form contained neither signature. Emilio Megna, the oncoming cateye shift foreman for 9North, did sign the nearly blank page, indicating he had read the report. It would be the last time Megna entered the mine.

The Last Shift

....

When 99 men on No.9's cateye crew headed underground Wednesday, November 20, 1968, the outside temperature was below freezing, the humidity level and the barometric pressure were still low, and the wind had not stopped blowing.[1]

That morning, three of the regular section foremen were absent, and the company had replaced them with contract foremen. Most of the men were laboring on the mine's west side. One crew was mining coal on the east side at A-Face. Two teams of motormen were pulling trips of coal cars over the rail system from the west side to the east side, unloading the full cars at the bottom of the slope, then returning the empty cars to the working sections to be filled again.

As the men worked, their families slept.

9North. A mining machine was down on 9North with a faulty hydraulic hose. At some point, Emilio Megna's crew, who normally worked that section, was sent to 6Right-7South. Two mechanics, Edward A. Williams and Jack D. Michael, probably were in 9North repairing the machine.

Slope Bottom. By 3 a.m., the winds were gusting at about 20 miles per hour.[2] Soon, mainline motormen Walter Slovekosky and his buddy Nathaniel "Smokey" Stephens arrived at the slope bottom with a trip of coal. When Slovekosky noticed that the power was weak on the slope bottom, he reported the problem to the dispatcher, Charles Moody, who was working in an underground office directing traffic on the rail system. The power problem was not unusual. Power substations on the surface kicked out two or three times a week.[3]

Moody reported the problem to Russell Foster, who was on duty in the lamphouse. Foster, in turn, called the coal company's go-to man, Alex Kovarich, who had shortened his last name to "Kovar." A mechanic, he lived near the mine and could be there quickly, day or night, to deal with mechanical or electrical problems.

Outside the Slope. When Alex Kovar arrived at the mine around 3:30 a.m., he found a circuit breaker was out at the power substation at the top of the slope. He put it back in and drove to the No.1 fan, also on the east side of the mine near the slope.

He found the No.1 fan running. While he was there he changed the fan chart, a paper record of the fan's operation that spanned a week. When a fan was running, a needle marked the circular chart with ink. If the fan stalled or stopped, the needle reacted, dropping down the paper to leave a telltale line.

After checking the fan, Kovar said he talked with a couple of miners who were eating dinner in the bath house, where the men cleaned up and changed clothes before they went home. Still on the east side of the mine, Kovar went to the repair shop and began working on a piece of machinery.[4]

Mods Run. Early that morning, a loud noise woke Samuel Stout, who lived in Mods Run, a hollow that sat above part of the No.9 mine. His gas lines shook, and his windows rattled.

"That pump house blowed up," his wife said.

The couple pumped water into their home with a gas-operated machine that was in a building outside their house. Mr. Stout had just lit the gas the previous evening. He got up and looked out his kitchen window, but did not see a fire.

"What time is it?" Mrs. Stout asked.

Mr. Stout looked at the kitchen clock. It was only 4 a.m., so he went back to bed.

A few minutes later, his wife began having trouble breathing. "Something's smothering me, smoke from someplace," she said.

Mr. Stout got up again and looked for fire. The pump house still looked fine.

"The fan is down," his wife said, referring to No.9's Mods Run ventilation fan that sat a few hundred yards from their home.

"Well, the motor has burned up on that fan and throwed them blades off it. That's what made that racket," Mr. Stout said.[5]

He spoke from experience. The Mods Run fan had thrown off its blades before, creating a serious ventilation problem for the west side of the mine.

Railway Around 5 a.m., the power was still on in the mine. Walter Slovekosky and Smokey Stephens, were running another trip of coal from the west side of the mine to the slope bottom. They had 31 cars between their two locomotives. On their way, they passed Lester Willard and Charlie Hardman, who were hauling a trip of empty coal cars. Slovekosky and Willard started joking around over their radios.

"I'm a silent partner," Willard said.

"That's what I wish my wife would do, you know," Slovekosky answered. The men always kidded and "acted a fool," Slovekosky said later.

Headed in opposite directions, the two crews ended their banter. Slovekosky then heard Hardman report his location to the dispatcher who told Hardman to cut off 20 empty cars and take them to 7South. That was the last time he heard their voices.

When Slovekosky and Stephens arrived at the slope bottom, Slovekosky signaled his buddy to back the coal cars up to a loading area. Just then, all the power went down. It was about 5:30 a.m.

The outage lasted only a few seconds. The power came back on and so did the radios. But no one from the west side of the mine responded to their calls.

They knew something was wrong.[6]

Mods Run. Not far from the Stouts' home, about a third of a mile from the Mods Run fan, Jewell Simons was sitting in her living room sipping her first cup of morning tea. Her habit was to get up when the alarm sounded at 5:30 a.m.[7] Suddenly, she thought she heard her storm door slam shut. She had placed a stop in front of the door to keep the grandchildren from walking into the glass. Someone must have moved it, she thought. Her husband, James, a foreman and electrician at another nearby mine, heard the noise, too. Because they were used to hearing planes fly over, he thought it was a jet breaking the sound barrier.[8]

East Side. Alex Kovar had been in his shop working for about an hour when he, too, thought he heard a jet breaking the sound barrier. Then he felt a tremble. The lights in the shop went off and then came back on. He thought a fan might be down. Instinctively, he got into his truck and drove to the slope to use the company phone.

He called the Llewellyn station, but no one answered. He thought the Llewellyn fan had stopped. He called again and again. Still no answer. Then he called the chief maintenance supervisor, Cecil Selders, who lived in Fairmont.[9]

Llewellyn Run Portal. At about 5:30 a.m., the lamphouse shook and ceiling lights began to fall. A deafening blast followed, and all the lights went out. Debris rained down on lampmen Russell Foster, Edgell Wilson and Joseph Garcia.

Foster dropped to the floor and crawled along the wall until he reached a staircase and scooted under it to protect himself. He waited a few minutes, then made his way to the lamp rack and began turning on the cap lamps and yelling for his buddy, Edgell Wilson. He got no answer. Foster thought Wilson might be dead, so he went outside and looked for his body in the rubble. Wilson was not there.

Foster went back to the lamphouse and found Garcia, dazed with his arms folded, standing at the door. The two picked up lamps and resumed the search for Wilson, who had been struck by a ceiling light and had run from the building.[10] When the search ended, Garcia found his friend about

800 feet from the building. Wilson would have been underground that morning had a roof bolt machine not jammed and broken his arm a few weeks earlier.[11]

Llewellyn Parking Lot. Isaac Ray Kuhn was driving up to the Llewellyn portal when he heard the mine explode. The lights in the parking lot went out; he knew there would be no power or telephone. He immediately threw his truck into reverse, turned around and drove to Darrell Toothman's house and called Lockie Riggs.

"I was looking right at the shaft when the explosion come out," he said. "And all I could see, I couldn't tell whether it was dust or smoke because the instant it come out all the power went off. All I could see was electrical arcs and I didn't see any fire come out of the shaft at that time."[12]

His only light was coming from his headlights.

After he called Riggs, Kuhn drove back to Llewellyn Run to direct traffic away from the portal.

Lockie Riggs called Eugene Mauck, a Consolidation Coal official, who was shaving when the phone rang.[13] "Gene, we have got lots of troubles out at No.9," Riggs said.[14]

"Do you know what it is about?" Mauck asked.[15]

"I think you know as well as I do what it might be," Riggs answered.[16]

Mauck, who several times had been called in to solve ventilation problems at the No.9, jumped into his clothes and headed to the mine.

7South. Without warning, at about 5:30 a.m., the power went out in 7South on the mine's far southwest side. The youngest member of the crew, 24-year-old Paul Henderson Jr., was by himself near the dump, where coal was loaded into rail cars. Charles Crim, a masonry man, was laying cement blocks, making a permanent stopping in a crosscut.

Section foreman George Wilson and five other men were at the working face. Lewis Lake was on the mining machine, cutting coal. Ralph Starkey was operating the loading machine, dumping coal into the shuttle car, which was manned by Gary Martin. Nezer Vandergrift Jr. was sitting in another shuttle car.

The Consolidation No.9 Mine exploded on November 20, 1968, sending clouds of smoke into the winter air. Source: Larry Pierce and *The Charleston Gazette*.

Not far away, Bud Hillberry, who had been mortaring cement block stoppings, had stopped to talk to Alva Davis who was eating in the dinner hole. "Say, Bud, where are you going to go hunting on Monday?" Davis asked.[17]

There was no time to answer before the mine began to tremble, and the power went out. Davis felt the whoosh of the blast of air and watched as cement blocks blew past the dinner hole. His instincts kicked in, and he began gathering the self-rescuers.

The men at the working face barely had time to think before they realized they were in trouble. "What's wrong with the power?" Lewis Lake yelled from the continuous miner.

It might be a bad cable, he thought as he climbed down from the miner to check. He had taken only two or three steps before the force of the explosion swept over him. Full of dust and debris, the gust sounded like a strong wind that carries a fierce storm through the mountains. Blinded, Lake dropped to his stomach to find oxygen. But George Wilson yelled at him. "Lewis, get up out of there and let's get out of here because this is something we've never been in before."[18]

The dust was so thick that Gary Martin was lost the minute he stepped off his buggy. "What in the world is going on?" he thought as he pulled the hood of his sweatshirt over his face and sat down.[19]

Nezer Vandergrift tried to leave his shuttle car but gave up, knelt in the deck of the car and held onto the seat to brace himself against the fury.

Lake, Wilson and Ralph Starkey, the loading machine operator, crawled through the cloud of smoke and dust, moving along the miner and the loading machine until they reached Martin at his shuttle car. "We'll just follow my buggy cable back to the dinner hole," Martin told the men. He knew it was the only way they could travel without getting lost.[20]

Hand over hand, they moved along the cable. The men could not see, so they kept shouting at each other to make sure no one got lost. Along the way, they picked up Vandergrift, and together they made their way to the dinner hole.

There they found the other men on their crew, except for one man—young Paul Henderson.

Power Pull. After Alex Kovar called his boss, he went to the slope and started pulling switches. He pulled the oil switch in the little shanty. He pulled the AC power and the DC breaker. Then he drove to the Athas Run portal, another entrance to the mine, checked that fan and pulled switches there—oil switches, knife switches, all the switches. Then he went to Plum Run and pulled the power.

Next, he checked the Mods Run fan. The giant explosion doors at the end of the air shaft were open, and smoke was pouring out. The doors were designed to direct explosive forces away from the fan, which sat inside a building several feet from the shaft. "I didn't know what to do," he said. "I just backed the truck up and ran up to some people's house there, the Simons', and beat on the door."[21]

Mods Run. Jewell Simons was still drinking her tea when Alex Kovar knocked on her door. He asked to use the phone, as he had many times before. The Simons' rented their home from Mountaineer Coal Company, and, as part of their rental agreement, the Simons' gave the company's employees access to their phone.

This morning was different, though. Kovar was in a panic. He dialed a number incorrectly. He gave Jewell the phone, asked her to make the call and left. Jewell called the operator who put her through to Lockie Riggs.

"This is Jewell Simons, and there was a gentleman here at the house and he says there is some trouble at the mines and he asked me to get in touch with you and tell you that he was on his way to Llewellyn," she told Riggs. [22]

By then her husband, James, had looked out the back door and had seen smoke from the Mods Run fan shaft silhouetted against the dark sky. He put on his sweater, went down the road and got within about 100 feet of the shaft. The explosion doors were open, and smoke was pouring out. The fan was not running, and the lights at the fan house were not burning. It was not the first time James had known the fan to stop. It had been down other times, and at least once he had called the company to let them know about it.[23]

7 South. Like Marines, coal miners do not leave men behind. Ralph Starkey and Alva Davis left the dinner hole and went back to look for Paul Henderson. They searched the work area, but all they found was his dinner bucket. They feared he had run toward the Llewellyn portal at the point where they had entered the mine. It was the only functioning exit. Unfortunately, the explosion had come from that direction.

Hoping Henderson might find his way back to the section, the men scrawled a message in the dust on a coal car, telling him to come to the Mahan Run air shaft. Starkey and Davis had no choice but to return to the dinner hole. From there, the group of men started moving in darkness through the dust and smoke. Cold and frightened, they did not know where the blast had originated or if the mine would erupt again. With their self-rescuers in their mouths, they trudged about a quarter of a mile over rough terrain to reach what they knew was their only hope of survival—the Mahan Run air shaft. It had no elevator, but it had fresh air.

A-Face. At about 6 a.m., 30 minutes after the first explosion, one crew was still mining coal at A-Face on the east side of the mine. The men had no idea that, only a few miles away, the west side of the mine had exploded. A fan safety system should have cut all the power in the mine when the Mods Run fan threw off its blades. But the system had failed as it had failed before.

James Herron, A-Face section foreman, was checking for methane, using the light of his cap lamp to make his way through his section when the power flickered for a few seconds. Because he was not near any machinery, he did not notice the power dip. But his men did. They were not alarmed; power problems were common. They kept working.

When a belt that moved the coal broke down, Herron jumped into a jeep and headed to that part of the section. He saw the cap light of one of his men who was coming down the track. The miner hopped into Herron's jeep. Neither man had any idea the other side of the mine had become an inferno.[24]

Slope Bottom. When the west side of the mine blew up, Lewis Ray Parker was working at the bottom of the slope on the east side of the mine. He was dumping coal on the belt that carried it outside. Like everyone else at the bottom, he had no idea the mine had exploded. Also at the bottom of the slope, Smokey Stevens was unloading coal, and Walter Slovekosky was on a locomotive preparing to drive a trip of empty coal cars back to the west side of the mine.

At about 5:40 a.m., the slope bottom phone rang. The call was from Lockie Riggs who was still at home. He told Parker to contact Charlie Moody, the dispatcher. Parker got no response and called Riggs back. Riggs told him to try to contact someone, anyone, and get the men out of the mine. Parker knew the drill. He had been called out of the mine a few months earlier when a fan went down, and again when a compressor caught fire.

Parker told Slovekosky and Stevens to leave the mine. Stevens disconnected his locomotive from his trip of coal cars, taking time to secure it so it would not roll away. Parker, Stevens, Slovekosky and Robert Bland walked out of the mine, arriving on the surface at 6:15 a.m.[25]

Police Escort. After Lockie Riggs told Lewis Ray Parker to leave the mine, he called the county sheriff's department and asked for two radio cars. He followed one car out of Fairmont to the slope, where he found Lewis Ray Parker, Nathaniel Stevens, Walter Slovekosky and Robert Bland. The four men still had no idea what had happened on the west side of the mine. All phones appeared to be down, so Riggs began making calls from a patrol car's radio.[26]

7South at the Mahan Run Shaft. George Wilson's crew reached the Mahan Run air shaft at about 6:30 a.m. and began to yell through a metal pipe that led to the surface. When that seemed fruitless, they looked for something to use to hit the pipe. They knew using metal might create a spark, so they found a piece of wood and began pounding on the pipe, hoping to get someone's attention.

The air coming into the shaft had relieved enough pressure to save them from the blast's initial concussion, but it was not enough air to make the atmosphere safe to breathe. Too much carbon monoxide was coming from the mine. Some of the men began moving in and out of consciousness, making it hard to keep the self-rescuers in their mouths.

Gary Martin started to remove his self-rescuer, but Bud Hillberry looked at him, shook his head "no" and tapped on his self-rescuer. Martin knew Hillberry was a seasoned miner who had been on the rescue team when the No.9 blew up in 1954, so Martin left the self-rescuer in his mouth.[27]

Underground Motor Barn. At 6:30 a.m., Robert Mullins and Henry Conway were still working underground on the east side of the mine near the Athas Run portal and fan. Their power was still on. They neither heard nor felt anything and had no idea what was happening a few miles away. They were repairing a locomotive that was sitting on top of a pit that allowed them to get beneath the 30-ton and 50-ton locomotives. To test their repair, they hooked the motor up to one of their power sources. Nothing happened. Conway checked the phone to see if it was down, too. It was.

"It's time for us to go outside if we possibly can," he told Mullins. "If there's nothing wrong, why, we can come back in."[28] The two mechanics did not hurry. They cleaned up the shop, took time to lock their toolboxes, and walked to the nearest exit, the Athas Run portal, which was a few minutes away. They checked the phone there, and Lockie Riggs was on the line. He told them to get to the top as soon as possible; someone would be waiting to pick them up. He did not tell them they were in the middle of a disaster.

The two men reached the surface before 7 a.m., an hour and a half after the Llewellyn portal blew up and three hours after the Mods Run fan had blown off its blades.

A-Face. When the A-Face crew had loaded 45 coal cars, Roy Wilson called dispatcher Charlie Moody, but someone else was on the line. He was not sure who it was, but the voice told Wilson to gather the A-Face crew and bring them out of the mine as quickly as possible. He found his foreman, James Herron. They cut the power on the section and tried to take a jeep out, but it would move in only one direction—deeper into the mine. The backup plan was to take an empty coal car and locomotive out, but by that time the main power was down. With no other transportation, the men walked the mile and a half to the slope bottom and made it to the top at 7 a.m.[29]

7South at the Mahan Run Shaft. Gary Martin could not quit thinking about Paul Henderson. He was only 24 years old and had been mining for about two years. The young man could not have gone far, Martin surmised. Maybe he had passed out or was sheltering himself under a piece of equipment. Martin decided to go back and look for him one more time. He walked back through the dark tunnel, the light from his cap lamp cutting through darkness, dust and smoke. He encountered chaos. The heavy rails along the way had been torn from the floor and tossed and twisted like toys. The blast force had blown out cement stoppings and scattered them hundreds of feet in both directions. Overcasts, which were thick ventilation walls built to last 20 years, had tumbled to the mine's floor.

When Martin reached the working section, he walked through the entire area, looking for Henderson. He checked around the machinery, beside the coal cars, in the coal cars, under the coal cars. He began walking farther into the mine, past one block of coal, about 100 feet, then past another block and another block. He passed about 10 blocks before he gave up and returned to the Mahan shaft, where several of the men had passed out, overcome by carbon monoxide and noxious fumes. George Wilson, section foreman, was unconscious and so was Nezer Vandergrift. Then Lewis Lake went down.[30]

Martin took action. "Lewis, if you don't wake up and help me, we're going to lose two or three of these men," he said.

Lake could barely stand, but he did. He gave Vandergrift his coat and Wilson his gloves to ward off the cold air that was flowing into the shaft. Together, Lake and Martin lifted the men one at a time. They rubbed their wrists and pounded on the men to get their circulation going and to keep them breathing.[31]

The men did what they could to stay alive and waited for help in the frigid, dark hole inside the mountain. Eventually, they heard voices from above, but could not make out the words. They yelled back, desperately pleading for help.

Gary Martin (left), Bud Hillberry (right) and an unidentified man are hoisted from the No.9 mine. They were the last men to escape the disaster alive. Photo by Bob Campione.

At one point, someone dropped a few supplies down the shaft, including a phone, all-service gas masks and an oxygen resuscitator. Martin took charge, again, giving each of the unconscious miners a shot of oxygen. He did not know that too much oxygen would make them sick, but he found out quickly. Right after Martin gave oxygen to the last man, the first man began vomiting in his gas mask. He took the mask off, cleaned it and put it back on the miner. Then Martin threw up. Then everyone began vomiting.[32]

At about 7:45 a.m., a state and a federal official arrived at the top of the Mahan Run air shaft and made contact with the men. John Ashcraft with the West Virginia Department of Mines told Martin that the workers were going to turn on the No.1 and Athas fans. When the fans were turned on, a little after 8 a.m., the fresh air mixed with the methane and coal dust, which set off another big explosion in the mine. A cloud of dust and rocks and debris began rolling through the mine like giant tumbleweed. It hit 7South and blew over the men and out of the Mahan shaft.

Ashcraft called the men on the phone. "Hey down there. You guys all right? What's going on?"

"Shut the fans off! Shut the fans off!" Martin yelled back. Ashcraft told them to hold on; a crane was coming to pull them out.

On the Surface. Outside, coal company officials tried to get organized near the slope on the east side of the mine and at the Llewellyn portal on the west side.

Around 8 a.m. Lockie Riggs sent Cecil Selders and Alex Kovar to Mods Run to inspect the fan. The fan itself was set several feet away from the air shaft and housed in a metal building to protect it from an explosion. Two sets of doors on the air shaft coming out of the mine also were designed to protect the fan. If the mine exploded, one set of doors leading to the fan closed. Another set of doors, the explosion doors, opened, directing the forces away from the fan and into the atmosphere.

When Selders arrived at Mods Run, he saw the fan's explosion doors were open and smoke was pouring out through them. When he unlocked the fan house, he saw that the fan had thrown off its blades, just as James Stout and his wife had predicted much earlier that morning.[33]

7South at the Mahan Run Shaft. At about 8:50 a.m., rescue workers delivered a big bucket and a portable crane from a nearby coal mine. When they dropped the bucket into the Mahan shaft, it stopped about 20 feet above the floor. The cable was too short. Someone was sent to Fairmont to find a longer one. People at the top extended the reach of the cable using rope and sent down a jar of hot coffee in a small bucket. "Charlie, you want some coffee," Martin asked.

"Yeah," Charlie Crim said. It was the only word he said through the whole ordeal.[34]

Another hour passed before the rescuers began bringing the men out of the mine.

When the bucket finally reached them, they loaded the sickest men, Nezer Vandergrift and Ralph Starkey, first. They reached the surface at a few minutes past 10 a.m. An ambulance was waiting to rush them to the hospital. Lewis Lake, George Wilson and Alva Davis, who also were ill, were the next to reach the top. Finally, the bucket came back for Gary Martin, Bud Hillberry and Charlie Crim. About 15 feet from the top of the shaft the cable caught and the bucket stopped. The rescuers seemed stumped.

"Why don't you raise the crane boom up?" asked Hillberry, who feared another explosion would blast the men out of the shaft—it would have, too, had there been another blast.[35]

The rescuers raised the boom and hoisted the bucket and the men to safety at 10:40 a.m., more than five hours after the first blast roared through 7South.

The Disaster Hits Home

Had Wayne Fetty not been expecting houseguests, he would have died in the No.9 disaster. He was a welder and mechanic who worked the afternoon shift that ended at midnight.

He had been a metal smith in the U.S. Navy during the Korean War. He loved the work, loved the Navy. Sometimes he wondered if he should have made a career in the service. Instead, he came home and took a job with the Consolidation Coal Company. He worked a few other places, too, but came back to the No.9.

At first, he worked underground, then his bosses offered him a job outside. He worried that people with more seniority might be angry; jobs on the surface were prized. They were safer. His bosses wanted him outside, and so he made the move. Most of the time he worked in a repair shop, but he went underground when machinery broke and his skills were needed. He did a lot of welding, and welding in the tunnels had its risks. If methane was present, a spark could set off an explosion. For safety, he always hooked up a water hose near his underground work site and took a supply of rock dust to neutralize any loose coal dust.

The night before the mine exploded, Fetty had gone to Fairmont to pick up supplies. When he returned, his boss asked him for a favor: Would he stay past midnight to fix some equipment that had gone down on 6Right-7South?

Fetty agreed to stay. He put on his safety gear and headed underground. He burned the old bearings off the equipment, and he and some other miners made the repair. Everything went smoothly, and he was ready to leave at about 1 a.m. The midnight shift foreman stopped him and asked him to stay even later, offered to pay him double to get some brattice cloth and do some maintenance to prepare 6Right-7South for production.

Fetty declined; he had company coming and had to go home. He went to the surface, closed his shop, which was near the slope, and was home by about 5 a.m. He had just gone to bed when the windows in his house rattled. Thinking nothing about the rattling, he went to sleep.

A few hours later, his phone rang. His wife answered. Someone asked her if Wayne was home, but did not tell her that the mine had exploded. The company was checking to see if he was still in the mine. A company official called back a little later and asked him to come back to work; the mine had exploded. He returned immediately.[1]

Bad News Morning

John Brock was on his way to work for the day shift the morning the No.9 exploded. As he neared the Mannington Bank, he noticed one of the miners he knew standing outside. He thought maybe the men had gone on strike, so he pulled his truck over. "What are you doing?" he asked.

"No need to go up, Johnny. It blowed up," the man said.

"It blowed up? Oh, my god."

Brock, who was on the union's safety committee, drove as fast as he could to the mine to see what he could do to help. Police stopped him at a roadblock. After he identified himself, they sent him to the slope on the east side of the mine. As soon as he stepped out of his truck, one of the mine managers told him to take a company truck to the Llewellyn Run portal and gather all the breathing devices and lights he could find. Domenick Poster went with him.

When they arrived at the portal, they saw that cars in the parking lot had been heavily damaged. Smoke was towering from the shaft. Debris was everywhere. Brock drove to the first-aid building, and the two men began grabbing armfuls of cap lamps and other equipment and loaded them into eight boxes. They even found a set of clothes for one of the bosses. They did not waste any time. "Jump in Domenick, we're going," Brock said.

The smoke from the shaft was so thick Brock could barely see to drive through the parking lot. He was dodging large equipment tires scattered by the explosion. "We're going to upset," Domenick said, when they ran over one of the tires.

"Hold on, Domenick. We're going to get out of here," Brock yelled, as he gunned the truck and steered it back to the slope.[2]

Wives at Work

Joy Boone was working the day shift at the ice bucket plant when someone came in screaming and crying. "The No.9 blew up."

Her first thought was that her husband, Tom, might be in the mine.

"What shift is your husband on," someone asked her.

"I don't know."

"Well don't you remember if you went to bed with him or not?"

By then she was too hysterical to remember. All the other women in the plant were crying, too, crying and screaming. Everyone had someone connected to the No.9: a husband, a father, a grandfather, a son, a brother, a friend, a cousin, someone. The company shut down the plant, and Joy went home to look for her husband.

Going in at 4 p.m, Tom Boone had worked the afternoon shift the day before the explosion. He was supposed to come out at midnight when the cateye shift started, but he did not. He was one of the men who had worked over to try to uncover a mining machine in 5Right-8North. Two men from the cateye shift came to finish the job, and so at about 2 a.m., Tom Boone decided to go home.

When he got to the slope bottom, he heard a phone ring. He was nosey and picked it up and listened to the conversation. "I heard this guy talking to somebody outside and he said, 'I went over there and it wouldn't stay in, so I blocked it in,'" Boone said.

National and local reporters packed the back room of Consolidation Coal's company store during briefings from company and government officials. Photo by Bob Campione.

The company had been having trouble with the Mods Run fan, and Boone thought the man must have been talking about it. The fan often stalled or stopped, which meant someone would have to reset its circuit breaker. That night, Boone assumed, the circuit breaker would not stay engaged, so someone used a wedge of wood to keep it from popping out.[3]

Rookie Reporter

Robert Morris was getting ready to go to classes at Fairmont State College when his boss at WTCS Radio called and asked him to cover the disaster. Morris was only an intern at the station, but he knew what an explosion could do to a community. He was born in Monongah, West Virginia, where hundreds of men and boys had died in a 1907 mine explosion. Both of his grandfathers had been coal miners. One had been injured in the mines, losing a finger. A mine explosion was big news, serious news, life-changing news.

On his way to the mine, Morris came to the roadblock, and police sent him to the company store—the Champion Store—where a small group of people already had gathered outside. He was one of the first reporters on the scene. The store manager had offered his office with a phone as a media center. Morris immediately began gathering information and calling in his reports. At one point, he drove into Fairmont to buy a reel-to-reel recorder so he could tape his interviews and transmit voices over the phone that could be used on the radio.

As the snow fell, people gathered at the store. Many stood outside, huddled around large drums of burning coal. Others, mostly women and children, stood or sat inside, surrounded by Christmas decorations, dolls and toys. Some prayed. Some cried. Others were silent. Morris told their stories.[4]

At about 11:30 a.m., the company provided reporters with a list of 21 men who had made it to safety. At first, young Morris was not sure if he was supposed to share the names with those who had gathered. He felt he should not be the person to inform the families. But he did. Reporters from the large networks had not yet arrived, so Morris called the news into his station's affiliate, ABC radio.[5]

The West Virginian, Fairmont's afternoon paper, ran the news on the front page that evening with a list of the 21 survivors. Not all the names were spelled correctly, but the people in Marion County recognized them. At press time, reporters still did not know how many men were trapped in the mine. An estimate of more than 70 was the number that ran in the paper.[6]

Throughout the day, reporters from around the state, Pennsylvania and Ohio began to find their way to Farmington. The local telephone company rushed to install more lines near the mine. Within hours, workers had strung miles of cable. A trailer with coin-operated phones was placed outside the company store. The workload for the Fairmont phone operators doubled. Everyone wanted information.

Even the additional phone lines weren't enough, so Robert Morris asked to use the phone at a nearby home. The family had no problem allowing the young local reporter access to their line. Vic Miles, a reporter for KDKA television in Pittsburgh, caught on to Morris' trick and asked to go with him. Morris worried that the family might get upset, but when they saw

Frank Matish. Courtesy of James Matish.

Miles they recognized him. "Oh my goodness. It's Vic Miles from Channel 2." Their phone was then his phone.[7]

Missing Fathers

At school that morning, James Matish heard some of the older boys talking about trouble at a coal mine. A little later, he saw his mother and the school principal standing outside his classroom. His mother was crying, and he knew something was terribly wrong. Mary Matish explained what had happened and asked James if he wanted to go home. James decided to stay because he knew how important it was to his father that he receive a good education. Frank Matish always challenged his son to excel in his schoolwork. One day he picked up James's new spelling book and flipped to the final pages. He called out a word and asked James to spell it. James didn't know how to spell the word yet.

"It's all the way in the back of the book," James said.

"If I were your age, I'd know how to spell every word in the back of the book," his father replied.[8]

David Mainella Jr. was underground in the Pruntytown Mine in a nearby county when the No.9 exploded. When he came out, he heard about the disaster and headed to his parents' home. He thought his father had not gone to work that day because his father had tickets to attend a concert at the Fairmont Theater.

"I looked in the garage and didn't see his car there, and I knew he was in the mines," David said. David Mainella Sr. was 62. He already had filled out his retirement papers and had less than four weeks to work. Unfortunately, he was still underground in the No.9.[9]

No Good Answers

Bill Bunner had just finished his shift at the Williams Mine when someone told him about the No.9.

"I said, 'Jesus Christ,' and over there I went," he said. As he watched the smoke pour from the No.9, he asked miners he knew what was happening underground. They told him the air was shifting back and forth between the Mods Run and Llewellyn shafts, feeding the flames.

The wives of some of his old buddies looked to him for hope. "Bill, what do you think my husband's chances are of getting out?" they would ask.

"I couldn't answer them," he said.

Men came to him, too. With them, he was honest. "I told Andy, this one guy's brother, I said, 'Andy, they're dead. There ain't no way they could come out.' I knew they were dead because of the air shafts—they were working between them." There were no other ways out.[10]

That first afternoon, West Virginia's governor, Hulett C. Smith, flew into the area from Charleston, the state capital. He addressed the press in the back room of the Champion Store. His defeatist message reflected the close relationship between the state government officials and the coal industry.

"I should like to explain that this is an accident," Gov. Smith said. "I

The pregnant wife of a trapped coal miner waits for news in the company store near the No.9 Mine. Photo by Bob Campione.

have confidence that the mining industry is seeing the most improved safety measures are being taken. We have experienced tragedy here many times before. Mining is a hazardous profession."[11]

A few days later, when No.9 miners testified under oath, they did not call the disaster an "accident." Furthermore, their description of underground conditions would lead no one to conclude that Consolidation Coal had been taking all the safety measures available to the industry.

The Wait

The public and most of the media were kept away from the Llewellyn Run portal, as well as the rest of the mine. A couple of local reporters and photographers were allowed additional access. They saw close-up the devastation: the smoke billowing white, then grey, then black each time an explosion hit. The fire was spreading and burning out of control. Flames shot from portals where the men had entered the mine and from the airshafts they depended on for oxygen.

Ambulances from several funeral homes remained on call should more men need to be transported to a hospital. The Red Cross and the Salvation Army set up stations to aid anyone who needed their help.

At the company store, women and children waited all day for news of more survivors.

Sixteen-year-old Joe Megna and his family waited at the store, hoping his father, Emilio, would escape the inferno. Joe and some of the men stood outside in the cold on a nearby bridge. They could see the No.9's tipple, a coal cleaning plant, near the slope that led to the mine.

"They'll never get the bodies out; the rats will eat them," Joe heard a law enforcement officer say. Joe hit the officer. Someone grabbed the teen and took him to his mother.[12]

More Explosions

As the hours passed, conditions in the mine failed to improve. Company and government officials monitored each of the mine's ventilation shafts.[13]

At 2:40 p.m., smoke began pouring from an Athas Run shaft, which was near the elevator that had carried Robert Mullins and Henry Conway out of the mine earlier that day.

At 6:30 p.m., a powerful explosion blew debris up and out of the Mahan Run air shaft against the incoming air current that had been measuring 100,000 cubic feet per minute. Through that shaft, George Wilson and his crew had been rescued via the giant bucket.

At 9:30 p.m., the Llewellyn Run shaft, which had vented the first major explosion, sent flames shooting more than 100 feet into the sky. Then the intake and return shafts at Mods Run both exploded at 10 p.m. About the same time, company officials confirmed the names of the 78 men trapped inside the mine. The company had spent much of the day calling homes of miners to verify who had gone to work but had not come home. They made lists of the men known to be working inside and their possible locations.

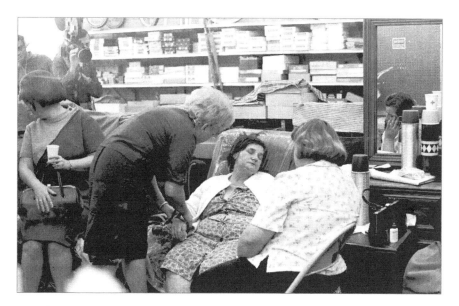

An exhausted woman is comforted as she waits for word about a loved one trapped in the No.9 Mine. Photo by Bob Campione.

The most reliable way to determine who was in the mine was to check the lamphouse board that held the metal identification tags. Of course, the lamphouse and everything at the Llewellyn portal had been destroyed in the explosions. Fire trucks had come to the parking lot to wet down the cars there; it was too hot and too dangerous to try to move them.

At 11 p.m., one hour after the company named the 78 miners, another violent explosion hit the Mods Run air shaft. The flames lit the night sky.

The officials all knew that the fire in the mine was out of control; the only way to stop it was to cut off its oxygen supply. They also knew that taking that step would be a death sentence to anyone who might have survived the explosions. One company official tried to inject some hope into the situation. The men might have been able to build a barricade against the fire, said William Poundstone, executive vice president for Consolidation Coal.[14]

Leslie Ryan, an inspector from the West Virginia Department of Mines, had lost hope. "There's not a chance in the world to get those men out," he told the Associated Press.[15]

A Paralyzed Community

Day 2: Thursday, November 21

No one went to school the day after the No.9 exploded. Marion County's 12 public schools closed. Many children joined their mothers and other relatives who gathered in the small red brick church nestled in a hollow not far from the company store. Their prayers drifted skyward all morning, moving beyond the steeple of the James Fork United Methodist Church, which would become the families' refuge in the days to come.

Two white candles flickered on the altar as the Rev. John Barnes told the people in the pews that God was with them. He asked them to sing "How Great Thou Art." Some did.

After a brief service, he invited people to kneel at the altar to pray. Many went forward. One young woman collapsed there. A miner picked her up. She cried into his chest, setting off more tears throughout the church. The hopelessness of the situation was becoming evident, even among the faithful.

When the service ended, the weary crowd trudged back to the company store over the rugged dirt road and against the bitter winter wind. Some stopped to look toward the coal mine.[1]

At the store, the company issued emergency paychecks to the families, and the vigil continued. The Red Cross set up trailers and provided hot beverages.

Red Cross volunteers were onsite after the explosion, serving hot beverages and snacks to those waiting outside the No.9 Mine. Photo by Bob Campione.

Throughout the day, reporters crowded into a storage room that had been cleared in the back of the company store. They came from the major television networks, the local stations, Charleston stations, and stations and newspapers from around the state and from neighboring states. Other news and news wire services—the Associated Press, United Press International, the British Broadcasting Corporation and Reuters—came, too.

Two Associated Press photographers rented an airplane and shot the scene from the air. The local paper, *The West Virginian*, allowed the men to transmit their photographs to all parts of the United States, to London, Paris, Rome and numerous other cities. Within a day, the tragedy had become not only national but international news. The No.9 was the worst mine disaster since 1951, when a mine explosion killed 119 men in West Frankfort, Illinois.

Writing for *The New York Times*, reporter Joseph A. Loftus told of the No.9's long history of safety violations and the violations found in most U.S. coal mines. The statistics were frightening. "Federal inspection records for 1967 show that 82 percent of the 5,400 underground coal mines were found in violation of the major provisions of the safety act," he wrote.[2]

Loftus put the safety issue in context. Legislation that would have improved mine safety had failed to make it through Congress during the session that had concluded just before the No.9 disaster. The proposed law would have made the federal law effective, for the first time allowing the government to fine operators up to $1,000 per violation (equivalent to about $6,200 per violation in 2009).[3]

Ironically, Stewart L. Udall, U.S. Secretary of the Interior, who oversaw coal mine safety, followed the traditional political line. He said the proposed law would not have prevented the No.9 disaster. That may have been true: It would not have gone into effect soon enough to force Consol to make the No.9 safe. However, after an even tougher law was passed in 1969, as a direct result of the No.9 tragedy, mines were forced to become safer. Udall did take some of the blame: "I don't think the industry people have done enough. I don't think the labor unions have done enough. I don't think my department has done enough."[4]

No one, in fact, had made sure the No.9 was safe. And none of the groups—not Consol, not the West Virginia Department of Mines, not the U.S. Bureau of Mines and not the United Mine Workers of America—knew how to save the 78 men who were trapped inside the mountain.

As televisions and newspapers carried the No.9 disaster into America's living rooms, Congress recognized that the public no longer would tolerate the high human cost of producing coal. It also became clear to many observers that the miners' union had become as ineffective as the government in keeping miners safe.

The day after the No.9 exploded, William Anthony "Tony" Boyle, international president of the United Mine Workers of America, came to Farmington to comment on the disaster and left the same day. He did not deliver a fiery speech on behalf of coal miners as his predecessor, John L. Lewis, had done when disasters struck. Instead, he told the people that he was "shaken" and shared their grief.

UMWA President, Tony Boyle, speaks to the media during a press conference following the No.9 Mine explosion. Photo by Bob Campione.

"I would be the last one in this group to give up hope; but it looks very dark to me," he said.[5]

He promised to push for more safety regulations at the federal level, but his industry friendly remarks called into question his sincerity and angered many who heard his comments or read them in the newspapers. He told the people that Consolidation Coal Company was one of the most safety conscious companies in the industry and the most cooperative with the union.[6]

Consol and Boyle's UMW were more than cooperative. Just a few weeks before the No.9 exploded, a federal jury in Lexington, Kentucky, found the UMW and Consol guilty of breaking federal antitrust laws. They were arranging illegal contracts to put small coal companies out of business. One small company, South-East Coal Company, sued. After a 6-week trial, a jury awarded South-East $7,231,356 and attorneys' fees of $335,000. Consol appealed the case. Ultimately, the U.S. Supreme Court refused to hear the case, and the judgment stood. The UMWA and Consol each paid half of the bill.[7]

Boyle had become so corrupt that later he would be willing to commit murder to protect his powerful union position. He also had adopted the same fatalistic excuse that was widely accepted in the industry, by politicians and often by miners and their families. "But as long as we mine coal, there is always this inherent danger of explosion," he told the No.9 families.[8]

While Tony Boyle and company representatives addressed the press, the No.9 mine continued to burn. Air from the ventilation shafts fed the fire, coal dust continued to ignite, methane and coal burned and black smoke towered into the sky. Once again, flames shot out of the Llewellyn portal. Earlier that morning, the heat coming from the shaft was so intense that at least two cars in the parking lot caught fire near the bathhouse. Fearing nearby residents were in danger from carbon monoxide and dangerous fumes, local officials evacuated nine families who lived within a half-mile radius of No.9.[9]

To control the fire, officials knew they must stop the air flowing into the mine. That evening, they capped the two shafts at Mods Run using a steel plate covered by steel beams that weighed 16 tons. Even with the shafts capped, two other fans continued to pump air into the mine.[10] To shut them down, everyone knew, was to seal the fate of the miners inside. Company officials promised not to stop the fans until every possible step to rescue the men had been attempted.

Day 3: Friday, November 22

At 2:48 a.m., not quite eight hours after the company sealed the shafts at Mods Run, the intake shaft blew its cap. The explosion was felt four miles away at the company store, where the lights flickered briefly, alarming the people who had spent the night there. One man said the blast sounded like a cannon and sent a big red fireball into the sky followed by "a big blue flame"—blue, the color of methane burning.[11] A teenager standing on a nearby bridge said he felt the explosion's concussion against his face.[12]

Two hours later, another explosion blew the cap from Mods Run's return shaft. That blast shot a 1,000-gallon steel tank up and out of the 600-foot shaft. Debris from the explosion was found almost a half a mile from the opening. At that point, officials decided they would have to fill Mods Run's shafts with limestone.[13] The explosions created a serious setback: another day that rescue teams could not enter the mine.

The third day of waiting also brought devastating results from underground air samples that had been taken the previous day. John Brock[14] and another coal miner had been collecting air samples by dipping glass tubes into the existing boreholes, which were small openings used to run power lines from the surface to the bottom of the mine. All but one of the samples taken from several areas of the mine indicated that the air could not support life. It contained too much carbon dioxide and too much methane. The only place that had good air was near the east side of the mine, which had not been affected by the explosions.[15]

Despite the bad news, families kept their vigil at the company store or gathered for prayer at the James Fork United Methodist Church. Schools reopened, but not all the children returned to class.

While many people continued to believe the men could still be alive, others began to waiver. Here and there, reporters heard the kind of talk common in the mining community. "It's terrible, but you have to accept reality and God's will . . . and people get killed in the mines as well as out of it, and none has assurance of when he will live or die," said Mrs. Walter Looman, a school teacher. Looman's husband had spent 38 years in the mines, some of that time in the No.9.[16]

The pessimism was founded in the reality of the profession. In 1968, coal mining was among the most dangerous industrial occupations in the nation,[17] but it need not have been. It was dangerous because laws were weak and enforcement lax. It was dangerous because the coal companies' push for production often short-circuited safety.[18] It was dangerous because miners needed jobs, and jobs went to people who would produce, even when conditions were dangerous.

Day 4: Saturday, November 23

Thirty trucks rumbled through Marion County carrying thousands of tons of limestone. By early afternoon, they had emptied their loads into the

Mods Run airshafts.[19] The sound of the trucks was the sound of defeat and one more step toward admitting that the men in the mine likely were dead.

Sealing the shafts was dangerous work. Large chunks of rocks were dropped in first. If they could not withstand the pressure in the mine, smaller limestone pieces would shoot from the hole like bullets, one official said.[20]

Workers also began drilling additional boreholes in areas where the miners might have sought sanctuary, but the drilling did not go quickly. At a press conference, William N. Poundstone, a Consolidation Coal executive vice president, announced that workers were drilling the first two new boreholes. One was nearly half way to the bottom of the mine, and another was about 60 feet deep, far short of the 600-foot destination.

The lack of progress angered some people in the community. Tony Megna, the brother of trapped miner Emilio Megna, and Emilio's mother, Mary Megna, began pressing for more information. *New York Times* reporter Ben A. Franklin captured the exchange:[21]

"Why aren't more drills being used?" asked Megna, who was a high school principal in Ohio.

"You realize we have an area of tremendous proportions," Poundstone said.

"Why aren't more holes being dug? There are not enough drills or something? Why couldn't we get more drills so we can get contact with them down there to see if they are alive?" Megna asked.

"Well . . ." Poundstone responded.

Megna's voice grew louder. "It seems to me there ought to be a drill over each spot where they might think there is a section of men barricaded in. We've got hundreds of drills in this state. Why don't they bring them in? It wouldn't take that much money."

"It's not a matter of money, I can assure you," Poundstone said as he began to walk out of the room.

"Is it that you don't think they're alive, anyway?" a reporter asked.

"You've got to try!" Megna shouted. "Those men are down there. I have a brother down there. We know he's alive. You've got to make contact."

"Yes, I know," Poundstone muttered.

"He's talking in circles, and we're tired of hearing circles," shouted Mary

Consolidation Coal official William Poundstone uses a No.9 underground map to brief the media on the workings of the mine. Photo by Bob Campione.

Megna, the trapped miner's mother in a heavy Italian accent. "My son is down there, he wants to get out."

"Can't you answer the question about drilling?" newsmen persisted.

"There's a limit to what we can do," Poundstone said. "There are other factors."

But he would not elaborate. Instead, he left the room, leaving Mary Megna to beg reporters to "call President Johnson."

The exchange did not speed the drilling.

Day 5: Sunday, November 24

Before God and all who had gathered at the James Fork United Methodist Church, John Corcoran, president of Consolidation Coal, promised the miners' loved ones that he would not order the mine sealed as long as there was any chance that someone could be alive.[22]

Late that afternoon, he sent two rescue teams into the mine. Neither came close to the areas where survivors might have been. Both teams entered through the Athas Run portal. The first team walked about two miles east on the main haulage road, traveling away from the west side of the mine, which had exploded. The men came out of the slope 38 minutes later. They saw no damage. The air was breathable, and so they did not need to wear gas masks.

The second team walked west toward the devastation, but traveled only about three-quarters of a mile before they encountered carbon monoxide and turned back. Along the way, the men saw some blackened surfaces and rock dust bags scattered about. The roof had not collapsed in that area, but they had barely reached the edge of the west side of the mine. Within 30 minutes, they had given up their search.[23]

The mission brought little new information and no hope for the families, some who had refused to go home, choosing instead to sleep in the church.

Day 6: Monday, November 25

Mine officials delivered bad news on the sixth day following the disaster. Test results of air samples taken from two new boreholes—one at 6Right-7South and another that at 3Right-7South—showed that the air there could not sustain life. Two and possibly three teams of miners were believed to be in those areas.

A microphone and light also were dropped down a borehole near the Llewellyn portal, where men likely were trapped. The listening device was sensitive enough to pick up a whisper within 100 feet, but the only sound it carried to the surface was the steady drip of water and the plunk of small rocks or pieces of coal. It picked up no voices, no breathing, no tapping a man might make to call for help—no sign of life.[24]

To those reporting the news, the situation appeared dismal. At a press conference, one newsman asked company officials what kind of benefits the

Fairmont Times Editor Bill Evans listens during a press conference after the No.9 Mine explosion. Photo by Bob Campione.

wives would receive. It was a question the families could not bear to hear. Some of the women broke into tears.

"The hell with this money situation," a miner said. "That's all these newsmen are worrying about. They should know better than to ask those kinds of questions in front of these grieved people."[25]

People in the community did what they could to help the families. They took up cash collections in church and held roller skating events to bring in some cash.

And they cooked. So much food was donated that the church groups had to ask people to stop bringing the casseroles and bread and cakes and pies.

The Red Cross began helping relatives of the trapped miners who were in the military service get emergency leaves so they could come home.

People from around the country began sending in suggestions for rescuing the trapped men. Some wanted the company to allow rescue workers to go into the mine if they were willing to take the risk. Others suggested blasting the mine with steam to put out the flames. None of the suggestions was deemed workable, and others could not even be taken seriously.[26]

One man wrote claiming he had had a vision and knew where the men were trapped. If someone would pick him up in an airplane, he would show him.

Another man showed up at a local church claiming God had sent him. The minister there answered, "The Lord sent me too, and I got here first."

Yet another man claimed he and his friend could walk into the mine. God would part the fire, and they would find the miners. A woman knew her dog could find the men.

Officials tried to guard the families from such people. They also decided to speed up the work of drilling boreholes by bringing in two additional rigs that were supposed to be faster than the two already at work.

Miners in other mines were becoming more outspoken about their working conditions. At the nearby Federal No.2, owned by Eastern Associated Coal Corp., 175 miners refused to go into the mine because they said it was unsafe. They demanded the mine be rock dusted properly before they would go underground.[27]

Day 7: Tuesday, November 26

Constant media coverage of the exploding mine and the excruciating video and photographs of the devastated families emboldened several politicians. In Washington, one West Virginia lawmaker, who would become a leading supporter of coal mine safety, held a press conference.[28]

Mine safety laws are "terribly weak and company-oriented," said Rep. Ken Hechler, D-W.Va. Hechler quoted a 34-year veteran of Logan County mines who had said that mine operators knew exactly when federal and state inspectors were coming. Once they left, operators forgot about safety.

A U.S. Bureau of Mines spokesman defended inspectors, saying they might call small, remote mines to make sure they were operating before arriving for an inspection.

Hechler accused the United Mine Workers of America of being more concerned about wages and job losses than miners' health and safety. Union officials denied his claims. Hechler vowed to introduce a mine safety bill that would change the status quo. U.S. Sen. Gaylord Nelson, D-Wis., also began blasting the No.9's poor safety record and admonishing the federal Bureau of Mines for doing little to enforce existing laws.

What was happening on the national level, however, was not the immediate concern of the families. They still looked to the company to bring their men out of the mine. Air samples, however, continued to show that no one could survive. Furthermore, the microphones and telephones dropped down the holes brought no response. One reporter wanted the company to drill a hole big enough to send down a video camera. That request was denied.

Another blow hit just after noon. The Mahan shaft, which had been smoking for four days, exploded violently without warning. Debris shot from the mine. The men monitoring it were covered with soot. The Mahan shaft was miles from the site of the main explosions, which led officials to conclude that the fires had spread throughout the west side of the mine.

Only moments before, John Corcoran, company president, had told families that the only safe way to bring anyone out of the mine would be through larger holes drilled into the tunnels. But he added that no larger holes would be drilled unless some sign of life was found via the smaller boreholes. The only sound coming from the seventh borehole drilled the day before was rushing water, a sign of flooding.[29]

Day 8: Wednesday, November 27

The day before Thanksgiving, a siren sounded inside the No.9, set off by officials to get the attention of anyone alive underground. The siren blared for 20 minutes before officials stopped it and lowered a microphone into the borehole. There was no reply, just the sound of dripping water in an otherwise silent, cold, dark world.

That day, West Virginia's governor-elect Arch A. Moore made a second

appearance at the No.9 mine. As others before him, he praised the Consolidation Coal Company. He said if he were a coal miner, he would work in the
No.9 because he had seen the inspection reports. "[T]hey showed we had
some adverse comment but, on balance, they also showed the mine was not
unsafe before the disaster."[30] He offered ideas on how to keep miners safe.
He suggested installing airtight safety chambers underground and making
sure a communication system was in place to allow the people underground
to talk to the people outside the mine.

To help the families, he said, he was trying to bring home soldiers from
Vietnam who had relatives in the mine.

That day, the United Mine Workers local 4042 handed out Thanksgiving
care packages for the families of the trapped miners. They included turkey
and all the trimmings. Mary Matish refused to accept one, saying she was a
good money manager and did not need it.

Her husband, Frank, was believed to have been working in the far west
side of the mine, operating a loading machine, which transferred the coal
from the working face to a shuttle car. The work would have put him in one
of the most dangerous areas of the mine—a particularly gassy area that was
far from any exits.

"We've been provided for," Mary said. "Frank brings home $189 every
two weeks. . . . We've had everything we've wanted. Our house is paid for
and we've owned three cars. We don't owe nobody nothing," she said.[31]

The one thing she wanted after the explosion was answers. "I want to
know something. I pray. I want God to give some sign. I want to hear a
voice," she said as she kept vigil with the other families.[32] The Associated
Press sent out a photo of her holding her rosary and wiping the tears from
her eyes with a handkerchief. It ran in newspapers around the world, and
letters and cards and cash poured in.[33] A letter from Canada contained a
page of Bible verses, but no signature.

Mrs. Charles Boyd sent a letter from Hollywood, Florida, recounting
her own grandfather's and father's time in the coal mines. Her grandfather
had been a mine superintendent in Pennsylvania. Her father would rise
early to go to the mine to help clear it of slate before he went to school.

Mary Matish received dozens of letters and sympathy cards after her picture appeared in newspapers around the world. Courtesy of James Matish.

"Your sweet face and full newspaper article of the tragedy appeared in the Wednesday, November 27th issue of the Miami newspaper," she wrote. She sent her prayers, as well.

Some people tried to use the tragedy to convert her to Mormonism.

Factory workers in Ohio sent $40 in a Western Union telegram. "Please accept this money as a token of our sympathy. Please use it in any way to help the families of the trapped miners."

Mrs. Elizabeth Golden of Elkhart, Indiana, sent her prayers and told of her father's death in a West Virginia coal mine. "I will never forget that.... He was crushed badly and they took him to the miner's hospital in Fairmont. I went to visit him. I asked him then, 'Papa, when you get well don't go back into the mine.' His words to me were, 'Darling, that's all I know.'

And he did go back to inspect a 'heading' as they called it on Sunday morning and was killed then. Jimmy O'Brien was his name."

Mary could not write well, and so she paid a neighbor who had pretty handwriting to write thank-you notes to the dozens of people who had sent cards and letters.[34]

Mary continued to pray, even though officials had no positive news to deliver.

Results from another borehole test showed the air in the 4Right-8North section was, like the air tested from all the boreholes, poisonous.

Day 9: Thursday, November 28

At 2:28 a.m. on Thanksgiving morning, another violent blast rocked the No.9, spewing flames and smoke from the Mahan shaft. It was a terrible sign.[35]

Air sample results from two new boreholes delivered more bad news. The air was deadly in two more sections in the far west side of the mine—9North and 5Right-8North—both areas where men had been working.

Apart from the news media, the company store was nearly empty. A Thanksgiving dinner was flown in from Washington D.C. by the American Broadcasting Company (ABC). The company found an airline caterer to fix the turkey, sweet potatoes, peas, cranberry sauce and pumpkin pie and brought it in through Clarksburg.[36]

Most of the families stayed home, but the James Fork United Methodist Church held a service for the families. The Rev. Melvin Risinger told the small congregation that they should be thankful that God supports people when they are grieving. At that moment, two women came through the doors with pies. The minister invited the women in.

"The other day, I heard someone say, 'Why on earth is God doing this?' The answer is in these two women who came in with the pumpkin pies or the volunteer policeman, his shoes muddy, directing traffic or nurses who come here straight from their jobs. These are God's people and we can be thankful for their help." [37]

The journalist who recorded the scene did not indicate how the families received this message.

Day 10: Friday, November 29

On the morning after that awful Thanksgiving, rumors were flying through the media and around the community that the company was going to seal the mine. Eighteen men, including federal and state officials and company and union representatives, were in a meeting, discussing the information they had been collecting for nine long days.

They knew the air on the west side of the mine was poisonous everywhere it had been tested. If men had survived the explosions—by then more than 20 major blasts and numerous smaller ones—they would have no air to breathe, even if they had built barricades following the first explosion.

The first rescue attempt had been fruitless, and the west side of the mine was still burning and exploding, too dangerous to send more men inside. The only way to stop the fire and the explosions was to seal the mine, which was what they did.

Sharing this gut-wrenching decision with the families began with phone calls to the next of kin, asking them to come to the James Fork Church, where so many had spent hours praying that their loved ones were alive. About 200 people came, filling the wooden pews and packing into the corners of the church, built to seat half that many.[38]

Officials would not allow the news media into the church. Instead, a press conference for them was held almost seven miles away in the company's Monongah office.

At about 6 p.m., John Corcoran, Consolidation Coal president, walked to the front of the church and said what had to be said. "When I first came here a few days ago I made a promise that when the time came I would be with you. That time has come," Corcoran told the families. Everyone knew the words that would follow:[39]

There was no way to reach the men.
There was no chance that any of the men were alive.
There was no other course to take but to seal the mine.

"The West Virginia Department of Mines and United States Bureau of Mines, who have governmental jurisdiction over rescue operations, concur in this statement and recommend that the mine be sealed promptly," Corcoran said, transferring some of the responsibility to others.

"There was never such wailing and crying and screaming; it's hard to imagine," said James Matish, who had turned 16 a few days earlier. On the hard wooden pew, he sat by his mother, Mary. Together, the two devout Catholics tried to make sense of what they had heard.[40]

Years later, he would call that evening the most horrifying time in his life. He said at one point, a Catholic bishop stepped up to the microphone and asked everyone to say the Lord's Prayer. Few joined in, he said.

"Who does he think he is? Does he think he's God?" James heard one person say.[41]

The comment took the teenager aback. He had never heard anyone challenge a man of God.

Outside the church, Tony Megna, whose brother Emilio was still in the mine, once again accused the company of doing too little to save the men and of caring more about production than safety. His teenage nephew, Joe Megna, was trying to protect his mother from reporters. When a television reporter put a big camera too close to her face, he hit the man, sending him and his camera down a hill.[42]

All the families were struggling under the weight of their grief.

"I'm trying to hold up," said Mrs. Juanita Mayle, the mother of 16 children, whose 51-year-old husband, Hartzell Mayle, was buried in the mine. "I must for the children's sake. He would want me to."[43]

Two days earlier she had told a reporter she was sure her husband would come back to her. Her husband had been a miner for 28 years, but to make ends meet, they had also taken up farming. She said they "didn't know the difference between a cucumber and a pepper" when they moved to a 56-acre farm in nearby Taylor County. There they raised chickens and pigs and corn to supplement his coal company paycheck.[44]

When the mine first exploded, she said her four-year-old twins, Cindy Sue and Linda Lou, would not eat. Only after she convinced them their daddy would be coming home did they begin to eat again.

After Corcoran made his announcement, the Mayles' 17-year-old daughter, Donna, said she had known they were going to seal the mine. But it still hurt.

Everyone hurt that day. The hurt spread across the coalfields. It was picked up by the media and spread around the world. As the families were being notified, limestone trucks rumbled toward the mine—90 trucks this time, carrying 1,600 tons of rock that would become a sort of temporary tombstone for Frank Matish, Emilio Megna, Hartzell Mayle and all the other doomed miners.

By 7:30 p.m., the cap lamps of the men sealing the mine could be seen from a distance, a macabre light show accompanied by the echoes of their labor. The work continued throughout the night. The men dumped about 1,000 tons of limestone into the Llewellyn Run shafts, the site of the first major explosion.

Day 11: Saturday, November 30

By 4:25 a.m., the work was finished. The slope was sealed with foam and all eight shafts capped. The two large ventilation fans were silent, no longer pumping millions of cubic feet of air into the mine each day.[45]

Condolences and contributions began to flood the community. Preachers talked of forgiveness and reconciliation.

President Lyndon Johnson issued a statement from the Texas White House calling for new laws.[46] "These laws will help, and they must be passed. But no number of laws, no amount of inspection and enforcement can ever eliminate the hazards that confront our mine workers every day. The only safeguard against these dangers is the daily concern of the employee and worker, the constant concern of management and labor to value protection as well as production."

Mrs. Peter Bota of Pittsburgh saw Mary Matish's photograph on the front page of *The Pittsburgh Press* and wrote to her. "My son has some dairy stores he manages. He has openings for cooks, dishwashers, janitors, waitresses, counter girls and etc. I myself am looking for an elderly middle aged couple to take care of a small apartment building for janitorial work."[47]

The words and offers were kind, but did not ease the pain the families felt. They were worried about their futures. The families of the men buried in the mine found little peace.

"The hurt will remain until the mine is opened again," said Mrs. Delores Forte, whose husband, Virgil, was believed to be working on the far west side of the mine. "There will be no Christmas. There will be no holiday until the mine is opened." [48]

Bungled Investigation

Both West Virginia and federal government officials claim to have investigated the No.9 disaster. However, their methods were flawed and their "official" findings were too little and too late to benefit the families of the dead or the safety of future miners.

An inquiry began a few days after the No.9 was sealed. The state summoned 84 people to testify,[1] but only 47 people took the oath and answered questions over a period of three days. The hearings were scheduled to continue another week, but they were canceled. Although officials announced that a final, formal inquiry would take place in the spring of 1969, none was ever held.[2]

Stay Home

Before the hearings began on December 5, 1968, a Consol official called No.9 section foreman Pete Sehewchuk and told him not to appear at the courthouse in Fairmont.

"I have to go because I got a summons," he said. "They'll arrest me."

"'You disregard that. We'll take care of it,'" Sehewchuk said he was told. Consequently, he did not go.

"I was going to tell them the truth. Any question they asked me, I was going to tell the truth," he said.[3]

His superiors knew he was not happy with the conditions in the mine, particularly on the gassy Main West Headings where Sehewchuk's crew was breaking off 10North, a new entry. He knew too much, and that, Sehewchuk always has believed, is why they did not want him to testify.

Section foreman Joseph McNece also was called to testify, but did not appear. Had he taken the stand, investigators could have asked him what was happening in 9North on the afternoon shift before the explosion and why he did not fill out and sign the section fireboss report after he left the mine.[4]

Intimidation Factor

The hearings, conducted under West Virginia law, were far from neutral. Men from Consol who themselves should have been under investigation were the investigators, as were men from the government agencies who had allowed dangerous conditions to persist in the No.9. Witnesses were interrogated by West Virginia's two top mine inspectors, two federal mine safety officials, three UMW officials, and a Consol lawyer.[5]

Also in the room was a state-appointed board tasked with listening to the testimony and determining what caused the disaster. That board included four Consol executives, two state officials, two federal officials and two UMW representatives. No unbiased coal mine experts sat on the board—no coal mine engineers from universities, no independent consultants—just the people who had profits or professional reputations at stake.

None of Consol's top executives was called to testify, but they were present while union miners and mid-level managers testified. Those who swore to tell the truth had to worry about their jobs. With the No.9 mine closed, there would be 368 fewer mining jobs in northwest West Virginia.

That testifying before their bosses intimidated some miners was clear. Long-time miner and motorman Robert Cook made a statement before he was questioned: "I have thought this darned thing over. It's a tragic thing to happen, but this I do know. From the testimony I'm going to have to give here, I know that my job is going to be in jeopardy with this company, if not within the whole coal area, but we got 78 men in there that sacrificed their life and I think I can sacrifice my job. And I will tell the truth and nothing but the truth to anyone."[6]

He told the panel that neither the No.9 crosscuts nor parts of the main haulage line were rock dusted properly. Operating a rear locomotive, he often ate a lot of dust, and he always wore a respirator.

Cook also testified that during one Saturday shift he had worked, the No.1 ventilation fan stopped running but the power did not shut down automatically. "So my buddy said to me, we better get over the hill because there'll be a knock in the power pretty soon," he said.[7]

However, an automatic knock in the power did not occur. Instead, a shift foreman had to take a jeep inside the mine and manually take the power down, he said.

A UMW official asked, "You've never experienced the fact that a fan would go down and within 12 to 15 minutes the power would automatically cut off?"

Cook, who had worked at the No.9 since July 1966, replied, "No, if it ever done that, it was something new that I didn't know anything about."

At the end of the questioning, Consol's lawyer assured Cook that his job was not in jeopardy.[8]

Alva G. Davis, who escaped the disaster by way of the Mahan Run air shaft, had no faith in the hearing process. When he testified, he answered a few basic questions but refused to discuss details about what had happened the day the mine exploded or what he had experienced while working in the No.9. He told the panel that he planned to submit a written statement to Congress. "I don't want it whitewashed before it gets there," he said.[9]

"Do I understand you that you don't want to talk about these things here, that you're afraid that somebody's going to whitewash them?" asked Lewis Evans, the UMW's safety director.[10]

"Yes sir, absolutely sir."

Evans tried again to get Davis to make a statement. Davis refused again. "This is a tragedy I'll never forget. I've got 78 fellow workers below and their families have my deepest sympathy, but I think there has been several failures toward safety features and if we would bring it to their attention, the company, there was different times that they would look down their noses at us. I haven't been proud the way Consol has treated me, although I went ahead and made money off Consol. I had a family to support, and

I don't like to be a rolling stone, but I certainly don't want my testimony whitewashed before Congress can hear it."[11]

Those who did testify revealed unsafe mining practices, any of which easily could have blown up the mine.

Two Men, 22 Square Miles

The testimony of George Glover Jr., Consol's contract fireboss, revealed major lapses in Consol's firebossing. He told the panel that when he and another man examined the mine on Sundays, he usually inspected seven sections, moving from place to place by jeep. His buddy helped him with the rest of the work.[12]

By law, that fireboss run had to be completed within four hours of the beginning of the cateye shift at 12 a.m.[13] In other words, in four hours, they had to inspect a 22-square-mile mine that had ten working sections, a long haulage road and a slope.

"The two of you did this whole mine?" asked Lewis Evans, UMW's safety director.

"Yes sir," Glover said.[14]

Evans read the law out loud, reiterating all the areas that must be checked:

"Each person . . . in making his examination shall examine all active working places . . . make tests with a permissible flame safety lamp for accumulations of methane and oxygen deficiency; examine seals and doors; examine and test the roof, face and ribs in the working places and on active roadways and travelways, approaches to abandoned workings and accessible falls in active sections."[15]

Then Evans asked, "I want to know how is it possible for two men in four hours in a mine as extensive as this to carry out all these duties that are placed on a fire boss under the law. How can you possibly do this? How can anybody possibly do this?"[16]

"I was busy," Glover said.

"You must be flying," Evans said.[17]

There was no reply.

Thomas J. Whyte, a Consol lawyer, tried to downplay the testimony, but Evans brought the subject up again, when Mountaineer Coal's safety director, Jess G. Bowers, testified.

Bowers, too, said that only two men made the four-hour run. He said the two could probably fireboss the working sections in four hours, but it would be "pretty rough" to cover the entire mine.[18]

"You know as well as I do that this is an utter impossibility. . . . [T]his mine isn't being firebossed," Evans said.[19]

Bowers did not reply.

When a few fireboss record books were produced, the investigators discussed them off-the-record with Bowers. On record, Evans then made a statement to summarize the panel's understanding:

"The only two men in the mine on Sunday who have been instructed to make fireboss examinations are the two men that I have spoken of, and I say again that the provisions of the West Virginia mining law cannot be complied with in firebossing of this mine by two men. . . . I would suggest to the state officials who are here, that if and when this mine ever reopens that they examine this problem because it is very vital and that presently they examine it at other mines operated by this company."[20]

The fireboss books produced during the investigation showed that on the Sunday before the mine exploded, Glover and his buddy started their fireboss run at 7 p.m., an hour before they should have. They walked out of the mine at 11:45 p.m. The records showed they examined the working sections, but none of the abandoned areas, escapeways or bleeder airways.[21] The books also lacked evidence that anyone had examined the mine's main haulageway between the Athas Run fan and 5North. This section contained about 4,000 feet of what Fay Casseday called "dead space" because so little fresh air reached the area.[22]

Bowers told the panel that Mountaineer Coal's Eugene Lieving was the company's safety inspector for the No.9. When Lieving testified, he said he was responsible for overseeing the mine's ventilation. The panel, however, did not ask him about ventilation issues. Instead, their questions focused on the timing and predictability of federal and state mine inspections.[23]

Blocked Bleeders

When officials questioned No.9's general mine foreman, Fay Casseday, they discovered what Consol had known for years: Most of the mine's bleeder airways, which ventilated its vast gobs, were not functioning at all. Casseday testified that the bleeder system on the west side of the mine had so many roof falls and obstructions that it was, in effect, useless, which was a serious violation of the law.[24]

William Park of the U.S. Bureau of Mines pressed Casseday about that bleeder system: "[W]ere you able to get air of any type or kind in that area?"

"To my knowledge, no," Cassedy said.

"Well, what you're actually saying then, Mr. Casseday, is all you're doing is ventilating the very edge of that gob, that you can actually get air only at the edge?" Park asked.

"I would have to say, yes," he answered.

Park could not let the point go.

"Is it your opinion that these gobs are loaded or do you think that they are rather free of methane?"

"I think that in any of these gassy mines, there's a lot of gas on the gobs, yes," Casseday said.

"Do you consider that you have a bleeder system in this mine, an adequate bleeder system?" Park asked.

"No. I have no way of getting back there to check this in any of these sections, see. Now I may have made a misstatement there. I had no idea of whether there would be air pulled through this or not, as you can't get back there, and an adequate bleeder system that you can actually travel, we don't have," Casseday said.

Casseday's direct supervisor, No.9's general superintendent, Lockie Riggs, had told the investigators a different story. Riggs said the firebosses walked the bleeders frequently. He said he himself checked them quite often.[25]

"I will go from one section to another in the returns myself just to double check the ventilation, falls, pipe lines, etcetera," he said.

"Did you have any occasion in the last month or so to question the amount of methane in your bleeders or gobs?" asked Leslie Ryan, a top mine inspector for West Virginia.

"No, not necessarily, I have been in all the return areas from the Mods Run shaft down to the extreme end of the mine in the last month, myself," Riggs said.

UMW's Lewis Evans asked Riggs if the bleeders were blocked by roof falls.

"In some areas they're congested by falls. We have emergency escapeways that have recently been run, and they're all open," Riggs said.

"Is this restricting the air in the bleeders?" Evans said.

"No sir. You can have pretty large falls and still be able to pass over them, and air is still able to pass over them," he said.

If state or federal inspectors noticed problems with the bleeder system, none noted them in any reports.

West Virginia inspectors examined the No.9 six times in 1967 and 1968. Not once did they cite the company for its dangerous bleeder system. Only once during those two years did a state inspector note any ventilation violations—in October 1967, inspectors found a section that did not have enough air.

Federal officials inspected the mine five times in 1967 and 1968 and did not note any violations related to the bleeder system. In fact, they did not cite the mine for any ventilation violations during their inspections.

Ventilation clearly was compromised by the lack of permanent stoppings, which was documented in the fireboss books and corroborated by testimony.

Park asked Casseday if he realized that the men on 7South were working with four or five open crosscuts on the right side of their section.[26]

"As I say, we were in the process of moving back to the left side and we had plastic curtains. We had masons up there on ventilation, two masons that night this thing happened, and I also had 10 metal stoppings that was someplace between the bottom and this section. We was going to get all this caught up the next day," Casseday said.

Testimony confirmed that the mine's fan system malfunctioned and ventilation laws were broken on a regular basis.

General superintendent Lockie Riggs admitted that the company routinely bypassed the alarm systems on its fans and its methane monitors. According to Riggs, the FEMCO fan safety system often sent off false alarms. He said company bosses always checked the fans to make sure they were running. If they got a false alarm, common practice was to disable it until they could get one of the two maintenance men to fix it.[27]

They'd just "block it out" at the substation, Riggs said.

His testimony should have set off alarms throughout the coal mining industry and the mine safety enforcement world. But it did not. The investigators did not ask the most obvious questions:

- Were any of No.9's fan safety alarms "blocked out" in November 1968? On November 20, 1968?
- How long does it take to get a maintenance man to come to the mine?
- How long does it take to fix the system?
- What can go wrong?
- How do you monitor a fan when the system is "blocked out?" What records are kept that document "blocked out alarms?"
- How did the workers "block out an alarm?"
- What else do you "block out?"

The panel members returned to the topic briefly when they questioned Cecil Selders, No.9's maintenance supervisor. He told them that the manufacturer's men were called out to do FEMCO system repairs, and they had been there in July 1968, testing the system. No.9 men could do only minor repairs, like changing a fuse, Selders said.[28]

Many important questions went unasked.

A case in point was the panel's handling of Alex Kovar, the man who was called to the mine at 3:30 a.m. on the day the mine exploded. When he explained his job, he told the investigators that he repaired parts and took care of the No.1 fan (slope) and Athas Run fan. He said he checked those fans once each day. He added that he checked the Mods Run fan "once a week unless it's down or there is power trouble or such."[29] No one asked

Kovar what he did when he checked the fans or what kinds of records were kept about the fans.

The law required then, as it does now, that someone—a real human being—physically check each fan once a day. None of the investigators asked for, and no one produced, evidence showing that the checks were being made on the Mods Run or Llewellyn Run fans.[30]

Kovar told the panel that he changed the No.1 fan's chart about an hour before the mine exploded and gave the chart to Foster Turner. No one asked him if he changed any other fan charts. No one asked him what the chart looked like, even though the chart held a week's worth of information about the fan. No one asked Foster Turner about that chart or any other charts or records that would have held important clues about No.9's ventilation system during the months, weeks, days and hours before the mine exploded.

Kovar must have known the importance of the charts. He mentioned them in his testimony and in a written statement he submitted to the panel.[31] Because Kovar was called when trouble arose, he may have been able to offer a lot of information about the mine's operation. Nonetheless, the panel asked him few questions beyond those specifically about the morning of the explosion. As it was, Kovar was so shaken physically and emotionally that two people, one on each side, had to hold onto him as he left the courthouse.[32]

Strangely, no one asked Consol managers for any of the mine's fan charts or fan record books. Most certainly they held information that would have explained a great deal about the mine's ventilation problems.

The 379 pages of transcribed sworn testimony show that federal, state and UMW officials were not skilled interrogators. Not only did they often fail to ask the right questions, they often fed answers to those being questioned.

For instance, when section foreman and company man Arthur Merrifield testified, federal official William R. Park, asked him what he did on the afternoon shift before the explosion. Merrifield answered that his crew moved from 6Right-7South to 6North.[33]

PARK: Did you find it in first-class shape when you arrived or did you do some work to get it in shape to start working?

MERRIFIELD: Found it in shape to work.

PARK: By this, you checked the air, checked the faces, checked your rock dusting, and the roadways?

MERRIFIELD: Watered the roadways.

PARK: Cables and equipment?

MERRIFIELD: Right.

PARK: And found everything satisfactory?

MERRIFIELD: In working order.

Rather than list what Merrifield should have done, Park should have let Merrifield explain what he did do. Otherwise, the panel had no way to know if Merrifield really knew how to fireboss a section before starting production. In fact, little information was gathered from Merrifield, even though he opened the door for a line of questioning that should have been followed.

PARK: Did anything at all unusual or out-of-the-ordinary occur on the section the last Tuesday you worked?

MERRIFIELD: No, nothing unusual any more than we broke down about the middle of the shift and moved to another section.

Neither Park nor anyone else on the panel followed up by asking what "broke down?" How often does equipment fail? What happens when it does? Was gas found on 6Right-7South that shift? Were there open crosscuts when Parks left? What, exactly, was happening on that section and what were the conditions there before Parks left it?

Despite the ineptitude of those conducting the interrogations and the biased nature of the entire process, the officials did gather enough information to conclude that the mine was unsafe. The hearings demonstrated that the coal company had broken numerous laws, including those that regulated mine ventilation, firebossing and coal dust control. Sadly, as time passed, it became clearer and clearer that neither state nor federal officials were going to use that information to hold anyone accountable for the deaths of 78 men.

Failure to Report

State officials did not even bother to produce a fatal accident report follow-ing the No.9 disaster,[34] even though state law required them to write one. The federal mining agency did not release its report until 1990. Its author, James D. Micheal, had submitted it to his typist on November 29, 1969, a year after No.9 was permanently sealed. When the report was made public, officials called it an "informational report," distancing themselves from any controversy.[35]

The only reason the federal Mine Safety and Health Administration (MSHA) released any report was to silence the UMWA and J. Davitt McAteer who continued, year after year, to ask for one. Finally, in July 1986, McAteer, then a lawyer with the Occupational Safety and Health Law Center in Wash-ington D.C., penned a Freedom of Information Act request for the federal report, which, he noted, "has been in draft form for a number of years."[36]

MSHA's Ronald J. Schell's response made it clear that the government never intended to release a final investigation report. The No.9 investiga-tion had never been completed because the mine was sealed, Schell wrote in his reply. He admitted a "draft report" existed, but said no decision had ever been reached on whether to finalize it. He told McAteer that a meeting would be convened to decide if the agency had the resources to finish it. At that time, McAteer's FOIA request would be processed.[37]

Even though the report had been finished for years, almost four more years passed before McAteer's request was "processed." It was done then only reluctantly.

Drafts of an internal "Briefing Outline" were produced and circulated that clearly show MSHA's damage-control plan. Handwritten notes on the outlines reveal the motivation behind the release: "If MSHA doesn't eventu-ally release a report, the last draft of record will be subject to FOIA." More notes show MSHA officials feared being forced to produce their "notes, records, etc." if they did not release something to keep people quiet.[38] The plan then became one to "release the printed report, quietly," without a press release.

In the outline, officials noted their fears of criticism from Consol and the families for waiting more than 20 years to issue a report. They feared outrage by the UMW, the widows and families, and Davitt McAteer because they failed to reach any "hard-hitting conclusions of responsibility for the disaster." They feared that their "editing" of the original report would cause former federal employees to accuse them of "whitewashing the report."

Indeed, had these parties been privy to the hearing transcripts and recovery documents held by federal and state officials and the depositions of Consol's managers taken after the mine was closed, they would have had good reason to be angry.

Widows and Wildcat Strikes

"Death in the mines can be as sudden as an explosion or a collapse of a roof and ribs, or it comes insidiously from pneumoconiosis or black lung disease. When a miner leaves his home for work, he and his family must live with the unspoken but always present fear that before the working day is over, he may be crushed or burned to death or suffocated. This acceptance of the possibility of death in the mines has become as much a part of the job as the tools and the tunnels.

"The time has come to replace this fatalism with hope by substituting action for words. Catastrophes in the coal mines are not inevitable. They can be prevented, and they must be prevented."

–President Richard M. Nixon, introducing his coal mine legislation March 3, 1969[1]

Two weeks after President Nixon told Congress to make mines safer and four months after her husband, Pete, died deep inside the No.9 mine, Sara Lee Kaznoski put on a black suit and a pair of black gloves[2] and asked Congress to stop the slaughter. By that time, 44 more coal miners had died underground in the United States.[3]

Mrs. Kaznoski told the U.S. Senate Subcommittee on Labor: "Each and every one of the widows and mothers that lost the same as I have lost and the children in losing their fathers through this terrible tragedy do not want a repetition of what we have gone through.

"Then, too, not only in a mass form of 78, but one by one taken, burned to death, crushed to death. My sister lost her husband and was left a widow with five children. Her husband was crushed to death some years ago.

"There are men whom I know well and their families who have lost one or both legs. They have lost fingers, they have lost so much, so many parts of their body which God gave them which, if you would only stop to think, the coal operators and the Federal Government and these State legislators could help how important all these things are to humanity.[4]

"My husband was a coal miner since the age of 14. He put many, many years in the mines. My father was a coal miner. My grandfather was a coal miner. My husband was injured twice in the mines. But still he was brave because he had a job to do. It is very necessary that we have a good administration and definitely a strong legislation."[5]

She was not an eloquent speaker, but on that March day, Sara Lee Kaznoski became a spokeswoman for the widows of the No.9 disaster and for thousands of families who had lost and would lose their loved ones in the mines.

New Jersey Sen. Harrison Williams Jr. thanked her for her testimony. "It helps us, Mrs. Kaznoski, to do what our Nation is now demanding, the right thing for people working in the mines and for their families," Williams said. "Certainly it is much too late for you, particularly, Mrs. Kaznoski."[6]

"You are right, Mr. Chairman, negligence is a crime. The company has caused the wrongful deaths of our spouses," she responded.[7]

Two other No.9 widows appeared with her, Mrs. Mary Kay Rogers and Mrs. Norma Snyder. They had few words to say. "I feel our cochairman, Mrs. Kaznoski, has explained everything. We would like to see all these safety and mine health bills passed," Mrs. Snyder said.

Mrs. Rogers asked for the same. "Of course, my husband is gone. Today is the fourth month. He is entombed in the No.9 mine but I still feel that a bill should be passed for more safety for all miners. Thank you."[8]

The widows sat beside their host, U.S. Rep. Ken Hechler, a West Virginia Democrat, who had become something of a hero to thousands of West Virginia miners.

Mary Matish (second from left), Sara Kaznoski (third from left) and other No.9 widows lobby in Charleston, West Virginia, for stricter coal mine safety laws. Courtesy of James Matish.

Hechler; activist Ralph Nader; Dr. Isadore E. Buff, a Charleston, W.Va., cardiologist; Dr. Donald Rasmussen, a pulmonary specialist from Beckley, W.Va.; and Dr. Hawey A. Wells, a pathologist from Conemaugh Valley Memorial Hospital in Pennsylvania, had begun a campaign to fight black lung disease.[9]

The doctors started the Physicians' Committee for Miners' Health and Safety (PCMHS). All three doctors had treated and studied coal miners with black lung. In fact, Dr. Wells and a U.S. Public Health Service researcher, Dr. Werner A. Laquerur, who was chief of pathology at the Appalachian Regional hospital in Beckley, had published their research in 1966 in *Science News*.[10]

The two had studied the bodies of hundreds of bituminous coal miners. In one study of 150 miners, they found that the right side of the heart for 40 percent of the miners was enlarged as a result of the strain of circulating blood through diseased lungs. The doctors also studied living miners and found the same strain among these individuals as well. That black lung did more than cause life-threatening and disabling breathing problems was clear to these physicians.

Local union leaders and miners joined Nader and Hechler to form the West Virginia Black Lung Association, and they began to travel through mining country gathering support. Three weeks before Hechler and the No.9 widows went to Washington, Hechler stood in the Charleston Civic Center waving a hunk of bologna as he denounced a West Virginia Medical Association report that claimed cigarettes, not coal dust, were damaging miners' lungs. About 2,000 miners were in the crowd, part of a growing wildcat strike that had begun when miners walked out of the East Gulf Mine in Raleigh County, West Virginia.[11]

"The greatest heroes are you coal miners who have taken your future in your hands and said: 'No longer are we going to live and work and die like animals,'" Hechler proclaimed. Speakers belittled the national leaders of the United Mine Workers (UMW) for ingratiating themselves with the coal companies and ignoring miners' working conditions.

James Wyatt, a 60-year-old miner with black lung disease, struggled for his breath as he sang a miner's song:

A young miner's lungs may be hearty and hale
When he enters the mine with his dinner pail
But coal dust and grime
In a few years time
Fills up his lungs and they begin to fail
Black lungs, full of coal dust
Coal miners must breathe it or bust.
Black lungs, gasping for breath
With black lungs we are choking to death.

After the rally, the miners and their supporters marched to the steps of the state Capitol, carrying placards that read: "No law, no work." "No law, no coal."

One of the marchers, Mrs. James Hall, told a *Charleston Gazette* reporter that her husband was disabled by black lung, but a doctor told him it was "all in his mind."

When the picketers reached the Capitol steps, then-Governor Arch Alfred Moore Jr. came out and spoke to them. He said he supported black lung legislation, but he scolded the miners for striking. Miners had a right to strike, he said, but their families would be left without necessities if they did not work.

That Moore was indebted to the coal industry for his political success was well known then and would become more obvious in the years to follow. A Republican lawyer, he was elected as governor in 1968, 1972 and 1984. In 1990, his debt to the coal industry became transparent. He was sentenced to almost six years in a federal prison after pleading guilty to five federal charges, including:

- accepting more than $500,000 to help Beckley coal operator H. Paul Kizer obtain a $2 million refund from the state's black lung benefit fund
- filing a false income tax return in 1984 by not reporting $10,000 in cash received from an official of Island Creek Coal Co.
- filing a false income tax return in 1985 by not reporting $50,000 received from an agent of Marrowbone Coal Co.

Moore later tried to withdraw his guilty pleas, but was unsuccessful. He was released from prison in less than three years based on his good behavior.

Wildcats

In 1969, the striking coal miners did not heed Moore's industry-driven warning to return to the coal mines. By March, about 20,000 West Virginia coal miners had walked out of the mines, refusing to work until their lawmakers took action. West Virginia legislators could not ignore them, nor could the lawmakers in Washington. *New York Times* reporter, Ben A. Franklin, covered the story, just as he had covered the No. 9 disaster. National television news teams broadcast it, too, giving the public an education about the coal mining industry and the laborers who brought them the coal that sent electricity to their homes.

Frank Reynolds reported the wildcat strike on the "ABC Evening News." He interviewed a West Virginia Coal Association spokesman and Dr. Hawey Wells. The Coal Association spokesman maintained that no evidence showed that lung diseases were related to coal mining. Dr. Wells countered flippantly that between the ages of 60 and 64, 800 times as many miners die of lung disease than gin.[12]

Before the strike ended, an estimated 40,000 miners were on strike, idling almost every mine in West Virginia. The movement spread to Pennsylvania and Kentucky. UMW president, Tony Boyle, ordered the miners back to work. They refused. Boyle was losing support, and a power struggle was underway within the UMW.

By mid-March, "NBC Evening News" anchor David Brinkley reported the West Virginia legislature had passed legislation to compensate miners with black lung, but until Governor Moore signed the bill, the miners refused to go back into the mines. The governor signed the bill.

Boyle Goes Ballistic

The day after Hechler waved the log of lunchmeat in Charleston, Tony Boyle exploded before the U.S. Senate subcommittee.[13]

He explained that he had come from a family of coal miners. He knew all about black lung; his father had the disease and had died in his arms. Then he began a tirade against Rep. Hechler, Ralph Nader, and Buff, Wells, and Rasmussen, the three physicians. He did not call them by name; he called them names: "instant experts," "do-gooders," "false prophets," "self-appointed saviors," and "bologna experts." Where had they been all these years while he has been working for the good of the miners?

After he had ranted for some time, Sen. Winston Prouty from Vermont interrupted him: "Mr. Boyle, I wonder if you would care to identify some of these so-called experts you have been referring to."

For a few minutes, Boyle discussed the pending legislation. Then he blasted the nameless "ballyhooers," the "cheap politician," the "professional fakers." Boyle never named the men he ridiculed.

When the subject of Consolidation Coal and the No. 9 explosion surfaced, Boyle again defended the coal company, saying it had supported mine safety legislation in the past. He said he did not agree with the coal miners who were striking. They were blackjacking Congress; something he would not do.

He said he had solicited the coal industry's support, and it was that support that helped him strengthen the coal mine law in 1966. His fight did not get into the "eastern papers," he said. "I will get a bologna, too, and I will stuff it down somebody's throat if necessary, if they keep on."

His threats were not idle. By the end of the year, he would do something much worse.

When Boyle quieted down, Sen. Williams thanked him for his written statement and the "other illuminating comments that were made in response to questions and without questions."

The senators and everyone else had learned a lot that day. Tony Boyle had lost control of the union and of himself.

Hechler had disparaged the UMW, but he was not a latecomer to coal mine safety. In 1968, he had carried President Lyndon Johnson's coal mine safety bill, but it died without a hearing. The No. 9 explosion triggered something in him. He was so angry that he sat at his Royal typewriter and hammered out his own bill, which moved through the House. He knew that the time was right to make changes. The public was angry. The coal miners were angry. Hechler, the former college professor, spoke out. He called federal laws weak, mine inspections all but useless, and the conditions in the mines criminal.[14]

The truth was his bill was stronger than the legislation the UMW offered, and Richard Nixon's legislation was stronger than the UMW's. Hechler's bill called for the highest civil penalties against coal mine operators who violated the law: $1,000 minimum with $20,000 maximum per violation. The Nixon administration bill, a form of the former Johnson administration bill, and the UMW bill each called for fines of $500 minimum and $10,000 maximum.[15]

All the bills called for criminal penalties, but Hechler's and the Nixon administration's bills were the toughest: $10,000 and six months in prison for the first offense and $20,000 and one year for the second offense. The UMW bill's fines were half that.[16]

The fines were a huge step forward, but coal miners wanted more than fines; they wanted rules, specific rules. Two West Virginia coal miners who worked for the Consolidation Coal Company, Elmer Yocum and Elijah Wolford, told U.S. senators they were tired of federal inspectors who could only make recommendations. They wanted inspectors who could protect them. They said many of their state inspectors ignored violations because of conflicts of interest: they had been company men and owned company stock.

"'Recommendation' is a dirty word to me," Mr. Yocum told the senators. Inspectors should be able to go into a mine and say, "Do this," or "Do that," he said.[17]

"We don't like the word 'sufficient' inasmuch as ventilation is concerned. . . . We want so many feet, cubic feet of air per minute spelled out," he said.[18]

"We don't want 'adequate' clearance, we want so many feet and inches of clearance," he said, referring to rules that dictate how close machinery can come to the ribs and roof of a mine or the electrically powered lines along the roof.

"These words such as 'adequate,' 'recommend,' and 'sufficient' are too loose. They are as wide as a mountain," Mr. Yocum said.[19]

Such terms had not been effective, and everyone knew it. Even specific recommendations about the amount of air that must pass through a working face had failed because the machinery of mining had changed. Continuous miners were faster, bringing down more coal, as much as eight tons a minute, testified West Virginia's Sen. Robert C. Byrd, the son of a coal miner.[20] The faster the coal fell, the faster methane was emitted. What once had been considered an "adequate" amount of face air no longer was adequate or safe.

Mr. Wolford had counted the number of times the word "adequate" appeared in the federal coal mine safety law at that time: 34 times.[21] Safety was not taken seriously at his mine, he said. When people were hurt, everyone in the mine was penalized financially. But even that was not taken seriously.[22]

He shared a letter from Consolidation Coal to its employees at the company's Arkwright and Osage mines in West Virginia. It detailed three lost-time accidents from August, two resulting from "inadequate" clearance between a coal miner and the mine's roof.[23]

Edgar W. Statler, a shuttle car operator, suffered a neck injury when his hat caught a roof bolt and he was knocked from his shuttle car. Lewis Snow, a shuttle car operator, suffered a fractured vertebra after he was thrown against the roof when his shuttle car hit part of the mine floor that had buckled into a roll. Charles Haas, a mechanic, sprained his back while lifting part of a machine. The penalty for sustaining injuries: Miners at both mines would not receive their 400 S&H Green Stamps that month. Four hundred stamps would have filled about a third of an S&H Green Stamp book. A whole book was worth about $3. A person could trade in books for merchandise. For instance, an electric shaver cost 9 1/4 books.[24]

If a mine had a perfect safety record all year, miners could expect to collect S&H Green Stamps worth $24.50, Mr. Wolford said. But he had never known that to happen.[25]

He also told the senators that Consolidation Coal officials routinely underreported the number of accidents in his mine. Nevertheless, thousands of injuries were reported each year. In 1968, coal companies had reported 3,845 nonfatal mining accidents in West Virginia, Rep. Hechler told the committee.[26]

Underreporting by the companies and the state and federal governments' lax safety inspections could explain how Consolidation Coal claimed a "good safety record."

Such claims did not prevent the No. 9 disaster, which at last had prompted Congress to take action and the federal government to take a hard look at its mine inspection program.

During the hearings in the House, John F. O'Leary, director of the U.S. Bureau of Mines, testified that he had issued new orders to federal mine inspectors, concerning both the "method and the rigor of inspections." Spot inspections had been increased manifold and the Bureau had revised its interpretations of the existing law to utilize "every ounce of authority inherent in that law," O'Leary said.[27]

The Bureau also had begun "intensive investigations to find methods for improving ventilation in abandoned areas of underground mines," he said. No doubt, this work was prompted by Consolidation Coal's lack of ventilation in its abandoned gob areas, which were seriously hampering the mine's ventilation but never cited by federal inspectors.

Hechler and others were pushing for safety and for a set of coal dust standards that would protect miners from pneumoconiosis, or black lung disease. In 1969, the law did not specify how much coal dust could be in the air of a coal mine. The language of the federal law was vague, or as Elmer Yocum put it, "as wide as a mountain."[28]

The law passed in 1952 read: "Where underground mining operations raise an excessive amount of dust into the air, water, or water with a wetting agent added to it, or other effective method shall be used to allay such dust at its source."[29]

How much was "excessive?" What about dust that had drifted far from its source?

Many in the coal industry did not even want to recognize pneumoconiosis as a disease separate from silicosis, another deadly lung disease caused by breathing in silica dust from rocks and sand. The surgeon general, however, recognized it as a separate disease and, in 1969, estimated that 100,000 coal miners were afflicted.[30]

The former Johnson administration bill, the Hechler bill, and the UMW bill each called for no more than 3 milligrams of coal dust per cubic meter of air. That level, scientist believed, would begin to reduce the incidence of black lung disease. The Nixon bill was the weakest, allowing 4.5 milligrams of dust per cubic meter of air and a reduction to 3 milligrams "as soon as possible."[31]

The coal industry wanted no regulation. Coal companies did not want to pay for equipment to measure dust levels or adopt new practices that would minimize dust. Cloyd D. McDowell, president of the Harlan County, Kentucky, Coal Operators' Association, argued that a lung specialist from

Great Britain had told doctors at a UMW hospital in his state that breathing coal dust alone would not cause black lung disease. Another substance had to be present, such as cigarette smoke, he said. The doctor's visit was in 1958, when people still thought cigarette smoke was safe.

"Coal dust per se may or may not be harmful to the health of miners," McDowell said. He wanted more research before Congress imposed "arbitrary limits."[32]

No one had proof that the modern mining machines created more respirable dust, argued James R. Garvey, vice president of the National Coal Association. He said the machines reduced the amount of dust miners breathed because some machines were equipped with water sprays. He also argued that some of the dust particles were too big to stick in the lungs. His solution: more study.[33]

Huda Bailey, a former West Virginia coal miner, wanted more than a study. At 62, he had spent 50 years working in the mines, and he could barely breath.

"When I first started I was in the horse-and-mule days. There wasn't so much dust at that time. But when this new equipment arrived and went into production it stirred up all the dust, which is what is causing so much black lung and silicosis," he told the senators.[34] "About 10 years ago my breathing went dead on me little by little."[35]

The dust is too thick for a respirator to handle, Bailey said. A miner could take two or three breaths through a respirator and it would clog up with the dust.

Bailey testified that he was totally disabled because he could not breath. His income was limited to Social Security disability and the UMW's Mine Workers' Fund, which together gave him $267 a month.[36]

Henry Mann, also a retired West Virginia coal miner, told the senators that he ran a cutting machine for 25 of his 42 years in the mines. The machine had made him almost deaf and filled his lungs with coal dust. "At times you can't see nothing or hear nothing or nothing else," he said.[37]

Former West Virginia coal miner Otis Ratliff told the senators that he had to pay $1,332 for his own rib biopsy and hospital stay before the workmen's compensation board in West Virginia would believe he had silicosis.

The board would not accept two doctors' reports with the diagnosis of silicosis. At that time, the board did not recognize black lung as a disease.

"I thought if we could get something done about this, although if I didn't benefit, maybe it will help someone else," Mr. Ratliff said. "I thank you all."[38]

Sen. Robert C. Byrd described the slow and painful deaths of miners suffering from black lung disease. If they do not die from heart failure, they develop pneumonia or simply suffocate. "One out of every 10 soft coal miners working in the coalfields of Appalachia has a radiographic evidence of coal workers' pneumoconiosis," he told them, quoting a U.S. Public Health Service study.[39]

He also explained that although West Virginia had just passed a law to compensate miners disabled by the disease, it was not retroactive. Thus, none of the miners who had the disease before the law was passed would receive any help. He asked his colleagues to adopt a benefit program that would last for at least 20 years.[40]

West Virginia Sen. Randolph Jennings, who sat on the Senate subcommittee on Labor and had carried the UMW's bill, was not particularly optimistic about putting tough controls on coal dust. He was worried about the economic effect on the industry. He always had catered to the coal companies.[41]

President Nixon threatened to veto the bill because of the black lung compensation costs. Republican House Leader Gerald Ford moved to strike the black lung provisions. Then, just after Christmas, Rep. Hechler brought his most powerful allies back to Washington, a group of No.9 widows.

The coal industry had political contributions on its side, but the coal miners had the ghosts of 78 men who accompanied their widows to Washington. The dead men and the wildcat strikes proved to be more powerful than the coal money behind many of the politicians.

Years later, Sara Kaznoski would credit Hechler for inspiring the widows when they were at their lowest. "He taught us to be angry; he taught us to stand up and speak out. He taught us what direction to go," she told an Associated Press reporter.[42] She and other No.9 widows formed their own group, the Farmington Widows Mine Disaster Committee, which supported the legislative battles and a few battles of their own.

In the end, Congress passed legislation that required mining companies to keep coal dust under control so that no more than 3.0 milligrams of respirable dust per cubic meter of air circulated in the active working areas of the mine. Within three years, the limit dropped to 2.0 milligrams. But there were loopholes in the law. Any company could apply for a permit of noncompliance if it could prove it could not meet the standard. After a year, the company could renew its permit for another six months. The permit allowed companies to operate with as much as 4.5 milligrams per cubic meter of air.

Congress passed the legislation, but President Nixon was ready to veto it. He said the provisions for compensating coal miners with black lung disease were too expensive. The Farmington Widows Mine Disaster Committee and the West Virginia Black Lung Association and their supporters were not going to let that happen. On December 29, they asked miners to protest, and a smattering of wildcat strikes began. The miners said they would not stop in West Virginia or Pennsylvania or Kentucky.

On December 31, President Nixon signed the bill, delivering a much different speech than the one he had given following the No.9 disaster. He called the 1969 Federal Coal Mine Health and Safety Act a "historic advancement in industrial practices." But he had reservations about the workmen's compensation program. He did not say the words "black lung" or "pneumoconiosis." He said workmen's compensation was the job of the states, and the new law should in no way lead anyone to believe that the program would be continued forever. "[A]ll Federal responsibility in this area will expire within seven years," he said.[43]

President Jimmy Carter, however, saw the issue differently, signing the federal Black Lung Benefits Act, that included an excise tax on coal to compensate miners with black lung disease. As he signed House Bill 4544 on March 1, 1977, President Carter made this statement:

"Coal miners have a right to working conditions as free as possible from dangerous coal dust. The black lung program recognizes that miners and their families also deserve compensation under a fair system when they contract this terrible disease and die or are disabled as a result of their work in the mines."[44]

Body Production

"Now, concrete seals are broken, chipped away by chattering jackhammers. . . .
It probably will be spring before the bodies of the trapped miners six miles down are
reached, brought out and put to rest. No one can tell how long it will take the living
to find peace."

—*Roger Stuart, reporter,* The Pittsburgh Press, *Sept. 14, 1969.*[1]

While the battle over coal miners' health and safety raged in Washington and Charleston, W.Va., in 1969, Consol officials began putting together a plan to reopen the No.9.

David H. Davis sent a "personal & confidential" memo to his top managers in March asking them to formulate their own ideas but to keep everything confidential. He told them not to "discuss matters that pertain to No 9 with any Tom, Dick or Harry with whom you meet. . . . I expect you to treat all these matters in confidence because we cannot afford to be giving out any information to anyone."[2]

The biggest challenge was the same one the mine officials had faced before the explosion: how to ventilate a mine that was full of methane gas. Much would depend on where they first entered the mine. Company officials considered several options before meeting with federal, state and UMW men.[3]

Plan A: Enter the mine through the Mahan Shaft, explore that area and move to the 7South faces, then 6Right-7South, then north to the Main West Headings, eventually reaching 8North and 9North.

Plan B: Enter the mine through the slope on the east side and move west.

Plan C: Enter by the slope and Mahan Shaft simultaneously.

Two schemes were possible for ventilating the mine during the early stages of recovery. The older method used "airlocks," which meant sending in a recovery team that would advance by about 1,000 feet, stop and seal the area, and move slowly in front of the seal taking the available air with them. The teams would then erect another seal and repeat the procedure as they moved through the mine. It was a slow and dangerous method.

A faster and safer method required the drilling of large boreholes through which blowers attempt to clear out the methane from a tunnel about 3,000 feet long. Then the men would build a seal, drill more holes, and advance.[4]

By June 1969, almost seven months had passed since the disaster. UMW officials, activists and the families wanted the dead men out of the mine. Ralph Nader called James Westfield, with the U.S. Bureau of Mines, to find out when the mine would be opened. Westfield told him the fires were out, but hot spots could still be an issue.[5] Temperatures measured through small boreholes into mine had dropped to between 58 degrees to 63 degrees Fahrenheit, which meant there were no fires in most areas of the mine. Still, the gobs and caved-in areas might have been burning, and the Llewellyn Run portal temperatures were too high.[6]

When Consol and the officials met on June 16, Westfield took control. The mine would have to be opened from the east, and Consol should follow its plan to drill two 22-inch boreholes into the mine that could be used to flush out the methane. No one would go into the mine until the methane came out.[7]

William Park, also with the U.S. Bureau of Mines, insisted that the east end of the mine be opened and restored before moving west. "We must produce bodies soon," Park said.[8]

Consol's William N. Poundstone did not want to reopen the east end until crews were ready to move west.[9]

Park accused Consol of a deliberate delay.[10]

Consol's C.R. Nailler countered that their reopening plan had been ready for weeks, but the company had not been able to get all the government officials to come to a meeting. Finally, Consol and government officials agreed to start drilling and meet again the next month.[11]

Consol officials met with the families and briefed them on the plan; then the drilling and outside preparation began. The drilling was not cheap. The estimate to drill one 770-foot hole was about $68,000, or more than $390,000 in 2009 dollars.[12] The coal company told government officials that it was self-insuring on the equipment it lost underground. Not discussed was insurance for lost production or the type of tax write-offs the company might be able to use to cover its costs.

The company had made lists of the 15 rescue teams it would need and numerous supplies, including: track wrenches, wooden cars, locomotives, tractors and trailers, air pumps, air saws, mobile radio units, walkie-talkies, mine phones, steel ties, telephone wire, inflatable stoppings, 100 rolls of brattice cloth, 5,000 solid cement blocks, 5,000 wedges, 2,000 roof bolts, mason trowels, timber jacks and a live pony with rubber horse shoes and a harness. Consol also made a list of the unthinkable: 10 stretchers, 80 white sheets, and 80 plastic mortician's bags.[13]

The company had consulted "confidentially and unofficially" with a mortician for the handling of the bodies. A temporary morgue would be established on the surface, where morticians could pick up the bodies "as usually contracted for by the family."[14]

Consol officials wanted the morticians to form a corporation and furnish "technicians" to go underground and prepare the bodies for transfer to the surface. "Families should be relieved and should appreciate a more professional treatment of bodies. Recovery personnel will be less likely to be emotionally affected," the plan stated.[15]

Ultimately, that step would not be realized. The miners on the recovery teams handled all the underground work and the bodies. Many of the men were deeply affected. John Brock, who was on a recovery team, still cannot talk about finding and bringing out the bodies. Forty-some years later, he immediately chokes up.[16]

Methane Check

As Consol employees began readying for the opening of the mine, they were hit with a reminder of the dangers of methane gas. On the July 29 cateye shift, Frank Sanders was painting the inside of the lamphouse near the Athas Run intake air shaft when he saw a flash near a water sink. An explosion followed that knocked Sanders to the floor and set the lamphouse ablaze. His boss had driven away to get him more paint, so Sanders covered the two miles to the slope office on foot. He was taken to the hospital and treated for minor burns, and the fire was put out by 5:30 a.m. No one could blame him for the explosion because he did not smoke. However, the authorities could blame his foreman for not checking the lamphouse for methane before leaving him alone to paint. As it turned out, the miners who had been painting inside the building two shifts before Sanders had found 2 percent methane leaking into the building and opened doors and windows for ventilation. Allegedly, the power to the building had been disconnected prior to the painting. Federal investigators, however, said they could not determine the cause of the methane ignition because the explosion and the fire had damaged the electrical circuits.[17]

August Meeting

When Consol and government officials met again in August, they estimated that once in the mine, crews would take one to three months to work their way to the Mods Run Shaft. They debated whether to start the recovery of the east side before or after the 22-inch boreholes were drilled.[18]

Consol's executive vice president, William Poundstone, asked U.S. Bureau of Mines' Westfield if he had any misgivings about the temperatures or carbon monoxide readings in the mine. "To be real safe, the mine would have to remain sealed for another year, and even then you would find hotspots," Westfield responded.[19]

Poundstone redirected the questions to John Ashcraft, director of the West Virginia Department of Mines. Ashcraft said, "I have some misgivings. I'm not one to run hurriedly, but the longer we wait, the safer it becomes. I'm just as anxious to get those men because many of them were my friends. It is better to wait a little longer."[20]

The consensus was to wait.

When the boreholes were finished, the group met again in September and finalized a plan for unsealing the No.9. Public relations people were briefed. The work would begin at the Athas Run shaft, which was far from any homes. The work would be dangerous. When the crane lifted off the seal, methane would gush from the shaft. No one would be allowed on the property. Someone would need to notify air traffic controllers so they would not allow planes in the area. If the weather cooperated, the work would take place on September 12, 1969.[21]

The Unsealing

As Consol prepared to unseal the mine, No.9 widow Mary Rogers watched trucks carrying ventilation fans and equipment to the disaster site rumble past her two-story home. Freelance photographer and journalist Jeanne Rasmussen was there, sitting with Mrs. Rogers in her semi-dark living room, listening to the widow talk about her husband, Fred.[22]

Fred was a handsome man who resembled Errol Flynn, Rasmussen noted. That day, as on many days, Mrs. Rogers was crying. "To me, he went to work and he hasn't come home. I never gave up hope," she said. "I still— even to this day—I still feel it. I think maybe somewhere he's still livin.'"[23]

Her husband would, in fact, come out of the mine, but not in 1969.

The day before the seals came off the Athas Run shaft, John Ashcraft asked people to pray the reopening plan he and the other officials had chosen was the right one.[24]

People did pray. The United Mine Workers and its 120,000 members in the United States and Canada stopped working for one hour to remember the dead.[25] In the UMW union hall just a few miles from the No.9, a few miners listened to the Rev. Wesley Dobbs ask God to keep the workers safe.[26]

"We must strive to make things better in the mines, so man won't have to fear; so he can go into the mines with peace of mind," said Dobbs, himself a miner. Dobbs did not stop there. "We must not question why they were taken from us. It was God's will. He has a way of coming into our lives."

Then the miners prayed: "Lord, let the miner face death and not be afraid."

Then the men left, some on their way to work. That day, September 12,

Recovery workers unseal the opening to No.9's slope. Photo by Bob Campione.

recovery workers used nonsparking beryllium jackhammers to chip the concrete from the shaft as giant fans blew fresh air over them to carry away the methane.[27]

Once the seal was off, the Athas Run fan was started by remote control at 10:55 a.m. After four hours, the air coming from the mine at Athas Run still contained 44 percent methane.[28]

The next day, following their plan, the men turned on the No.1 fan near the slope, which cleared the mine enough that men could begin exploring the east side. When John Ashcraft and two other men were lowered by bucket into the Athas elevator shaft, James Westfield called after them: "Take it easy, boys."[29]

Underground, the men walked westward as far as they could. They found the mine's walls had been burned black. There was no white rock dust. "It's blacker than Hell in there!" said federal official William R. Park, whose face was covered with soot as he left the mine.[30]

Recovery teams spent more than a month sealing the east side from the west, establishing a fresh air base, restoring ventilation and power, clearing roof falls, and pumping waist-deep water out of the mine. That preliminary work was the easy part. Once they pushed into the west side of the mine, they found massive roof falls and unspeakable destruction. The worst part was finding the bodies.

At about 4 a.m. on October 23, a crew discovered Lester Willard's remains floating in approximately three feet of water near his derailed 50-ton locomotive. He was about a half a mile from the Plum Run overcast, about the place where officials thought they would find him. He had been stopped cold on the rail tracks as he brought up the rear of a trip of empty coal cars.[31]

He had joked with Walter Slovekosky at about 5 a.m. the morning he died. Slovekosky probably was the last person to hear his voice.[32] Lester Willard was only 49 years old, a World War II veteran, a Navy man, who came home to the mines. He and his wife, Eva, ran a small printing company out of their home. For extra income, Lester worked part-time as a custodian at Fairmont State College. The couple had three sons.[33]

State Police troopers identified his body by the number on his electric cap lamp and his artificial leg. The clothing on Willard's body was burned, but not his hair even though his miner's cap had fallen off his head.[34]

To prepare for body identification, troopers had researched all the miners' backgrounds and collected details that would help them identify each man. They knew the bodies would be in bad shape after so many months in the mine, most under water.

Dr. Charles H. Koon, the Marion County Coroner, examined Lester Willard's body, but he told the prosecuting attorney, Frank C. Mascara, autopsies were not needed because all the men had died in an explosion, regardless of the specific cause of death.[35]

Knowing the specific cause, however, would have been useful to investigators trying to determine the location of the first explosion. The extent of damage to the internal organs could indicate how close each man had been to the explosive forces. Death by asphyxiation would place the miner

A recovery crew prepares to go underground at the No.9 to begin looking for bodies.
Source: Technical Information Center and Library, National Mine Health and Safety Academy.

far from the source or sources of explosions. Analysis of the types of gases in the body tissue also could have given investigators clues about the conditions in the mine during the explosions and after it was sealed. Autopsies also could have shown the condition of the miners' lungs and whether they had black lung disease.

Autopsies were not performed.

A huge roof fall had separated Lester Willard's locomotive from the rest of the trip of cars and the lead locomotive. Just before midnight on the same day Willard's body was located, coal miner John F. Floyd scaled the roof fall and found a gap in the coal. When he looked through, he spotted the 30-ton lead locomotive. He immediately contacted his boss at the fresh air base.[36]

"Is anyone in the motor?" his boss asked.

He kept looking.

"Is anyone in the motor?"

Floyd was not sure. The tunnel had been filled with water. He could not distinguish one thing from another. Years later, Floyd compared the scene to autumn, when the leaves are down and everything looks the same.

"Is anyone in the motor?" the voice asked a third time.

Floyd focused on the locomotive where Charles F. Hardman was still sitting in the deck, his head bowed and resting on his folded arms.[37] His wristwatch had stopped at 5:27. The controls on Hardman's motor were in the normal operating positions for traveling down a slight grade, indicating that he and Willard were on the move and had no warning before the explosion hit them.[38]

The Search Continued

As fall turned to winter, the crews worked their way through the mine, moving 1,000 feet at a time. They also battled methane buildups in the explosive range, especially as the barometric pressure began to drop. The farther they walked, the more damage they found. The explosions had blown out stoppings and destroyed overcasts, the concrete walls used to control airflow. Between 2North and 3North, the men encountered roof falls and 2 percent methane throughout the area. Between 3North and 4North, they removed more roof falls. In 4North, fires had left heavy coke deposits, some six inches deep, and ashes were piled 10 inches deep along the Main West Headings.[39]

By December 4, officials decided to stop all work except the firebossing and water pumping until the Mods Run return airshaft was open. An outside contractor began mucking out the shaft, which had been filled to stop the fires after the explosion. For six days, 10 hours a day, a large bucket and clam reached into the shaft and scooped out the rock and crushed stone. It took the rest of the year and into January to ready a new Mods Run ventilation system. No recovery work was done during that time, and no more bodies came out of the mountain in 1969.[40]

In Search of Justice

No.9 widow Sara Lee Kaznoski's testimony before Congress helped forge a new law, and it emboldened her to join the revolt against UMW president, Tony Boyle. Kaznoski began attending Jock Yablonski's rallies in his bid to overthrow Boyle.

During a student and miners conference at West Virginia University, she urged attendees to support Yablonski. She called Boyle a "cold-hearted man" who had broken his promises to the widows. Promises, she said, were like pie crust, easily made and easily broken.[1]

Dr. I. E. Buff, who had testified before Congress with the widows, was with Sara that day. He criticized the university for spending $300,000 on Astroturf for its football field instead of adding classrooms and a black lung clinic for miners.[2]

The two reportedly got the meetings off to a "rousing start."[3]

Sara was used to speaking out. When she was a child, her father was president of the local UMW. She went to rallies with him, stood on a stage, and sang in support of a striking union leader:

Van Bittner will win the strike,
The scabs will hit the pike,
As sure as the world goes 'round.[4]

Joining the Yablonski campaign took her to a new level of political involvement and put her in danger. She received a telephone death threat, but did not meet that fate. Boyle had a bigger target—Yablonski—and he told two of his men that his opponent "ought to be killed or done away with." His friend and UMW official, William Turnblazer, made it happen. Three union leaders—Albert Pass, William Prater and Silous Huddleston—concocted the assassination plan, using $20,000 in union funds to hire three hit men.[5]

They were not the brightest killers. They followed Yablonski and Ken Hechler as they took their campaign through the Appalachian Mountains and across the Midwest coalfields. They failed at least three times to make their hit, once when Yablonski and Hechler were twisting through the mountains on their way to the Huntington, West Virginia, airport. The killers did not get their work done before the UMW election. When the votes were tallied on December 9, 1969, Yablonski had lost, 80,577 to 46,073, but he would not concede. Instead, he asked the U.S. Labor Department to investigation the election.

UMW politics were dirty and deadly. On December 31, 1969, just hours after President Nixon signed the 1969 Federal Coal Mine Health and Safety Act, Paul E. Gilly, 37, Claude E. Vealey, 26, and Aubran "Buddy" Martin, 21, sat in their car on a hillside overlooking the Yablonski's three-story stone farmhouse.[6] The two young drifters and the older house painter and slum-district restaurant owner waited for the Yablonski's guests to leave. They waited for Jock, his wife, Margaret, and 25-year-old daughter, Charlotte, to turn out the lights and fall asleep. After drinking a few beers, they sneaked to the house, cut the telephone line, slipped in through a side door and up the stairs. Armed with a semiautomatic carbine, Vealey took the master bedroom, and Martin found Charlotte's room.[7]

The plan was to shoot at the same time, but Vealey's carbine jammed as Martin pulled his trigger twice, sending two bullets into Charlotte's curler-topped head. A college graduate, she had quit her job with an antipoverty program in West Virginia to help with her father's campaign. The shots woke Charlotte's parents. Margaret screamed, and Jock rose and tried to load the shotgun he kept by his bed. Martin drilled two bullets into Margaret, and Jock took three rounds from a rifle. Jock was still alive when

No.9 widows Sara Kaznoski (middle) and Mary Matish (right) became close friends as they lobbied for stronger coal mine health and safety laws. Photo courtesy of James Matish.

Vealey reloaded Martin's revolver and shot him two more times, once in the back of the head.[8]

Local Action

The Yablonski deaths slowed Sara Kaznoski's activism at the national level, but not at the local level. She already had launched a campaign for the No.9 widows. Shortly after the disaster, Sara, Mary Rogers and Mary Matish formed the Widows Mine Disaster Committee as a way to support each other and to make sure the company found their husbands' bodies so they could give them decent burials. Some of the widows liked Sara. Some did not.

Sara was a natural organizer. When the kids in her neighborhood began getting into mischief, she gathered them on her front porch and told them they were a city council. At each porch meeting, they said the Pledge of Allegiance to the American flag, and she gave them their assignments for the day. She kept them so busy they had no time to get into trouble.

She had been the manager in her own home, too.

Her husband, Pete, brought his paycheck home and gave it to her.

"If he needed money or anything, he'd ask her for it," Pete Kaznoski Jr. said.[9]

His father was soft-spoken, easy to get along with.

"He was a guy that . . . " Pete Jr. paused. "Everybody wanted a father like him."

Pete Sr. did not like to hunt, did not like to kill animals. But when Pete Jr. wanted to hunt, his father bought him a .22 rifle. The weapon was accidentally fired one day, shooting Pete Jr. in the big toe. The young man tried to pass it off as a dog bite. The doctor knew better.

Pete and his two sons chose a safer hobby, fishing, to enjoy together, and the entire family liked card games. They played 500 rummy, hearts, spades and pinochle.[10]

As a couple, Pete and Sara loved to dance the polka and the jitterbug. They could do all the ballroom dances. They were good dancers, too, light on their feet. She weighed only about 100 pounds. He was taller than she and thin, too.[11]

Pete Jr. did not always get along with his mother. He left home when he was 16, lied about his age, and joined the military. His mother was not happy with his decision. Nonetheless, she wanted neither of her sons going into the mines.[12]

She was not happy about her husband going underground every day. In the days before the mine exploded, he told her the mine was going to blow. It was getting gassy, he said. Many No.9 widows said their husbands had come home and complained about the gas in the days before the disaster. That was unusual. Many miners did not talk about their work at home. They did not want to worry their families.

"I asked him not to go back, and he said he'd sleep on it," Sara told a reporter.

On the day her husband died, Sara Kaznoski set the table for his breakfast. Pete had gone to work on the cateye shift and would come home hungry in the morning. Coffee was ready. His orange juice poured. Vitamins laid out. The newspaper was there, too, but it did not carry the news Sara was about to hear on the "Today Show."[13]

She was working on an afghan when a broadcaster began talking about a mine explosion in West Virginia. The words hit her hard: "Farmington No.9 mine." "Men trapped." "Rescue operation underway." Sara dropped her needlework, ran to the telephone and called Pete's brother, Frank. Then she ran out of the house screaming.[14]

Pete Jr. heard the news on television, too, in Stillwater, Oklahoma, where he was stationed.[15] He and his brother, John, came home. Family from both sides came into town. One of Sara's nieces, a nurse, gave her a shot to sedate her. When hope was gone, John and his wife, who were expecting their first child, went home. He had a teaching job out of state. Pete Jr. returned to Oklahoma and asked for a transfer to Ohio to be closer to his mother.[16]

As the shock of the disaster began to wear off, Sara and the other widows knew they had to start thinking about money. How were they going to support themselves and their children? After the mine was sealed, the state quickly processed workmen's compensation payments for the survivors, but they were relatively small. Each widow received $300 for funeral expenses and began receiving payments of $90 a month, which would stop if she remarried or died. Each dependent child received $25 a month. In 2009 dollars, the $90 payment was equivalent to about $525 and the $25 to about $146.[17] Unless the widows had been carrying significant life insurance on their husbands, they were in trouble.

The UMW Welfare and Retirement Fund kicked in $5,000 per widow to be paid over time, but most of the widows soon found they did not have access to their husband's union pensions, even though their husbands had reached retirement age. That information was a hard blow.[18]

A Pittsburgh television station raised $70,000 that was distributed to the families. Donations also came in from 42 states, the District of Columbia, South Vietnam and Nova Scotia. Two local groups were formed to accept the money, the Citizens Mine Disaster Committee and the Farmington No.9 Disaster Committee. As often is the case when it comes to money, not everyone agreed about how it should be shared. The money began to divide the community.

Together, the two groups held $304,732. Some widows, including Sara Kaznoski, thought the sum should be divided 78 ways. Others thought women with children should receive more. Finally, a judge had to make the decision. One-third of the money was divided among the widows, with each receiving $1,319. The other $200,000 was deposited in a trust fund to be shared by the 144 dependent children as they reached 21.[19]

Another fund was available, too. Most of the coal miners at the No.9 had been paying into the Monument Fund of the Employees of Mountaineer Coal Company No.9. When a miner died, the money could be used to buy a gravestone. It was a much smaller fund, with not quite $12,000. A judge determined that 62 people could claim the money and divided it equally among them.

Richard T. Cooper, a reporter for *The Los Angeles Times,* flew to West Virginia in April 1969 and wrote a story about the money disputes. He said the people in the Farmington area lived in isolation and carried strong traditions and fundamentalist religious views. Their community was a place where people accepted the danger of the mines with stoicism and silence. Many people in the small mining towns did not like the "agitators," women who would speak up about money or even move on with their lives and find new husbands. One miner Cooper interviewed criticized a widow for buying a new car, wrecking it, and buying another. Widows were supposed to mourn and be quiet.

"For some," Cooper wrote, "the abrupt loneliness is unbearable. Private emptiness must be filled with public activity."[20]

That interpretation underestimated the many levels of tragedy created by the No.9 disaster. Loneliness explained very little. Many, if not most, of the widows and their families, whether they spoke of it openly or kept silent, were angry. Many wanted compensation for their losses. If the only compensation possible at that time was money, they felt they at least deserved that.

Once the short-term money debates were settled, the bigger issues resurfaced. Consol, many believed, should accept responsibility for the preexplosion conditions in the No.9 and the deaths of 78 men. Seeking justice, some of the wives contacted Jock Yablonski's son Kenneth Yablonski, whose law practice was in Washington, Pennsylvania. In 1962, he had successfully represented widows from the Robena No.3 coal mine disaster in Pennsylvania that killed 37 men. In that case, he won a court order for autopsies that would show the men had black lung disease, which increased workmen's compensation payments to the widows.[21]

While Yablonski and the No.9 widows were putting together their case, Consol officials had been coming up with their own plan for dealing with the families of the dead. The company teamed with a local Catholic priest, Rev. Everett F. Briggs, and a few of the widows. Some reports say the priest and his group approached Consol with a settlement plan, but drafts of documents later produced in court show that the coal company's lawyers penned the agreement.[22] Who knows whether Briggs truly believed Consol's offer to the widows was just. One point is certain: The deal was carefully crafted to the advantage of the coal company. If the widows accepted Consol's money, they had to agree not to sue the company or attempt to block the company from mining coal during the recovery of bodies.

The initial document surfaced in mid-November 1970, after the company had recovered two bodies. If the widows signed, Consol agreed to make a "special compensatory payment" to the families of $10,000 in three annual payments beginning in 1971. Or the company would:

- make $1,000 annual payments for 10 years, with the running balance in an account earning 8 percent interest
- continue looking for bodies as long as it could start mining coal, too
- look for bodies only in 6North and 7North, areas the company knew would not uncover the source of the disaster

- seal off most of the underground area where the other 76 dead were believed to be and make it a cemetery[23]

The agreement said that the union, state and federal officials already had agreed that it was too dangerous to proceed. This was not true.

When Ken Hechler heard about the agreement, he was horrified that the search for the cause of the disaster would not be thorough. He immediately wrote to the U.S. Secretary of the Interior, Walter J. Hickel. "Many working miners at this mine and all over the Nation quite possibly could receive untold safety benefits, once your Department recovers this area of the mine and investigates the cause of that terrible accident."[24]

Dr. I. E. Buff immediately criticized the plan because the agreement stripped the widows of their right to sue the company or take any other action against it. It also could have ended their access to the state's workmen's compensation benefits.

Federal and West Virginia officials told *The New York Times* that the deal had been kept a secret from them. The agreement "would keep us from finding out what caused this disaster, and I would never approve of that," said John Ashcraft, who had become the director of West Virginia's Department of Mines.[25]

The agreement also required the signatures of at least 60 of the "bereaved families." Furthermore, Consol would communicate only with its handpicked "Memorial Committee," whose president was Father Briggs. The committee had four members: No.9 widows Elizabeth Skarzinski, Genevieve Gouzd, Josephine Muto and Della Walter.

The most unreasonable term was that Consol would not honor the agreement unless the UMW, the West Virginia Department of Mines and the U.S. Bureau of Mines approved the plan and agreed not to take any legal action against the company. This stipulation would have protected the company against criminal charges if the investigators found the company had allowed dangerous conditions to exist in the mine. In fact, the sworn testimony already had provided the state with enough evidence to file criminal charges had it chosen to do so.

Instead, the "investigation" continued, and Father Briggs became

Consol's "water boy." By saying the agreement originated with the priest and widows, the coal company could use him to convince the UMW and the government agencies to give it their blessings.

Two days after the agreement became public and began drawing criticism, Consol added two amendments. First, the $10,000 would not affect the widows' workmen's compensation payments. Second, if the company happened to be mining coal near one of the tunnels that held any of the 76 bodies, recovery of some of the dead might be attempted.[26]

With encouragement from Father Briggs, 70 widows signed the agreement. The priest then began his next assignment—to convince the government agencies to approve the agreement. Coal company officials, of course, knew the UMW would not go along with the deal as long as the dead were not recovered. The company knew, too, it would not be appropriate for the government agencies that were investigating the disaster to make any kind of agreement with Consol. The plan was perfect. The coal company could stall the widows, hold on to the money and blame it on the union and the government officials who would look bad for rejecting both a man of the cloth and grieving widows.

The company had nothing to lose, including its coal. If the plan fell through, company officials knew they still could access No.9's coal reserves simply by expanding its mines that were adjacent to the No.9.

Perhaps out of naivety, or perhaps for some other reason or part of some other deal, Father Briggs began his campaign. He told the media that the widows were living "under the pall of death. . . . There was this fantasy that widows couldn't remarry because their husbands weren't buried."

On December 11, 1969, Father Briggs began a letter-writing campaign to convince the union and state and federal officials to approve the agreement. Governor Arch Moore did not reply.[27] The U.S. Department of the Interior told the priest that it could not be party to or play any role in the agreement. It denied that the Department had ever said it was too dangerous to continue the recovery, as stated in the agreement.[28]

The UMW also bristled in response to the priest's letter and at the agreement's statement that the union already had decided it was too dangerous to continue the recovery effort. "We do not believe that at this time that every reasonable effort has been made to recover the bodies," responded UMW's Lewis L. Evans. He added that no one had consulted the UMW about the agreement.[29]

Father Briggs shot back, accusing the union of "depriving the deceased miners' families of the beneficial provisions of that Agreement." In the same letter, he defended the recovery effort, supporting the company's stand that it had made every reasonable effort to find the other 76 men.[30]

Father Briggs sent a copy of the letter to John Corcoran, president of Consol. Corcoran replied: "Certainly we are hopeful that your letter will result in indications from the other three agencies permitting early implementation of the arrangement with the bereaved families. As for Consol, we continue to believe in the soundness and good sense of this program covered by the agreement. . . . I will be most interested in learning the nature of the responses of the other three agencies to your registered letter of last Friday."[31]

Three More Men

In the summer of 1970, Sara Kaznoski began her own letter-writing campaign. She asked the U.S. Bureau of Mines to take total control of the No.9 recovery effort because the coal company was moving too slowly. The Bureau's James Westfield replied that it was satisfied with the work that was being done. (She probably did not realize it then, but James Westfield had been fighting behind the scenes to make sure No.9's dead were recovered from the mine. He was not making any friends in high places.)

Sara also wrote to then-Governor Arch A. Moore, expressing her concerns that the recovery was moving too slowly. The company was mining coal and making a profit while it recovered bodies, which the governor had openly opposed. Gov. Moore answered Sara's letter in July.

"No one is more concerned than I or as anxious as I am to recover the bodies of the victims of this disaster as quickly as possible," he wrote.[1] He assured her that the company and state officials were doing everything possible to find the men. Only coal that had to be removed to reach the dead was being mined. He received weekly reports on the recovery and had seen photographs of the devastation, including large roof falls that would require the miners to drive new entries, mining coal as they moved forward.[2]

The recovery work was moving slowly. The Federal, state, UMW and Consol officials, known as the Four Agencies, met several times, trying to agree on how to avoid massive roof falls and keep enough air circulating to prevent another explosion.

Explosions inside the No.9 uprooted railway tracks throughout the mine. Source: Informational Report of Investigation, Underground Coal Mine Explosion and Fire, Consol No.9 Mine, U.S. Department of Labor, Mine Safety and Health Administration.

Consol had three of the four large ventilation fans running most of the time. That summer, however, one or more fans failed or malfunctioned 11 times.[3] The FEMCO fan alarm system malfunctioned several times, too.[4]

On July 23, the No.1 fan malfunctioned, ripping off its own blades. The incident was reminiscent of the failure of the Mods Run fan. The one difference—the alarm system worked in 1970, cutting off the power in the mine.[5] Five days later, an electrical storm knocked out all three of the fans.[6]

In September, the Four Agencies met to discuss Consol's plan to drive new tunnels from the Main West Headings all the way down to the Mahan Run air shafts. James Westfield objected.[7] "What we should do is go in 6North and recover those bodies," he said.[8]

UMW's Lewis Evans said he would never agree to driving the new tunnels, which would require mining coal.[9]

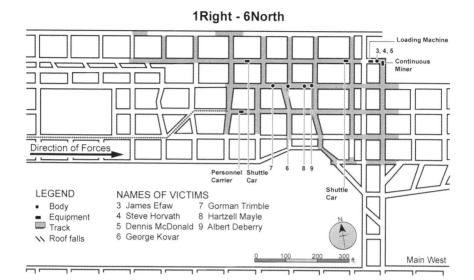

1Right - 6North

The men at 6North were at the end of their day. The evidence shows these men were killed instantly and without warning. Three bodies were discovered here in 1970 and six more in 1971 (see Chapter 18). Map by Rachel Davis.

Westfield also insisted that a ventilation study be conducted "to find our trouble spots and not waste time or create other hazards."[10]

The meeting adjourned, and Consol abandoned its idea, at least temporarily. When the ventilation survey was complete,[11] the group met again and decided to adjust the ventilation, drive a new tunnel parallel to 6North in order to avoid roof falls, and find the men who had died there.[12]

On December 1, 1970, crews believed they were near the place the men had been working on 1Right-6North. The recovery crews began driving through a wall of coal into that section. "Nothing held them back. They worked very diligently since everyone had one thought in mind—how many of the men might we find?" wrote Consol manager Eugene Mauck in his report of the day's work.[13]

"It's a shuttle car," one of the men shouted as the crew broke through the barrier.[14]

The area was black with soot, which hung in streamers from the roof and covered the floor. The recovery crew's cap lamps were no match for the deep darkness of the mine. They did not see the bodies at first, but the "sweet nauseating odor" of death was unmistakable. As they neared the loading machine, they saw a man's head jutting up though the chunks of coal. Then they saw his body, then a stray shoe, then another shoe and a third shoe. Most of the recovery team stayed clear of the area because the stench was so strong.[15]

"Brother, that is it," one man said. He later quit.

What the men discovered demonstrated the violence of the explosive forces that had hit the section. The control panel on the mining machine, which had been secured with ½-inch bolts, had been torn from its mounting. The machine's hoses were charred, and so were the bodies. The men cleaned the areas around the dead, beginning with the first man they had found. His face was in full view, but carried no identifiable features. His

This jeep near the Llewellyn shaft was swept off the railway by the violence in the mine. Source: Informational Report of Investigation, Underground Coal Mine Explosion and Fire Consol No.9 Mine, U.S. Department of Labor, Mine Safety and Health Administration.

nose was missing. His head was shrunken and burned black, the skin tight and hard.[16] "The body was dehydrated and small and the legs were bent backward as though a strong wind had windrowed it," Mauck wrote.

The second man's right arm was draped over part of the loading machine and fell away from the torso when it was moved. The body was badly decomposed; its skull was separated from the body and broken into pieces. The lower jaw had neither flesh nor teeth.

The third man was lying under the second, his body "wrapped around the head of the loading machine, again indicating the force" that blew into the area. "As a matter of fact, the right arm of this body was trapped under the loading machine head. How was this possible?" Mauck wrote. "But this is the way it was found."

The third man was wearing insulated underwear, which helped preserve his body.

Before they died, the three men in 6North had been winding down for the day. One man was backing a mining machine out of a crosscut. Its pump motor was on, but a roof fall had covered much of the machine. The men had turned off the loading machine and may have been preparing to grease it.[17]

Workers found no self-rescuers in the area and no evidence that the men had any warning that they were about to die. The scene indicated that a blast wave from the initial explosion over-pressurized everything in its path. When the wave reached 6North, it likely killed the men almost instantly, penetrating their bodies and causing many of their organs to implode. The blast wave trauma explains why the men's belts, hats and shoes were found stripped from their bodies.[18]

"There is a great force that is created when there is an explosion like that," Eugene Mauck said later.[19] "I think it compresses the body and it comes back out again and when it does, it sheds this stuff. The shoes—we find them without their shoes, on most of them, not all of them. Maybe they would be missing one shoe. Very few of them still had their belts on where they were affected by pressure."[20]

Recovery workers deodorized and numbered the bodies.

"They were difficult to load into the carrying bags. Two of the bodies had to have a leg broken free in order to bag them," Mauck wrote in his report.

Outside the mine, only one man was identified quickly. Forty-two-year-old Dennis N. McDonald had his metal check tag, #235, in his pocket.[21] His cap-lamp battery with the same number was near his body. He wore false teeth, too, further evidence of his identity.[22] McDonald, who was serving as the section foreman, had just three years of mining experience.

Officials had to use dental records and X-rays to confirm the names of the other two miners. World War II veteran James Efaw, 46, had been a miner for six years. Steve Horvath, a 42-year-old roof bolter, had 17 years of experience.[23]

Finding the three men gave the recovery teams hope that they would find the other 73 men still in the mountain.

Hidden Evidence

In November 1970, just days before recovery workers found her husband's body, Ethel McDonald joined 34 other widows in two lawsuits against Consolidation Coal.[1]

Kenneth Yablonski, the son of slain Jock Yablonski, had agreed to represent the widows and filed a lawsuit in Marion County, West Virginia. An identical lawsuit was filed in Pennsylvania, where Consol was headquartered. The widows were each seeking $113,000 for a total of just under $4 million. They claimed the company and its president, John Corcoran, "negligently, carelessly, recklessly and willfully" operated an unsafe mine.[2]

The money they sought would have been nothing to Consol or its corporate owner, Continental Oil. In 1969, Continental netted more than $146 million, which in 2009 dollars equals about $805 million. Continental's president anticipated even greater yields in 1970, in part, because the market and price conditions were favorable. Continental expected to sell 60 to 65 million tons of coal in 1970, up from 53.9 million in 1969.[3] In short, business was good.

The odds, however, did not favor the No.9 widows. From the beginning, they were at a disadvantage because West Virginia's workmen's compensation law did more to protect employers than employees and their families. Any employer who paid into the state's workmen's compensation fund could not be held liable for damages if an employee was injured or killed on the job. How the person died or was hurt did not matter; neither individual employees nor their families could sue. Dependents of the dead could do no more than collect the meager payments available through the state fund, with one exception. If someone could prove that an employer had deliberate intention to cause death or injury to an employee, then the person's dependents could sue for any excess damages not covered by the workmen's compensation law.

In their lawsuit, the widows accused the company of:

- hiring and failing to fire incompetent supervisors who knowingly disobeyed coal mining laws
- putting production before safety
- knowingly sending men into a dangerous mine
- allowing dangerous conditions to exist
- failing to ventilate and fireboss the mine properly
- failing to rock dust the mine adequately
- failing to maintain equipment

"Willfully" operating an unsafe mine, however, did not meet the "deliberate intent" stipulation. Yablonski, therefore, argued that West Virginia's workmen's compensation law was unconstitutional because the money it paid the widows was not equal to the earnings their dead spouses brought home.

Their case lingered in court as their lawyers tried to negotiate a settlement with the coal company. What neither the widows nor their attorney knew was that more than a month before they filed their lawsuits, a federal official had discovered the evidence they needed to win their case.

The Memo

On September 5, 1970, federal coal mine inspector Larry L. Layne and a recovery crew of nine men were working near the Mods Run airshafts. That day, for the first time since the disaster, they re-energized the Mods Run substation, a power unit on the surface that sent electricity underground.

A few days later, the electrician who had re-energized the substation told Layne that someone had deliberately disabled the Mods Run fan's safety alarm before the disaster. The electrician had found jumper wires bypassing both the fan alarm system and the mechanism that would have automatically shut off the power to the entire mine within minutes after the fan stopped or stalled.[4]

Immediately, Layne sent a handwritten memo to his federal district supervisor, James D. Micheal, in Morgantown. Micheal initialed the memo three days later and wrote at the bottom: "Copy to W.R. Park, Marshalek" and "Enter in notes." Joseph Marshalek was a federal supervising inspector at the No.9. William R. Park was a federal district supervisor in Mount Hope, West Virginia.[5]

Almost two more weeks passed before a copy of the memo was sent to William R. Park.[6] When Park received the memo, he made this note to "Montana," presumably someone in his office: "Keep with other material on No.9 explosion."[7]

What Marshalek did with the memo is unknown.

Several times, Layne asked his superiors what had happened to his memo, but no one ever gave him an answer. Not long after he wrote it, Layne was transferred to Wheeling, West Virginia. When he saw a copy of his memo in 2009, he remembered the incident well.[8] When the electrician came to him, Layne said he knew that the chief electrician, a company man, must have rigged up the bypass. A higher-level company manager would have given him orders to do so.[9]

In his sworn testimony after the disaster, Lawrence Riggs, No.9's general superintendent, admitted that the company had on occasion "blocked out" the alarm systems on fans, but no one asked him if any of the alarm systems were blocked out on the day the mine blew up.

"They wanted to continue mining coal when the fan was down. That had happened. They mined, according to testimony and reports; they had mined an entire shift with one of the fans being down. It was all about greed," Layne said after reviewing the hearing transcripts.[10]

Layne was familiar with Consol's mines in the area because he had inspected them in the 1960s. "Their attitude was if you have enough work for seven men, you send five and a boss. The boss is supposed to do work for two men," Layne said. The foremen were so busy that they did not have time to fireboss their sections properly.[11]

When the No.9 was reopened for recovery, a No.9 miner informed federal inspector Larry L. Layne (third from the left) that he had discovered evidence that the safety alarm on the Mods Run fan had been disabled prior to the disaster. Photo courtesy of Larry L. Layne.

During one inspection of Consol's Williams mine, which was near the No.9, Layne had to shut down two sections. One had so much coal dust and loose coal that the men had to load seven 10-ton coal cars to clean up the mess. On another section, the miners had driven through coal for 90 feet without stopping to spread any rock dust. After that inspection, Layne said the coal company tried to have him transferred to another district, but the UMW safety committees prevented the move. Layne said that the union men knew he was looking out for them.[12]

Later, Layne, a ventilation specialist, became a federal investigator in criminal and civil coal mine cases. He was a chief accident investigator before he retired in 1992.[13]

If state officials knew about his memo, Layne said, they should have filed criminal charges against Consol. They could have made the charges stick. The evidence also would have given the widows stronger grounds for their lawsuit.[14]

The Fan Charts

Inspector Layne had questions about his memo and about other documents that disappeared the day the No.9 exploded. Layne was at the mine that morning. When he arrived, he immediately went to the Mods Run fan shaft. He saw the explosion doors on the fan shaft had blown open, just as others testified later. At that point, his experience told him he needed to find the Mods Run fan chart, which would show him when the fan stopped running.[15] The chart was important because it held a week's worth of information about the fan's operation. As long as the fan was running, a pen drew a line around the circular chart. If the fan stopped, so did the line on the chart, which would indicate the exact time the fan failed.

Layne found the fan chart box, but someone already had broken into it. The glass face was smashed, and the chart was gone. The explosion did not break the glass, Layne said. Like the fan, it was kept a safe distance from the shafts and any explosive forces. Someone without a key had taken the chart.[16]

Layne asked his boss, Joseph Marshalek, who had the fan chart, and Marshalek told him state officials had it.[17]

Layne asked John Ashcraft with the West Virginia Department of Mines if he or his people had the chart. Ashcraft told him federal officials had it.[18]

"According to my boss, we don't have the chart," Layne told Ashcraft.

"You have the chart," Ashcraft said.[19]

Someone had the chart. Several people could have smashed the glass and taken it. The most motivated, of course, would be someone who could be held responsible for the disaster, most likely within the company; someone trying to protect the responsible party; or someone who was ordered to retrieve the chart.

People on the Scene

Several people were known to have been on the west side of the mine, with easy access to the Mods Run fan chart, after the 5:30 a.m. explosion. A list follows. Times are approximations.

6 a.m. Alex Kovar went to Mods Run and saw the fan shaft's explosion doors were open and smoke was pouring out.[20]

7 a.m. Alex Kovar went to Athas Run to pick up the two mechanics who had come up the elevator and out of the mine.[21]

Fay Casseday was at Athas Run and entered a building there to make a call. How long he stayed or where he went after making the call is unclear.[22]

7:30 a.m. Cecil Selders and Lockie Riggs came up the hollow at Athas Run.[23] Riggs sent Kovar and Selders over the hill to the Mods Run fan. They drove to the site.

8 a.m. Cecil Selders and Alex Kovar arrived at Mods Run just after the mine exploded a second time. They waited for the smoke to clear. Kovar went to a nearby home to make calls.[24]

Kovar notes that "Alda Freeman and Buck Fluharty" were at the Mods Run airshaft.[25]

8:15 a.m. Freeman, Fluharty and Kovar left to take the bucket to Mahan Run to rescue the men in 7South.[26]

Cecil Selders, who had keys to the Mods Run fan house, said he opened the door and saw the fan had thrown off its blades. He did not mention the fan chart box or the chart.[27]

9:05 a.m. Cecil Selders went to the slope and reported that the Mods Run fan was demolished.[28]

During the hearings, none of the interrogators asked the men who had been at Mods Run whether they saw or changed the fan chart. Nor did they ask to view the fan record book, which the men signed whenever they checked on the fan. In fact, fan record books were not mentioned during the hearings. No evidence was found in state and federal files to suggest that any fan record books were produced during the hearings. No doubt, both state and federal officials would have known that coal mine fans had charts and miners kept fan records.

Cecil Selders and Alex Kovar discussed their activities at Mods Run. However, officials did not ask Fay Casseday or Lockie Riggs if they had seen the fan, the fan chart or the fan record book.

Neither Mr. Freeman nor Mr. Fluharty was called to testify.

Two key participants at the mine that morning who had access to every part of the mine were David H. Davis, president of Mountaineer Coal, and Kenneth K. Kincell, Mountaineer Coal's manager of mines. Instead of being questioned, they sat on the board that was supposed to determine what caused the disaster.

Years later, during a deposition for a second lawsuit by the No.9 widows, Consol executive H. Eugene Mauck talked about the Mods Run fan chart. He was at the No.9 the day it exploded. He said Consol did not know when the Llewellyn fan had shut down the day the mine exploded. The company did know when the Mods Run fan stopped running.[29]

"Was the fan chart from the morning of November 20 kept?" asked the lawyer.[30]

"I am sure it is somewhere but I don't know. I personally never saw the thing but it's bound to be among the collector's items," Mauck said.[31]

There was a discussion off the record, then Mauck continued: "I never personally saw it. Kencill and those guys had the thing."[32]

State officials did not summons H. Eugene Mauck to testify during the No.9 investigation hearings.

Other Clues

In 2009, in response to a West Virginia Freedom of Information Request, four fan charts turned up in a cardboard box of No.9 documents at West Virginia's Office of Miners' Health, Safety, and Training in Oak Hill.[33] The charts raise even more questions about what happened before the explosion and on the morning of the explosion.

No.1 Fan. Two charts are labeled #1, indicating the No.1 fan near the slope on the east side of the mine.

The first chart is dated "11-13-68," its starting date.[34] Alex Kovar signed the chart. It is smudged in places, and the thin ink line is jagged, with a dip at about 3:40 a.m. on November 20, about the time Kovar said he changed the chart. Kovar testified that he put the chart in his vehicle and gave it to Foster Turner before he went home that evening.[35]

The second chart for the No.1 fan is dated "11-20-68," with a starting time of 4 a.m. and Kovar's signature.[36] It, too, has smudges and a thin ink line that shows more irregularities than the first. The chart appears to have been removed a week later on Wednesday, November 27 at 7 a.m.

Athas Run Fan. The third chart is labeled "#2," for the Athas Run fan. Alex Kovar signed it on "11-13-68," indicating he put the chart on at 7:15 a.m.[37] The ink line dips on the Saturday before the explosion. On November 20, the day of the explosion, the ink line dips again at about 3:45 a.m. It comes back up at about 4:15 a.m. and makes a bigger dip at 5 a.m., indicating at least two interruptions. After the 5 a.m. dip, the ink line remains below its normal level until about 8 a.m. or 9 a.m. At this time, it stops as someone apparently removed it.

Kovar did not say he removed the Athas Run fan chart. His initials, however, and what appears to be the word "testing" appear on the chart near the time of the dips. Yet Kovar's testimony does not place him at the Athas Run fan during those hours. Cecil Selders was in that area between 8 a.m. and 9 a.m., but his signature is not on the chart.

Federal official Joseph Marshalek made a note about the Athas Run fan at 9:25 a.m. He wrote: "Fan chart changed. Fan chart showed irregularity some time before explosion. This is a weekly chart. Close examination not possible as chart was removed by company employee."[38]

Mods Run Fan. The fourth chart is the most troubling. It is labeled "#3," for the Mods Run fan. It is dated "11-18-68," the Monday before the mine exploded, off schedule with the other fan chart changes, which were made on Wednesdays.[39] Alex Kovar testified that he checked the Mods run fan on Mondays, but was not responsible for changing its charts.[40]

The chart marked "#3" has a starting time of 8 a.m. with a signature in handwriting much like Alex Kovar's. It reads "Oral Huff," who, according to a newspaper account at the time, had already retired.[41] The ink line on the chart is thick and solid, unlike the thin, jagged lines on the other charts. The line stops abruptly at 5 a.m. on the morning of the explosion. It is not smudged with black fingerprints like the other three charts.[42]

Was this chart fabricated? Was the signature authentic? Most, if not all, of the people who could answer those questions are dead. Clearly, though, West Virginia's state inspectors had obtained a few of No.9's fan charts.

Also in Oak Hill Box D33 is a list with descriptions of photographic slides apparently taken by the state at the time of the disaster and during the recovery operations.[43] No. 12 on the slide list is "Mods Run fan chart." But the box at Oak Hill contained no slides.[44]

Questions arose about missing state disaster slides in November 1970, about the same time the No.9 widows filed their lawsuit. Dr. I. E. Buff, who had testified before Congress about black lung disease, accused government officials of hiding the No.9 slides.[45]

A memo to federal district supervisor William R. Park dated November 24, 1970, explains where at least a few of the slides had been: "Attached are the 17 slides taken underground at No.9. These slides belong to John Ashcraft. I feel that these are the slides which I. E. Buff is reporting as being hidden. Last night's paper said he knew exactly how many the State was withholding and that if any were destroyed, he would request a Federal investigation. What do you want done with these?" It was signed "Frances."[46]

Park initialed the memo and scrolled across the bottom: "Gary will return to Mr. Ashcraft."[47]

"Return to Ashcraft," was scrolled below that, dated "12/2/70" and initialed by another writer, whose handwriting is illegible.[48]

The tray apparently was returned to Ashcraft, but whether all the slides were returned is not clear. Upon his retirement, Ashcraft gave the tray of slides to Joe Megna whose father, Emilio Megna, died in the No.9 disaster.[49] The slide tray, which is not full, contains dozens of images—smoke billowing from the Llewellyn portal, maps of the mine, and massive coal cars thrown from their tracks—but there is no image of a fan chart in the tray.

A photo of a fan chart taken at the No.9 disaster, however, was found in 2009 at the National Mine Health and Safety Academy's Library located in Beaver, West Virginia.[50] The image is blurry and apparently copied from a slide. No legible date, signature or fan number is on the image. The pen that marks the chart with ink has stopped at about 1 p.m. on a Friday. Two dark lines dip on the chart at about 9 p.m. the same day. Is this an image of the missing Mods Run fan chart slide? Could it be a photograph of the chart from the Llewellyn Run fan? Somebody knew, and somebody may still know.

Ungodly Work

....

When Pete Kaznoski did not come home from the mine, Pete Jr. asked for a hardship leave from the military and moved into a house near his mother.[1]

He applied for a mining job with Consol, but he got the sense the company did not want him in its mine. His mother intervened, talked to some people she knew, and it wasn't long before two coal-company men came to his door.

"We've heard you're looking for a job, Pete."

"Yeah," he said. "I'm having a hard time."

They asked him to come to the Morgantown office for an interview. The morning of his interview, Pete asked his wife to make him a sandwich to take along because he was not sure when he would be home. He did not need the sandwich. When he arrived at the office, a company manager took him to a hotel restaurant and ordered him a steak and a couple of martinis. Pete ate the meal, but wanted to get down to business.

"Hey, when are we going to have this job interview?" he asked. "I need a job. I haven't worked in a couple of months and I need to earn some money."

"Oh, you're hired," the manager said.

Pete reported to work the next week, but the company did not have anything for him to do. He had an office but no assignments. Finally, after about two weeks, he asked for work and began to get assignments. One of his first jobs was to revamp the company's college recruitment program. Pete gathered names and data from schools with mining programs. He wrote a report, and his boss presented it to upper management. They liked it. His boss took credit for the work, Pete said.

Pete also began collecting production and man-hour data from the district offices, which he presented to the top officials in the Pittsburgh office.

Then something happened. Another company manager came to him and asked him about the lawsuit his mother had filed against the company. He wanted Pete to "talk to her about it." Pete said he would not interfere in his mother's business. If his job depended on that, he would give the company his resignation and two weeks notice.

"You don't need to resign," the manager said. "We'll pay you for the two weeks and you can leave right now."

That was that. Pete went back into the military, the widows pressed forward with their lawsuit, and the coal miners kept digging out the dead while Consol managers looked for ways to begin mining coal at the No.9.

More Men Out

In January 1971, recovery workers found the rest of the men who had been working on 1Right-6North, an area that had been hit by the force of the explosions.

First, they saw a seat from a rail car, then pieces of a dinner bucket, part of a sweater, then more of the dinner bucket, then George Kovar Jr. His identification number was on his body. No. 98.[2]

Later the same day, they discovered Gorman Trimble. The recovery men took his identification tag from beneath his body, tied it to his left leg, and took him out of the mine.[3]

The next day, workers found a rubber boot, a "torn up" dinner bucket, and the top of a battery for a cap lamp that belonged to Hartzell Mayle. No. 118.[4]

The crew did not find Mayle for three more days. When the men did, they found part of his jacket and then the liner from a boot. He had no shoes on his feet, but was fully clothed and still had a belt on his body. He was badly decomposed.

John Brock (far left) and other trained miners spent years recovering bodies from the No.9 mine. Courtesy of John Brock.

James Herron, who had escaped from the mine the day it exploded, helped bring Mayle's body out. Mayle's wife and son identified him by his wristwatch and the green shirt he had worn to work. An X-ray confirmed two old fractures in one of his arms.[6]

The next day, the last man on that section came out of the mine. Albert Deberry was fully clothed. He still wore his belt and even his cap. The poisonous gases had killed him. His check number, wristwatch, clothing and wedding ring proved his identity. [7]

Request to Mine Coal

At a Four Agency meeting on February 12, 1971, Consol asked state and federal officials to lift their mine closure orders on the No.9 so the company could begin mining coal again in A-Face, on the east side of the mine. The company, once again, wanted to drive tunnels from the Main West Headings to 7South, mining coal along the way.

Internal memos show how important mining coal was to Consol. Prior to the Four Agency meeting, Consol executives had held their own meeting in January to discuss various ways to ventilate the mine. In his notes about the meeting, David H. Davis wrote: "Regardless of the next step we are facing several weeks or a few months work without accomplishing much in the way of producing any coal."[8]

At another private meeting, the executives decided to use their $10,000 "agreement" with the widows to try to force the issue. The "agreement" still required the UMW and state and federal officials to allow the company to mine coal before the $10,000 would be paid out. The agreement also called for sealing the disaster areas and declaring them a graveyard.

Davis wrote in his notes on that meeting: "We should tell the agencies that we have a commitment to the widows, dependent upon certain points. Namely, we will be permitted to mine coal and recover sections if and when practicable to do so. . . . Let them tell us what their ideas are about in regard to what we can do in mining this area. Then tell them we have decided it is too dangerous and we are not willing to continue to take chances—under the circumstances."[9]

The meeting did not go well for Consol.

"The Governor does not want a cemetery in any West Virginia mine as long as he is governor and will not lift the closure order at this time," said John Ashcraft, director of West Virginia's Department of Mines.[10]

Lewis Evans with the UMW said that he did not care what Consol paid the widows. The company could pay them $50,000 or $10,000, that was Consol's business. The union would not approve mining any coal except to get to sections to recover bodies.

James Westfield, with the U.S. Bureau of Mines (USBM), said that any agreement between Consol and the families was Consol's problem. When the work became too hazardous, the USBM would recommend stopping the work, but making the mine operable was "a hell of a big job and a far way off," he said. Until that day came, the USBM would not remove the closure order or seal off any section that could be recovered, he said.

Shilling for the Coal Company

When the outcome of the Four Agency meeting reached Father Everett Briggs, he was outraged. He chastised UMW leaders, telling them that Consol should be allowed to mine coal before they recovered all the dead bodies. That was only fair, he said, so the company could recoup its costs.[11]

The idea that the company could be permitted to make money while it looked for the dead infuriated many people, including Sara Kaznoski and many other widows. At a Widows Mine Disaster Committee meeting in early 1971, the women discussed the "inhumane act of Father Briggs and Consol" who were trying to seal their husbands in the No.9 mine forever in order to avoid finding the cause of the disaster.[12]

In April, Father Briggs was trying to set up a meeting with the governor, but told Sara and her group that they would not be included—they could set up their own meeting.[13]

Westfield Gets the Boot

The power of the coal lobby during a Republican administration could not have been clearer than it was on the last day of March 1971.

James Westfield was on the ground in Nemacolin, Pennsylvania, directing the rescue operation for two miners who had been missing for five days after the mine caught fire, when his superiors ordered him to retire. He was only 67 and physically fit.[14]

Even though he was considered the country's leading expert on the cause and prevention of coal mine disasters, the decision had been made months earlier.[15] Edward D. Failor, a special assistant to the director of the USBM, was credited with instigating Westfield's departure and that of another top official with the USBM, Henry Wheeler, a few months later.[16] Even though he had no mining experience, Failor, who already was earning as much as his boss, was promoted into Wheeler's position. He had been a Republican fundraiser in Iowa, a judge, and a lobbyist for the Iowa Association of Coin Operated Laundries. Despite his inexperience, he became the chief assessment officer, whose job it was to determine how to levy fines against errant coal companies.[17]

The Bureau of Mine's practices came under scrutiny by the U.S. Government Accounting Office (GAO), which began investigating how the agency was enforcing the 1969 law. The GAO announced its finding in 1971. It had found that the Bureau of Mines had not been doing the number of inspections required by law, having completed only 31 percent of the required safety inspections and 1 percent of the health inspections related to black lung disease.[18] Many of its inspectors had not been issuing notices of violations even when they found the same hazardous conditions over and over again at the same mine.[19]

Failor was credited with adopting his own abbreviated methods for determining penalties and arbitrarily setting extremely low fines schedules. For instance, a violation resulting in imminent danger could be assessed at $20 instead of the $500 the agency had originally set for initial violations.[20] The 1969 law allowed penalties of up to $10,000 per violation.

The GAO's report also pointed out glaring problems in the way coal mine accidents and disasters were investigated. For instance, individuals who were responsible for the inspections of specific mines were conducting the investigations in those mines, which created a clear conflict of interest. What if the disaster was caused by a violation he missed during an inspection? What if the inspector found that a ventilation plan his supervisors had approved was inadequate? The GAO recommended instituting an investigation process that was not riddled with conflicts of interest.[21]

Back to Washington

Shortly after James Westfield lost his job, four members of the Widows Mine Disaster Committee—Sara Kaznoski, Mary Matish, Mary Rogers and Mildred Hardman—made another trip to Washington D.C. to meet with Ken Hechler, other Congressional leaders and federal mining officials. They told their stories again and asked for help to speed the recovery of their husbands' bodies.

They were promised that James C. Westfield would be in charge of the recovery. "We were thankful to hear this for we believe in Mr. Westfield," Sara wrote in her notes.[22]

Of course, Westfield was not placed in charge.

They also lobbied for changes in the Social Security laws so widows younger than 50 could receive payments from their husbands' accounts. Washington leaders encouraged them to contact every widow in every state of the union to gain more voices on the mining issues.[23]

At one of their meetings, the women discussed traveling to Hyden, Kentucky, to meet with the widows of 38 miners who died in a Finley Coal Company mine in December 1970, two years after the No.9 disaster and one year after the new federal law had been signed.[24] The notes do not indicate that any were able to make the trip.

Conditions in the Finley mine were much like those in the No.9 prior to its disasters. The Finley mine was not rockdusted properly and had excessive accumulations of coal dust. Miners there did not have access to water to keep the dust down at the working faces. They also were using their explosives illegally.[25] Investigators said coal dust had been thrown into suspension and ignited, killing the 38 miners.[26]

During that investigation, federal officials also discovered that the company was not firebossing its mines regularly. The company "could not locate" many required records. Officials also found matches and cigarette butts in the mine.[27] Sadly, federal inspectors had cited the Finley mine for the same violations a month before it exploded. Unfortunately, the government did not have enough inspectors to recheck the mine and make sure the company had eliminated the hazards.[28]

The disaster drove the 1970 U.S. coal-mine death toll to 260, not much lower than the 311 deaths of 1968.[29]

Years later, the Finley Coal Company pleaded no contest to charges of violating the federal law. A federal judge fined it $122,500.[30]

Relatives of 25 of the dead miners and a miner who survived but was seriously injured tried to sue the federal government for negligence. The courts ruled against them.[31]

More Bodies

David Mainella Sr.'s body was found in June 1971, along with a crew of six men. Another man, Louis Boros, should have been recovered, but his body was never found.

The crew had been mining coal in 3Right-7North. The men had survived the initial blast, found their self-rescuers, and walked (or ran or stumbled) away from the working face. They left behind a loaded shuttle car of coal at the face and a string of loaded coal cars on the tracks.[32]

Frank Tate Jr. had made it the farthest, almost three-quarters of a mile. The others were found here and there along the 7North entry. Mainella and Goy Taylor brought up the rear. Jerry Stoneking and Raymond Parsons had gone a few hundred yards farther, and David Cartwright and Dennis Toler were lying near each other in a crosscut about 200 feet behind Tate.[33] Some of the men still wore their identifications. One man was missing all his clothing.

The men had made a valiant effort to escape, but they had nowhere to go. There was no way out and no way to be rescued.

Forces of the explosion were evident. A conveyor belt was wrapped around a coal car. Other coal cars were twisted from the tracks. Stoppings were blown out. Flames had been minimal in the area, which might have brought some comfort to Toler's wife, Barbara. In 1968, she had waited for him outside the mine after the explosion, refusing to leave even though she was overdue with their third child. She had brought her husband a clean shirt, just in case his clothes had been burned off. The Tolers were almost out of debt at the time, she told an Associated Press reporter. Her husband earned $270 every two weeks, but almost all of it went to the company store. Dennis Toler, who was 26, also worked another full-time job digging graves at a cemetery.[34] "He only gets about two hours of sleep a day," she said.[35]

By the time they found her husband's body, Barbara was seeing another coal miner, and they planned to marry. She had signed the agreement with

Consol after the company told the widows it could take three or more years to find their husbands.[36]

As bodies came out, the miners were identified, funerals were arranged, and a few families could put their men to rest. The Mainella family happened to be having its reunion the day they brought David Mainella out of the mine. Nearby relatives were present, and others had come in from other states. He had a big funeral. "Cars were lined up it seemed for miles," his son David Patrick Mainella said. "He was a pretty well-known person and well-liked."[37]

Mr. Mainella was a religious man, a Catholic, who took his family to church every Sunday, David Patrick said as he reminisced about his father and his family.[38]

"You would never think my father was a coal miner," David said. "He was just so sophisticated, he and my mother. They looked like royalty when they went out." Mr. Mainella always wore a coat and tie. "He was always dressed up and was always persnickety about that," David said.

He was a sports fan; he listened to games on the radio, and he bought his family a television. It had a 10-inch screen, great for watching Notre Dame football. He also loved baseball. He played ball with his son and was the president of the Sandlot League in Fairmont. When the grandkids came along, he liked to watch them play, too.

Mr. Mainella loved the 4th of July. One year he loved it too much and blew off part of his fingers when he was lighting some fireworks.

Mr. Mainella had been a company man, a section foreman. He earned more than a union worker, but just enough to support his wife, five children and one grandfather who lived with him in a small, one-bathroom, three-bedroom home. It was tight, and times were tough, said his son, David. "I don't know how we did it," David said. "I remember Dad, one time, said, 'If I could make $10,000 a year, I'd be on the easy street.'"

Even when there was not much food in the refrigerator, Mrs. Mainella could put together a five-course meal. "I don't know where she got it, where it came from. I don't know how she did it," David said.

A lot of food came from her garden, where she also planted flowers. Some of the older Italian men used to tease her about her flowers. "You can't

Coal mine foreman David Mainella, a family man, died with his crew in the No.9.
Courtesy of David Patrick Mainella.

eat them," they'd say. "They take up too much of the hillside. You should
plant more tomatoes and peppers." She planted flowers anyway, every year.

Mrs. Mainella went into shock when the company sealed the mine with
her husband inside. She was never the same after that experience. She never
remarried. Mr. Mainella's death hit the family doubly hard because he had
already filed his retirement papers. He had less than four weeks to work. He
was 62. He almost made it.

3Right - 7North

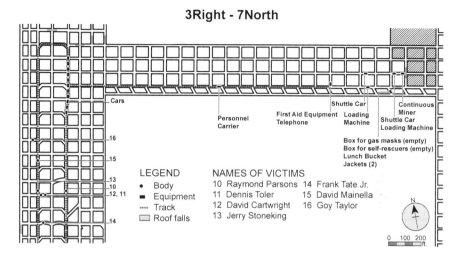

David Mainella Sr.'s body was found in 3Right-7North, along with his crew of six men. Map by Rachel Davis.

The Widows Mine Disaster Committee sent baskets of flowers to the funerals, and the community went through another cycle of mourning. Everyone would mourn again near the end of 1971, when a runaway trip of cars derailed in the No.9 as two men tried to haul coal to the slope.[39]

It was November, and the men had just returned to work after a work stoppage as the union negotiated a contract. Bennie Tippner and Everett Huff were operating the two locomotives. Tippner was the lead operator on the 65-ton locomotive. Huff was bringing up the rear. Investigators said they failed to inspect their locomotives and were trying to haul too many loaded coal cars.[40]

When Huff realized the trip was out of control, he jumped from his vehicle. Tippner either jumped or was thrown from his locomotive when it derailed. Huff ran to his buddy and found him with no signs of life, pinned under the motor.

Recovery efforts slowed during the next few months. With the winter weather had come the curse of methane.

Inundated by Death

The No.9 was full of roof falls, some creating openings 30 feet high, blocking the tunnels with rock and coal. To clean them out, the men had to scale the falls and secure the roof with jacks and roof bolts. It was dangerous work. The rocks and coal could slide out from under a man or the roof could tumble in on him.

James Herron and his crew encountered a particularly large roof fall as they tried to clear the way to 8North. The union men refused to climb it, so Herron and other company men crawled up the fall and jacked up the roof. Not long afterwards, the company called the two men into the Morgantown office. Consol lawyers were present, and they wanted their foremen to say the mine was too dangerous to continue the recovery effort. Herron refused to comply. He had been a U.S. Marine. His father had died in a coal mine. "You don't leave men behind," he said, years later.[1]

The recovery continued, and Consol opened new tunnels to bypass roof falls and reach the dead in 8North. The work took time, but it allowed the company to mine coal and drain the section, which was flooded top to bottom. To get to the water, the company drilled boreholes from the surface and lowered pumps into the mine. It took weeks to remove the water, drive new tunnels and provide enough air to break through the wall and begin exploring the area. Nonetheless, the company had been able to mine coal as it moved forward.

In May 1972, a recovery crew entered 4Right-8North. Forces from the

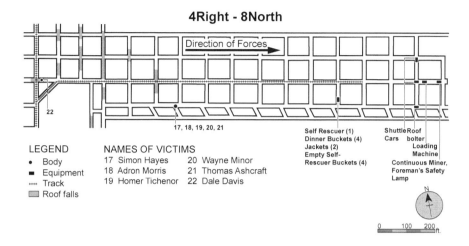

Despite having accessed self-rescuers and gas masks, the men working in 4Right-8North died of asphyxiation approximately 2,000 feet from the work area. Map by Rachel Davis.

explosions had torn the place apart. One machine had been blown into the side of a 16-ton steel mine car, denting the car and knocking it off the track. Belt lines that carried the coal through the tunnels were wrecked, and the supply track ripped from the floor and twisted into odd shapes. Metal and cement block stoppings were blown out.[2]

Four lunch buckets and two jackets were at the dinner hole, along with empty self-rescuer and all-service gas mask boxes. None of the men were there. They had survived long enough to walk 2,000 feet away from the working face. Five were lying near each other in a crosscut, their bodies well preserved and fully clothed. They were wearing their belts and cap lamps, too, which indicated they had died from asphyxiation. Each carried full identification.[3]

Wayne R. Minor was wearing a gas mask, and another mask was lying near Simon P. Hayes. Adron W. Morris, Homer E. Tichenor and Thomas Ashcraft each lay near self-rescuers. Their foreman, Dale E. Davis, was found about 500 feet away, partially covered by a roof fall. Most likely he had told the men to wait in the crosscut while he looked for an escapeway. He, too,

Explosions in the No.9 brought down the roof. Source: U.S. Department of Labor, Mine Safety and Health Administration.

was fully clothed, but missing his cap, which could have floated away when the water filled the section.[4]

Another Consol Disaster

Two months after Dale Davis' crew was found, nine men died in another Consol mine in West Virginia.[5]

The Blacksville No.1 mine in Monongalia County had been having trouble, lots of trouble. After it failed its April 1972 inspection, federal officials had been in and out of the mine 22 times on special "spot" inspections. In fact, they had been in the mine just two days before the nine men died.[6]

On July 22, 1972, 43 men were working underground at the No.1 mine. Some were trying to move a continuous mining machine. The tunnel was too low, and the top of the miner touched an electric power line and the machine caught fire. The fire, which should have been extinguished easily, was allowed to burn out of control, blocking the escape of the nine men who perished.[7]

All of the men could have easily walked out of the mine alive had the men in charge told them to leave before the fire got out of control. The managers were not managing well. Investigators found that coal company officials did not have a workable plan for fighting underground fires. Furthermore, they did not contact the inside men or the outside rescue teams in time to get everyone out alive.[8]

The fire led to an explosion and set the mine on fire. The next day, the company sealed the mine, entombing the nine men.[9] A few days later, John Ashcraft, director of West Virginia's Department of Mines, announced that the company had violated the state's law. Everyone already knew the company had been violating the new federal law.

Six months later, officials opened the mine and the bodies were recovered and returned to their families.[10]

The Men in 5Right-8North

No.9 officials thought they would find three bodies in 5Right-8North. After breaking into the section in September 1972, they discovered nine bodies. The additional men were still trying to free a mining machine that had been partially covered by a roof fall before the explosion.

Fifty-eight-year-old Henry Skarzinski, the section foreman that night, was found just outside the dinner hole. A utility man with 34 years of mining experience, Skarzinski may have been trying to reach the gas masks and self-rescuers that were found nearby, unopened.[11]

The forces of the explosion had wrecked the jeeps the men had driven to the section and thrown equipment around. There was little evidence of fire, some coking here and there. Flames had not touched sandwich wrappers, rock dust bags or the engineers' cardboard tags attached to the roof.[12]

Company officials thought Russell D. Snyder had been putting in timbers along the Main West Headings when the mine exploded.[13] However, he was found in 5Right-8North, lying near a loading machine. Forrest B. Goff and Walter R. Martin, who were part of Sharzinski's crew, were found along

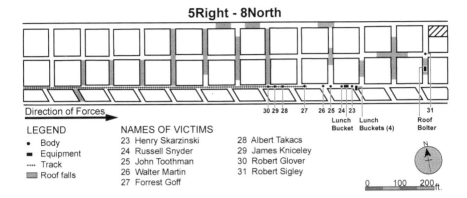

5Right - 8North

Direction of Forces

LEGEND
- Body
- Equipment
- Track
- Roof falls

NAMES OF VICTIMS
23 Henry Skarzinski
24 Russell Snyder
25 John Toothman
26 Walter Martin
27 Forrest Goff

28 Albert Takacs
29 James Kniceley
30 Robert Glover
31 Robert Sigley

30 29 28   27   26 25 24 23

Lunch   Lunch
Bucket   Buckets (4)

31

Roof
Bolter

N

0   100   200 ft.

Nine dead miners were found at 5Right-8North, six more than were thought to be in this area. The additional men were in the area to clear a roof fall that took place before the explosion. Map by Rachel Davis.

the rail tracks. James R. Kniceley was lying on the tracks, too, even though company officials thought he would be in 6North.[14]

One of the two highest ranking men in the mine that night, assistant mine foreman Albert Tackas, was on the tracks, too, a gas mask canister nearby. Most likely he was there to check on the mining machine. His jacket was still in his jeep along with maps of the mine and a copy of West Virginia's coal mining law.[15]

"He was a good mine foreman," said Stanley Plachta, a union man on the recovery team.[16] "We just discussed a lot of things that the company wouldn't want him to discuss with me."[17]

Tackas probably also was checking the Main West Headings that night, Plachta said, because the men had trouble there with gas the night before.[18] Tackas had a lot at stake: his 22-year-old son William was underground that night, assigned to do roof bolting along the Main West Headings. William had gone to work with his father every night until about a month before the disaster, when he married and moved away from home.[19] His body was never found.

Another 22-year-old died in the mine that night. Robert John Sigley, the youngest man on Henry Skarzinski's crew, was found with a self-rescuer

Recovery workers identified John W. Toothman's body using his miner's identification tag and the contents of his wallet, which were returned to the Toothman family. Courtesy of John Toothman.

around his neck near the mining machine. Like the machine, he was partly blanketed by a roof fall. All around him the roof had caved in, separating him from the rest of his crew. He died alone of asphyxiation.[20]

As he explored the section, Plachta found an open box of tools near the mining machine. Socket wrenches, crescent wrenches, a hammer, a punch, screw drivers—all the tools were there. The axle cap on the right side of the machine had been removed. The tools, no doubt, belonged to two mechanics, Robert L. Glover and John W. Toothman, who had been called to the section. After the explosion, Glover had made it the farthest from the working face and lay on the tracks. Toothman lay near a loading machine with a dust respirator on his face.[21]

The local undertaker who had grown up with Toothman took the bad news to the Toothman home. He told Toothman's son, John, that arranging a funeral for a friend was one of the hardest things he had to do. He gave the family Toothman's check number, his wallet with his driver's license and credit card tucked inside, and the watch someone had cut from Toothman's arm. Later, after studying the No.9 map, young John realized that 5Right-8North lay behind his grandmother's house, where his father had grown up. It was strangely comforting to know he had been so close to home.[22]

Mr. Toothman was a coal miner for only about a year and a half before he died. He had been a blacksmith and was good with his hands. He would not wear the leather apron when he pounded the shoes on horses. He said it was not safe because it could tie you to the horse.[23]

He liked to build things. He made go-carts and horse trailers and had turned an old ice-cream truck into a pick-up. When he went into the mines, those skills earned him a mechanic's job.

He was a family man. Some days he would come home and the whole family—three daughters and a son—would pile on top of him and his wife, laughing. They always ate at the table. No television during meals.

He taught his son how to fish and hunt, the things a father does. Young John went into the mines, even though his mother did not approve.[24] "You're 18," she told him. "I can't tell you what to do, but you know how I feel about it."[25]

John, a mechanic, received all the training that his father did not have. It does not bother him to go into the mines even though he remembers the trauma of the disaster. He was 12 years old at the time, but somehow made his way to the Mahan shaft and watched them bring out the last survivors. As each bucket came up, he looked for his father's face. One bucket, then two; men were coming up with pieces of brattice cloth and debris all over them. Then the last bucket.[26]

"The only thing I know was I stood there and watched for faces," John said years later.[27] "They quit bringing people out and that was the end of it. Dad's face wasn't one of the familiar ones . . . he didn't come up that shaft."[28]

They buried John W. Toothman in the Fluharty Cemetery, well off any main roads and high on a mountain where the deer like to graze. His wife, DeEtta, is next to him now. Their family visits often.[29]

He was 36. She was 72.

Who Can Stop Us?

....

By the end of 1972, recovery workers had reclaimed 31 bodies from the No.9. Widows of miners still entombed were frustrated and weary. Most had begun to believe the coal company officials when they said it was unlikely more bodies could be found.

As they had been from the beginning, Consol officials were more interested in coal production than finding the men who had died in their mine. The problem was ventilation,[1] the same problem the mine had before it exploded. The company was struggling to find a way to seal No.9's gobs or ventilate them to meet the law. Unable to convince state and federal officials to lift their mine closure orders, the company was forced to continue its recovery effort in order to bring more coal out of the No.9 with the hope that at some point they could move into full production.

The company also wanted the widows who had not signed their $10,000 agreement to do so and to drop their lawsuits. Sara Kaznoski and seven other widows refused to cooperate, and union miners were not ready to stop looking for the dead.

UMW Elections

On the national scene, the United Mine Workers of America was reinventing itself. The federal government had voided the 1969 election that kept

Tony Boyle in office and was overseeing a new election in December 1972.[2] Boyle still was favored to win, even though he was appealing his conviction for using union funds to make illegal campaign contributions. He had not yet been convicted of the murders of his former challenger, Jock Yablonski, and his wife and daughter.

Boyle lost the election to Miners for Democracy candidate, Arnold Miller. A West Virginia coal miner with black lung disease, Miller immediately cut his salary from Boyle's $50,000 to $35,000 and trimmed other leaders' salaries as well.[3] He also gave rank-and-file miners the right to vote in union elections, a right that Boyle had taken away and replaced with a 20-member voting board that he appointed.[4]

Another Disaster

Just days after the election, Miller was faced with his first mine disaster as UMW's president. A methane explosion in the Itmann No.3 mine in Miller's home county in southern West Virginia had killed five men and seriously injured three others.[5] Consol president John Corcoran, whose company owned about one-third of the Itmann mine, was on site along with Miller. The two had a face-off in the lamp house.[6]

Miller said he was sick of the disasters.

"Farmington, of course, shook the hell out of us," Corcoran said.[7]

The Blacksville explosion a year earlier forced the company to begin thinking about a "crash course" in safety training, he added.[8]

That statement was hard to take seriously, particularly when the two men stood before a sign that read: "Safety in '72 Can Mean a Turkey for You." Miller threatened strikes if safety didn't come quickly.[9]

Consol's "crash course" was not working at the Itmann No.3. Federal inspectors had been monitoring the mine, which had recorded a coal-dust explosion in January 1972 and a methane ignition five months later. Inspectors had withdrawn the men from the Itmann mine four times and written 89 notices of violation in 1972.[10] Notices of violations, however, did not mean much in 1972. Chaos in the U.S. Bureau of Mine's enforcement section had continued to draw criticism from members of Congress. U.S.

Rep. Ken Hechler, D-West Virginia, asked the U.S. Comptroller General for an update on the U.S. Government Accounting Office's 1971 investigation.[11] The Comptroller General reported that in 1972 the U.S. Bureau of Mines had improved its record somewhat. The number of required coal mine safety and health inspections had risen considerably, yet still fell short of the law's mandate. Inspectors had increased their use of the mine withdraw orders when they discovered imminent dangers, issuing 4,400 orders in 1971 and 2,800 in 1972.[12] The number of mining fatalities had dropped from 144 in 1971 to 122 in 1972, but the number of disabling injuries had risen.[13]

One of the biggest problems facing the enforcement program was the way it determined how much to fine coal companies for their violations. Although the law mandated specific conditions to be considered, such as how the fine would affect the company's financial stability, the Bureau was not always taking those conditions into consideration. The small mining companies challenged the civil penalties system, and in 1973, a judge ruled that the Bureau's procedure was unlawful.[14] That ruling relieved small companies of about $19 million in fines.[15]

Many factors complicated the Bureau of Mine's implementation of the 1969 law. Included were budgetary issues, staffing issues and the transmission of the law's requirements to the mining industry. The transition period was tumultuous, but over the years, both the fatality and injury numbers began to improve.

Eleven More Bodies

Safety at the No.9 was heavily regulated during the recovery of bodies. A federal mine inspector traveled underground with every crew and often a state inspector was present, too.[16]

In 1973, production crews mined coal as they drove entries parallel to 7South. Other workers began clearing the roof falls near the Llewellyn Run portal, where 11 men were found.

"The thrust of the explosion hit that shaft first. The very first one hit that shaft the hardest," said Consol's Eugene Mauck.[17] Everybody down there

Llewellyn Run Shaft

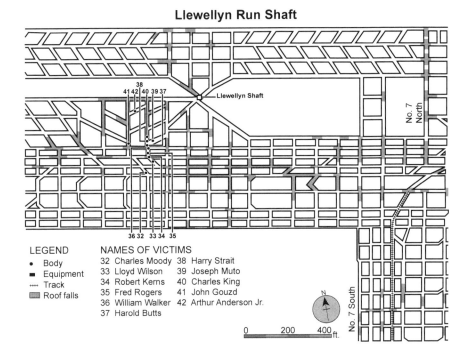

LEGEND

- Body
- Equipment
- Track
- Roof falls

NAMES OF VICTIMS

32 Charles Moody
33 Lloyd Wilson
34 Robert Kerns
35 Fred Rogers
36 William Walker
37 Harold Butts

38 Harry Strait
39 Joseph Muto
40 Charles King
41 John Gouzd
42 Arthur Anderson Jr.

0   200   400 ft.

The eleven men who died at the Llewellyn Run Shaft were killed instantly and without warning. Map by Rachel Davis.

"was killed that quick or quicker, probably the shock would have gotten them before anything else would have."[18]

Dispatcher Charles Moody was "right there at his job," when Mauck and others found his body in May.[19] Another eight men were uncovered in September, all near the elevator shaft.

Lloyd W. Wilson was lying in the Main West tunnel; Robert D. Kerns was found inside a personnel carrier. Mechanics Fred B. Rogers and William T. Walker were under a roof fall near the door of the mechanics shop. Supply men, Harold W. Butts and Harry L. Strait, also were found under slate piles. Finally, near the end of the month, two more mechanics, Joseph Muto and Charles E. King were brought to the surface.[20]

In February 1974, recovery workers continued their search of the Llewellyn Run area and found roof bolter John F. Gouzd,[21] whose nephew, Joe Manchin III, later became governor of West Virginia. The last body carried out of Llewellyn Run was that of Arthur A. Anderson Jr., a rockduster and motorman.[22] A miner for more than 30 years, he had worked the last shift before the No.9 exploded in 1954.

A New Agreement

Consol officials knew that federal, state and union officials were not going to sign off on their $10,000 agreement with the widows as originally planned. Therefore, they crafted a new one.

Drafts of the document clearly show the intent of the company was to stop the recovery effort and begin mining coal full-time. One draft stated that the recovery effort would continue only as long as it was "safe, reasonable and economically practical to do so, i.e., unless and until Consol experiences a substantial or material economic loss."[23] This language, of course, revealed that Consol was not losing money on the recovery effort. The paragraph was omitted from the final agreement.

The same draft stated that if the union or either the state or federal government tried to stop the company from putting the mine into full operation, the recovery of bodies would cease. That paragraph was marked out. A handwritten note on the side read: "Who can stop us?"[24]

The final agreement became vague, leaving the company lots of reasons to stop looking for bodies. The company said it would keep exploring the disaster areas as long as it was "safe, reasonable, feasible and practical."[25]

The compensation to the families remained at $10,000, which by 1974 had decreased in buying power to about $7,400, or about $43,000 in 2009 dollars.

Other than fairness and justice, the company had no incentive to offer a larger settlement. In January 1974, the Pennsylvania court dismissed the widows' lawsuit, and the West Virginia court was ready to do the same.[26] The company also had found 13 more bodies in March, giving the families of 55 recovered men reason to take the money.

3Right - 7South

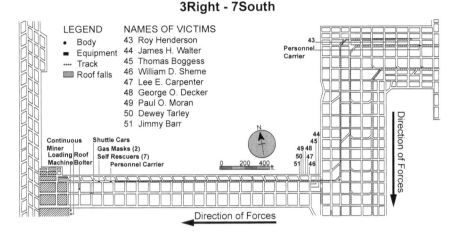

The men in 3Right-7South survived the initial explosion. Their bodies were found with gas masks and self-rescuers and they appeared to have been trying to find a way out. Map by Rachel Davis.

Nine of those men had survived the initial explosion in 3Right-7South Parallels. The crew there had found gas masks and self-rescuers, had walked about one-third mile away from the working face and were huddled together in a crosscut.[27] Assistant mine foreman Roy F. Henderson had taken a jeep and made it another one-third mile away, likely trying to find an escapeway for the crew.[28]

Henderson, an experienced 61-year-old foreman, had taken a lot of pressure from Lockie Riggs after he and section foreman Pete Sehewchuk brought two crews of men out of the mine a few months before the disaster.[29] The Llewellyn Run fan had gone down, and two sections were gassed up, including Sehewchuk's section. They could tell by the lack of air that a fan was down, but the power had not been cut off automatically. Sehewchuk cut the power on his section, sent his men to the dinner hole, called the dispatcher and took his men out of the mine.[30]

Stanley Plachta pulled his power and called Henderson to the section where he and another mechanic were working. Henderson told the mechanics to get in his jeep. They then headed out of the mine. Along the way,

Recovery workers found mining equipment covered with debris. Courtesy of
Joseph Megna.

Henderson stopped, threw a handful of dust in the air to check the ventilation. The dust blew in the wrong direction, signaling a reverse air pattern.[31]

When the fan stopped, a ventilation door that was supposed to close
automatically failed. Had the door shut, it would have prevented the
reversal of air, which sucked the methane out of the gobs and into the
working sections.

When Plachta later asked why a ventilation door had not closed itself,
he was told someone had blocked it open with a piece of wood. "That could
have blown the mine up or at least part of it," Plachta said.[32]

Although the men on the surface knew a fan was down, they did not
pull the power on the entire mine, nor did they call all the men out of the
mine. Sehewchuk was surprised that none of the other crews was called out
of the mine. He complained about it to Foster Turner.

"It went in one ear and it went out the other," he said.[33]

In fact, Plachta said, Lockie Riggs was angry because Sehewchuk and

Henderson had brought men out of the mine. He later overheard Henderson standing up for himself and Sehewchuk. "You should give him a medal instead of raising hell," Henderson told Riggs.[34]

A few weeks later, Henderson was demoted to the cateye shift, Plachta said. "That didn't serve him well because he got killed in the explosion."[35]

When Henderson's body was found, it was lying between the jeep and the side of the tunnel near the mouth of 7South Parallels. Nearly four inches of soot blanketed the area, indicating fires had ravaged that part of the mine. Damage was heavy. Three loaded coal cars had been derailed, and recovery workers had to scale roof falls to find the rest of the crew.[36]

James H. Walter was lying face up near the supply track. He had a self-rescuer under his head. Near him lay Thomas Boggess, face down wearing a gas mask.[37] Boggess had not been working that section long. He had switched jobs with Lewis Lake, who was rescued from the mine through the Mahan Run shaft.[38]

The other men were curled up in a crosscut of 3Right-7South. George O. Decker, also wearing a gas mask, was lying face down. William D. Sheme had a self-rescuer on his chest. The other men, Lee E. Carpenter, Paul O. Moran, Dewey Tarley and Jimmy Barr, were found lying face down.[39]

As the recovery crews moved to the working face, they found it much as it had been left. The mining machine "was standing there, looking like it was ready to go back to work," said Consol official John L. Rozance.[40]

After removing the bodies, recovery workers moved to 6Right-7South. From the mouth of the section, investigators could tell that explosive forces had blown both in and out of the section. The initial explosion that started the disaster could have come from the working face, Rozance said, but he did not believe that it had. The most immediate and intense damage had hit the Llewellyn Run portal, which would indicate the first explosion came from 9North or 10North.[41]

James Herron, who had escaped from A-Face in 1968, helped explore the mouth of 6Right-7South. He was shoveling debris near a rail track when he smelled decaying bodies. He scaled a roof fall and found Joe Feris, whose check tag fell off as his body was moved. Herron put the tag in his own pocket and brought it out of the mine with the body.[42]

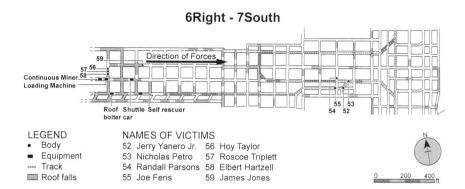

The explosive forces at 6Right-7South blew in and out. Eight men died here, including Randall Parsons, on the job for only eight days before the disaster. Map by Rachel Davis.

The crew also found three other trackmen nearby: Jerry Yanero Jr., Nicholas Petro and Randall Parsons. Parsons was 19 years old and had worked in the mine only eight days when he died.[43] Herron also found section foreman Emilio Megna's safety light, which had been torn in half. He probably was checking on the coal cars when the explosion hit.[44]

Take the Money

By the end of summer in 1974, most of the No.9 families had signed Consol's new agreement. Knowing that their case in West Virginia likely would fail, Kenneth Yablonski advised the 35 widows he represented to take the money, but seven widows did not sign the agreement at that time. Among them were Sara Kaznoski, Mary Rogers, Mary Triplett and Mary Matish.[45] Yablonski was surprised by their refusal.

"Your position regarding this leaves me in a quandary as to what you expect me to do regarding this case," he told Sara Kaznoski in a letter. "I also have some doubt in my mind as to whether or not I should continue to act as your attorney in this matter because your actions would at least create some doubt in my mind as to whether you trust my judgment as your attorney."[46]

As expected, the widows' lawsuit in West Virginia also was dismissed, but that did not stop Sara and other widows from seeking justice. They would continue lobbying for safer coal mines and black lung benefits.

To impede Sara, Consol's Eugene Mauck called her in April 1975 to "discuss the recovery of No.9" and the possibility of hiring her for some kind of job at the mine.[47] There is no evidence that she pursued the offer.

Business Is Business

....

No bodies came out of the No.9 in 1975 or 1976. Instead, Consol drove new tunnels—one parallel to 7South and another that opened a new path between 8North and 9North—which allowed the company to mine coal. In 1975, 64 miners were working underground, bringing out 600 tons of coal each day.[1]

In early 1976, Consol officials began getting estimates on the cost to make the No.9 totally operational. Reconditioning the coal processing plant would cost about $1.2 million, with about $200,000 of the total to be used to prepare the slurry dam, which was used to receive the wastewater from cleaning the coal. The dam, they estimated, was capable of serving the No.9 for "a number of years."[2]

Consol officials also were looking for ways to shorten the time it would take to make the No.9 operational. On March 9, engineering employees began looking for equipment that was available at the company's other mines that could be used at the No.9.[3]

The biggest problem, however, was ventilation. They were struggling to get enough air into the mine and would have to come up with a long-term plan if they wanted to mine more coal.

High Alert

To some extent, another mine disaster in March 1977 put the No.9 recovery officials on edge. The issue in that disaster, as in the No.9, was ventilation.

A Scotia Coal Company mine in Ovenfork, Kentucky, was fighting methane gas buildups without adequate permanent ventilation. Add improperly maintained electrical equipment to that malpractice, and disaster is inevitable. On March 9, an electrical arc set off an explosion that killed 15 coal miners. The initial disaster was bad enough, but two days later during the recovery effort a second explosion killed another 11 men. The tragic nature of the second explosion was compounded by the fact that the company had supplied the recovery team with inaccurate mine maps. Also, the officials planning the recovery failed to consider the likely hazard of using battery-powered equipment to explore the unventilated portions of a gassy mine.[4]

The disaster likely played into the tensions that surfaced during a No.9 Four Agency meeting on March 26. The officials were discussing what to do with the 7South Parallels. Consol's Eugene Mauck wanted to continue to ventilate the area. Federal official Jack Tisdale wanted the company to seal it. The men argued.[5]

"Alright, you may not seal 7South Parallels, but we will tell you this—you must improve the ventilation of this area or we will refuse to approve it," Tisdale said.[6]

"This we cannot do," Mauck replied. Then he asked, "Is this your final position?"[7]

"Yes," Tisdale said.[8]

Mauck turned to Lockie Riggs and said, "Seal her off."[9]

Too Many Problems

Ventilation continued to be a problem during the year, and on November 5, a bearing gave out on the Mahan Run fan and destroyed the fan's blades. The company put in a small centrifugal fan, but it was unable do the job. Methane levels at the fan exceeded 2 percent several times; each time, the men had to be withdrawn from the mine, slowing the work.[10]

In December 1976, Consol officials began serious discussions about closing the No.9 permanently. They decided they would not consult with union, state or federal officials. Instead, they would make their announcement quickly and quietly, notifying everyone who needed to know, including the widows, simultaneously. "There should absolutely be no press conference," the plan stated.[11]

June 29, 1977, would be the best date to make the notifications because the UMW election would be over, and the closing would not become an emotional issue for candidates to use. By then, the Scotia disaster would be "off people's minds," and the new administrations in Washington and Charleston would be in place.[12] Further, the miners would be in the middle of their first week of their two-week vacation and would not be getting together to discuss the closure, making a wildcat strike less likely.[13]

Consol executive Ralph Hatch reviewed the plan. He suggested that someone take the time to make sure the company could close the mine without state or federal approval. In light of the Scotia disaster, politicians could try to pressure the government agencies to find the cause of the disaster.[14]

Thinking It Over

Early in 1977, the Mahan Run fan caused problems again. Its pipes iced over, and the men outside shut the fan down. The men inside trying to recover 8North continued to work. They did not know the fan was down—the "train of communication failed."[15] The No.9 Safety Committee asked for a meeting of the Four Agencies, during which a better line of communication was devised.

Meanwhile, Consol officials still were mulling over their options. Even though they had a closure plan, they commissioned another study to see if it could bring the mine's ventilation up to federal standards. The study revealed two viable options. One would cost $5.2 million and the other $1.6 million.[16]

To move into full production, Consol had to ask state and federal officials to lift their mine withdrawal orders on the No.9. That was risky. Consol officials worried they would have to weather bad publicity for mining coal while bodies were buried in the mine.

Consol did not close the mine in 1977. Instead, as the crews mined coal, the company made weak efforts to look for bodies and no effort to find the cause of the disaster. Officials had no incentive to do either. In fact, they had not bothered to pump the water out of the flooded 9North and the Main West Headings, even though the cost to remove the water would have been relatively low had the pumping begun in 1970. By leaving the area flooded, Consol could and did claim that those sections had become too dangerous to recover.[17]

The excuse was convenient because they also knew they would find bodies in those areas. They had reason to believe that was where the disaster began.

6Right-7South

As the recovery work continued, Consol miners were bringing about 600 tons of coal out of the No.9 each day.

By autumn 1977, the crews had driven a new entry parallel to 6Right-7South, mining coal as they moved forward. They finally broke into 6Right-7South near the section's working face, where they encountered roof falls and water.

"It was hit awfully hard," said Danny Kuhn, a No.9 miner on the recovery crew.

Their first discovery was the continuous mining machine sitting at the working face. Its controls were in the "off" position, indicating that Emilio Megna's crew was not mining coal when they died.

To find the dead, the recovery crew followed the electric cables that energized the machinery. On September 26, they were using a cutting machine to break through the slate. The machine caught the cable and flipped it up, unearthing Hoy Taylor's body.

"It was sitting right up looking at me," Kuhn said. The body shook them all up. Taylor's body was intact, and his identification tag was hanging from his belt. Two days later, they found Roscoe M. Triplett and Elbert E. Hartzell, lying near one another next to the loading machine. They may have been cleaning up the loose coal there.

Feds Get the Picture

By November 1977, federal officials became suspicious about Consol's intentions to continue their recovery of the No.9. Mine specialist James D. Micheal wrote a memo to his boss suggesting "company officials were noncommittal on a timetable for completing any phases of the recovery operations." He noted that the company officials gave no indication of abandoning the recovery operations, but instead of submitting long range plans for approval by the Four Agencies, the company had begun to seek federal approval for short-range plans by phone.

"Obviously this method is unsatisfactory," Micheal wrote.[18]

Last Man Out

On December 2, 1977, recover crews found James Jones. Federal officials reported that he had been on his knees repairing a shuttle car cable with his knife. Kuhn said Jones had been carving a piece of wood.

"He had a penknife and was whittling. . . . [H]e didn't know anything was wrong," Kuhn said.[19]

Recovery work stopped on December 6, when UMW miners went on a strike that lasted more than three months, giving Consol officials time to plan No.9's closure. They decided to close the mine as soon as they could after the strike. Miners would be less likely to protest because they would need their paychecks. During one mine-closing strategy session, a Consol manager noted: "Driving entries in solid [coal] right now—wrong time to quit."[20] By the end of March 1978, No.9 crews were back on the job, working again in 6Right-7South. James Herron was operating a Joy cutting machine, chewing the coal away from a roof fall, when the cutting bar hit metal. He knew he had found a shuttle car. Hoping to find one of their buddies, the crew uncovered the machine. No bodies were in the area, but they knew they were close to uncovering Emilio Megna. He was there—they knew it, and they wanted to get him out. What the men did not know was that Consol was ready to close down the operation.[21]

Families of the No.9 miners who perished in the disaster gather near a makeshift memorial. James Matish (third from right, back row), Mary Matish (fourth from right, back row), Sara Kaznoski (fourth from left, front row). Source: Jeanne M. Rasmussen Collection, East Tennessee State University, Archives of Appalachia.

Herron was surprised when his bosses called him into the office and told him not to explore any more roof falls. At that point, he realized they did not care if more bodies were ever found.[22]

Herron was right. Shortly after the shuttle car was uncovered, Gene Mauck and another manager advised their bosses to announce immediately the end of the recovery effort. If they did not, he warned, the crews would be moving to the area where they believed Emilio Megna was buried.[23]

In one respect, the timing was not the best. Their parent company, Continental Oil, was holding a stockholders' meeting the same week of the closing. Consol wanted to make its announcement after the meeting so no one there would question the move. To wait even a few days, however, would allow the recovery crews to uncover more machinery and lead to more delays.[24]

"By Tuesday that area will be clear and the recovery teams would then begin working in another area since they believe there is the body of a foreman (Emilio Megna) still in the general vicinity. Thus, we would be committing to searching another area and this type of thing could go on indefinitely," wrote a Consol executive in a memo.

Consol took its managers' advice. On April 19, 1978, two days before the stockholder's meeting, officials made their closure notifications in unison. Some contacted federal officials; others called state officials and others union leaders. A special team was sent into the community to find the families of the 19 men who would never come out of the mine. Team members were equipped with written scripts and instructed not to deviate from them. They were to deliver their message and "depart as soon as possible." They were to go to the nearest telephone and call the company collect to report their successes.[25]

The company gave three "official" reasons for closing the mine: the chance of recovering all the bodies was extremely remote; it was unlikely that the cause of the disaster would ever be found; and further exposure of miners to the hazardous work was unwarranted.[26]

Consol's unilateral decisive action caught most people off guard. West Virginia officials stood behind Consol's decision. However, federal officials scrambled to determine what, if any, action they could take to make the company search the rest of the mine for the dead and for the cause of the disaster. They concluded that they had the authority to compel Consol to continue the recovery, and they had the authority to prevent Consol from sealing the mine so they could finish their own investigation. However, they did neither because they did not believe they could win if Consol challenged them in court.[27]

UMW officials immediately vowed to fight the No.9 closure.[28] Sara Kaznoski called that day "the second blackest day in her life." She and other widows immediately took action by contacting local lawyers.

Widows' Last Stand

When the No.9 exploded, James Matish was just a schoolboy. Ten years later, he was a lawyer who stood beside his mother, Mary Matish, and a few of the other widows. Their objective was to force Consol to find his father's body. James had come from a strong family.

Mary's parents, like her husband Frank's, had immigrated to the United States in the late 1800s. Her mother had died at a young age, and she and her two sisters were placed in a convent because her father, a coal miner, had a drinking problem. Eventually, she again lived with her father. At 14, she was sent to be a housekeeper for a wealthy family. In her early 20s, she met and married Frank, and 16 years passed before they had James.[1]

After Frank was entombed in the No.9, Mary stepped into the role of activist. She joined the Widows Mine Disaster Committee, and she testified on behalf of all miners before Congress and the West Virginia legislature. No one would have guessed she had only a third-grade education.[2]

When Consol notified the widows the recovery was finished, seven of the women whose husbands still lay in the pit, refused to accept that ending. By then, they had all signed Consol's $10,000 agreement, in which the company promised to look for the dead as long as the search could be done "safely, reasonably, feasibly and practically." (In the original draft of the agreement those words had been "safe, reasonable and economically practical.")

To seal the mine, the widows believed, was to breach that contract. They filed another lawsuit in the summer of 1978, asking the courts to force Consol to finish the recovery and to award them $1.4 million in punitive damages.[3]

The widows claimed that Consol had not done all it could to find their husbands. In fact, the company, they believed, had concealed the cause of the disaster from them and from state and federal authorities by not exploring the far west side of the mine. They claimed continuing the recovery could be done "safely, reasonably, feasibly and practically." They also claimed that Consol officials had issued false public statements and made false testimony during the investigation hearings.[4]

Contrary to documents that were uncovered during the legal discovery, Consol argued that in 1972, the company had decided it would never be able to operate the No.9 commercially again or discover the cause of the disaster. It said the only reason it kept the recovery going was to find bodies.

Officials used water buildup in the west end of the mine as an excuse to explain the failure to explore 9North and the far end of the Main West Headings, even though one Consol official swore under oath that the water could have been drained easily and inexpensively.[5] Consol officials claimed that they were unaware that water was accumulating at that location, even though they had been monitoring levels in 9North through test holes as early as August 1969, at which time they found no water had collected in 9North.[6] Consol officials also said they did not realize the effect water could have on the tunnels' roofs, even though they had seen how water had damaged many sections after draining them during the recovery effort.

Consol officials also claimed that recovery crews were in danger of being inundated with water if a coal barrier broke between the No.9 and the bordering, abandoned No.44 mine. In fact, the crews were in no more danger than the No.9 miners would have been if the mine had never blown up and Consol had continued its plan for mining the No.9. In 1974, Consol officials said they were worried that a barrier between a nearby abandoned mine might break and flood the No. 9. In response, federal officials called in special engineers who studied the problem. They determined that Consol had total control of the water and that the barrier was thick enough to withstand any amount of water that might build up behind it.[7]

When Consol received the report, Eugene Mauck responded by saying the company accepted the conclusion of the report, and the company would continue to monitor the water levels in the abandoned No.44 mine.[8]

Despite the report, Mauck told people during the recovery that he was waking up in a cold sweat because he kept dreaming that water had broken through the barrier and trapped miners. He used his dream to dramatize his deposition for the widows' lawsuit.[9]

Consol made many excuses for closing the mine. It claimed that it had spent $11 million on the recovery effort and was self-insuring, which may have been true in terms of covering workmen's compensation. However, records produced during the lawsuit show that it had insurance and was using it. For instance, in 1972, it listed $164,149 for "insurance recovery" and another $259,000 in "insurance recovery" that was credited to "Supply Lost in 1974." It also was able to "write-off" $515,000 in "plant and equipment loss."[10] The company also was bringing coal out of the mine and selling it.

During the court battle, which lasted almost four years, the widows' lawyers scoured the federal records and found Larry Layne's 1970 memo about the disabling of the Mods Run fan safety alarm before the explosion. During the depositions, the lawyers tried to pry loose details about the Mods Run fan safety alarm, but were not very successful. Consol objected to the widows' request for information about the FEMCO alarm system, contending that that information was irrelevant to the issue raised in the lawsuit.[11]

When the widows' lawyers tried to find out what had happened to the missing fan charts, Mauck testified that numerous documents related to the No.9 mine had been stolen from a vault that was near the Athas Run Portal.[12]

In sworn written statements, Consol executives said that the company's decision not to report the alleged theft to the police was based on past experience. The implication was that reporting such incidents did no good.[13]

The company wrote that it had kept no record of what had been stored in the vault. However, it did contain "a number of fireboss books" and "records relating to the maintenance and operation of various machinery utilized in the mine; and records relating to persons who went into the mine."[14]

Even if the widows' lawyers had been able to obtain the telltale documents—fan charts, fireboss books, work schedules, maintenance information—the statute of limitation for suing Consol for negligence was long past.

Case Settled

In late 1982, the widows reached an agreement with Consol, and the lawsuit was dismissed. As part of its settlement with the widows, the company gave them 246 acres of property above the mine site from which they could sell lumber and lease the gas rights. Consol also covered their lawyers' fees.[15]

The legal battle was a learning experience for the new lawyer, James Matish. It also forced him to relive the bad dream he experienced the morning the No.9 exploded.

Years later, as a circuit court judge in Harrison County, West Virginia, Matish would look back and realize that what Consol had allowed to happen in the No.9 could have been treated as a criminal act.[16] At the time, the federal government had no power to prosecute the company. The state of West Virginia did have the power, but did not use it. Given the sworn testimony taken during the No.9 hearings and the physical evidence discovered during nine years of recovery efforts, both the state and the federal governments easily could have assigned fault for the disaster. Neither chose to do so.

People still speculate about where the first explosion occurred. Some miners believe it started in 6Right-7South, where the men were killed instantly and where the explosive forces appear to have originated at the working face. However, evidence showed the forces moving both in and out of the section. Others are convinced that the disaster began in 9North, where gas had been a problem and two mechanics were working on a broken mining machine. They easily could have set off a spark. Or the explosion could have begun along the Main West Headings near 9North, where miners were securing the roof. No one will ever know for certain.

Even the violations that were known were never redressed. Neither the state nor the federal government issued a violation, levied a fine, or took any action against Consol or any of its employees even though conditions in the No.9 were so bad that 78 men died. Nor did Consol take responsibility for failing to maintain a safe mine. Not one Consol employee was disciplined, demoted or fired in the wake of the disaster.[17]

The widows may have been paid a paltry $10,000 and a few others also were awarded some property after a long court battle, but they knew they had not received justice.

If the families of the dead have found any peace, it has come from knowing that their loved ones made coal mining safer for thousands of men and women who would earn their incomes underground. The launch of the Federal Coal Mine Health and Safety Law of 1968 was difficult. Over time, it became a reality. Along with tougher state laws and stronger enforcement, it has helped reduce the annual death and injury tolls in underground mines. The changes in the laws and how they are enforced also have given coal mining families the ability to litigate successfully against companies who operate unsafe mines.

Since the 1970s, families have reached multi-million dollar settlements with negligent coal companies. Government agencies have begun to levy and collect fines. Sometimes criminal charges have even been filed against the worst offenders.

Among the early litigators was Gerald M. Stern who won a $13.5 million settlement for more than 600 clients following the Buffalo Creek disaster in Logan County, West Virginia, which claimed 125 lives.[18] The deaths and massive destruction of an entire valley occurred when a Pittston Company water and refuse retaining dam gave way. The catastrophe sent 130 million gallons of water and 1 million tons of refuse crashing 17 miles into the valley. Hundreds of homes and buildings were wiped out.[19]

Stern returned to the courtroom for the families of miners killed after two explosions rocked a Scotia Coal Company mine in Ovenfork, Kentucky, in 1976. Inadequate ventilation and too much methane explained the first blast that killed 15 men. The company's inaccurate mine maps, poor recovery planning, and the use of battery-powered equipment in an unventilated mine led to the second explosion two days later that killed 11 more men.[20]

Stern won a $5.9 million settlement from the coal company for the 15 families who lost men in the first explosion. He won another $2.1 million from the federal government for the deaths of five other miners in the second explosion.[21]

Other lawsuits have followed. Ten widows won a $10 million settlement for the deaths of their spouses in a 1981 methane gas explosion in a Consolidation Coal mine in Tennessee.[22]

Criminal charges were filed against a mine foreman and a coal mine operator in connection with the 1992 Southmountain mine explosion that killed eight Virginia miners. A judge sentenced the operator to six months in prison and ordered the company to pay the families of the dead $900,000.[23]

Three more prison sentences were handed down to coal company executives after 10 miners died in a 1989 explosion at the Pyro Mining Company's Williams Station Mine in Kentucky. The mine's general superintendent received the longest prison term of 18 months for allowing men to work in areas with dangerous accumulations of methane gas. The company also paid $3.75 million in fines and penalties for federal safety violations.[24]

More recently, some of the families of the 11 miners killed and the one miner seriously injured in the January 2, 2006, Sago Mine Disaster in West Virginia have reached undisclosed settlements with International Coal Group and Wolf Run Mining.[25] Settlement amounts for families of two miners who died a few months later in Massey Energy's Aracoma Coal Mine also were not disclosed. The company did agree to pay $1.7 million in civil fines for federal safety violations.[26]

The case of the Crandall Canyon Mine disaster in Utah offers another example of eventual requital. Six men were entombed in the mountain, and three rescue workers died trying to find them. Murray Energy reportedly settled the case with the families, paying out more than $20 million. The federal government levied $1.85 million in fines against the owners.[27]

At this writing in 2010, Massey Energy is under investigation for the deaths of 29 miners in its Upper Big Branch mine in Montcoal, West Virginia. No doubt lawsuits and settlements, citations and fines will arise. Perhaps even criminal charges will be filed. Whatever the outcome, one fact is certain: No amount of money will ever fully compensate the victims' survivors of this or any other coal mine disaster. Nor can money wipe away the trauma suffered by entire communities when the coal industry reduces men and women to numbers on metal check tags, easily replaced by others.

Every time a miner dies on the job, families who have lost loved ones in the mines are reminded of their own losses. In 2002, John Toothman

John Toothman and his family visit his parents' grave often. His father's body was recovered in 1972. Photo by Bonnie E. Stewart.

sat alone on his couch and cried like a baby when he watched the rescue of nine miners who had been trapped underground for three days in a Pennsylvania mine.

"I knew there were kids and grandkids. . . . I could just see their reactions on their faces when they knew their fathers were going to come home."[28] John Toothman waited four years for recovery crews to bring his father's body out of the No. 9. "You get to the understanding that he's dead, but you don't have a body, so you know the funeral is coming someday, possibly. You understand that. You prepare yourself for that."[29]

Four years after the disaster, he was in a room with four closed caskets. John Wesley Toothman was in one of them.

Who is ever ready for that?

"Forty years later, I'm still crying over it, so it just never ends I guess," said David Mainella Jr. His father did not want him to be a coal miner, but he became one anyway. David tried to get a job at the No. 9, but his father,

David Mainella Sr., told the superintendent not to hire him. David took a job with General Motors in Ohio. When he tired of driving more than 150 miles to come home on weekends, he took his first mining job, but not at the No.9. In the mines, he realized how much danger his father had faced every day and how much pressure coal companies put on miners to produce as much coal as possible.

"You went in there and it was a known fact that if you were a coal miner, you knew you was gonna get hurt or killed and accepted that. . . . A lot of times you go in there and say, 'Oh man, I just hope I can make it out alive today,'" he said.

When David was 43, he did almost die in a Consol mine. He was part of a crew moving some large machinery when a chain snapped, and he was struck in the forehead. The blow broke every bone in his face and destroyed his frontal sinuses. When he recovered, he returned to the mine, but he worked outside.

"When I got hurt, I didn't get a letter or a get well card or anything from Consol. If you didn't produce for them, you were done." Underground, he was a production hero. Outside he was a nobody.

Former Consol foreman James Herron felt that strange coldness of the industry when he retired. He and his family had sacrificed a lot for coal. His father had died under a roof fall at the age of 44. James escaped the 1968 No.9 disaster only because he was not working on the west side of the mine the morning the mine exploded. Still, he and others returned to the No.9 to help recover bodies, loading out thousands of tons of slate and rock, some of it lying on top of their friends. When they found men, they often recognized them by their clothing or numbers. They bagged them, one by one, and brought them out to their families.

After the recovery, Herron continued to mine for Consol until 1990, when he submitted his retirement papers. He was proud of the work he had done and was pleased when the company notified him that it had a gift for him, a ring. When he picked it up, he thought his bosses might give him a pat on the back or express their gratitude for his long years of service. When he arrived at the company office, a receptionist handed him a box with the ring. No other recognition was offered.[30]

Each year, the loved ones of the No.9 miners gather to honor them at a memorial park that sits atop the abandoned mine. Photo by Bonnie E. Stewart.

Herron, like many of the survivors, still lives near the No.9. He can tell you where the portals were, even though they are just green meadows now. He can give you directions to the tall, sleek, black tombstone that Consol erected as part of its agreement with the widows. The community gathers there once a year to honor the dead. The people study the 78 names etched in the granite. They pray. They flinch when the military rifles sound their salute. James Herron stays home on those days. He prefers to be alone when he stands atop the abandoned mine and honors his buddies.

"I'll think about those men the rest of my life," he said.

Many others will, too.

Acknowledgments

....

I owe a great debt to the families who lost loved ones in the No.9 mine disaster, particularly those who trusted me with their personal histories. John Toothman not only shared his father's story, he took me into a coal mine so that I could experience the world in which he works and in which his father died. Many thanks to James Matish, who guided me over the acres that cover the abandoned No.9 mine and became the final resting place for his father, Frank. A special thanks to Joseph Megna, for sharing his father's story and lending me the disaster slides he inherited from a state mine inspector.

I also am grateful to Pete Kaznoski, David Mainella and Gary Boros who were kind enough to relive that horrible tragedy and the sorrow it brought into their lives.

Understanding this story and delivering it accurately would have been much more difficult without the first-hand accounts of several miners who worked in the No.9 or were part of the recovery effort. They include William Bunner, Pete Sehewchuk, John Brock, Wayne Fetty, James Herron, John Floyd, Tom Boone and the late Stanley Plachta.

I am indebted to Larry L. Layne, the former federal coal mine inspector who authored the memo detailed in Chapter 17 and who spent several days examining and explaining hundreds of pages of state and federal documents concerning the disaster.

This book could not have been written without the assistance of Melody Bragg and Yvonne Farley with the National Mine Health and Safety Academy Technical Information Center and Library in Beaver, West

Virginia. Ms. Bragg spent many hours sifting through files and boxes of records to help me complete my work. W.Va. Department of Mines officials also helped me gather documents at the District 4 Office in Oak Hill, West Virginia.

Librarians at the following institutions helped me explore their holdings: West Virginia University Library's West Virginia Collection; the West Virginia Division of Culture and History at the West Virginia State Archives; and East Tennessee State University's Archives of Appalachia.

Numerous legal documents were provided by the late Brent E. Beveridge, and others were secured through the U.S. District Court in Clarksburg, West Virginia.

Many other individuals shared their wealth of legal and mining knowledge, including West Virginia University law professor Patrick McGinley; Dr. Ronald L. Lewis of the West Virginia University Department of History; and Davitt MacAteer, an administrator at Wheeling Jesuit University.

I must thank Associated Press reporter Vicki Smith for telling me that the No.9 mine disaster deserved a book.

I also am thankful for journalists who wrote the first stories about the No.9 disaster. They include Ben A. Franklin, Fannie Hoffman, Peggy Edwards, John Veasey, Niles Jackson and Joe Krovisky.

This book also benefited greatly from the photographs shot by Bob Campione.

Several former West Virginia University students also deserve my thanks, particularly Justin Weaver, who introduced me to the Farmington community and the miners who work there. Ivy Guiler Smith and Bailee Morris spent numerous hours transcribing audio interviews; Jesse Wright taught me how to edit photographs and helped me produce my first multimedia piece; Jon Offredo and Kendall Montgomery accompanied me with their cameras and Rachel Davis reproduced the No.9 maps.

Many thanks to Scott Finn who worked with me on the No.9 mine story that was broadcast on National Public Radio's "All Things Considered" on November 19, 2008, which energized me as I continued my research.

More encouragement and sound advice came from retired University of Illinois Press acquisitions editor Judy McCulloh and West Virginia University's Jackson Family distinguished chair, English Department chair and author, Donald Hall.

Generous grants from the West Virginia University Faculty Senate and the P.I. Reed School of Journalism supplied financial support for this work.

I am indebted to Carrie Mullen, director of the West Virginia University Press, for accepting this book and for guiding me through the publication process. Many thanks also go to her staff, including Than Saffel, Abby Freeland and Rachel King, for their design, marketing and editing efforts. Thanks, too, to editor MaryJo Thomas for her corrections and comments throughout this manuscript and to Michael Taber, who not only created the index but caught discrepancies in the text.

David R. Hirsh not only provided emotional support, he read two drafts of this book, offering invaluable comments and criticism. My friends Samata Taylor-Sturm and Maggie Delbon talked me through much of this work.

Without my family, there would be no book. They provided unconditional love and editorial assistance. Dale and Bobbie-Jo Harris read and reread each chapter of this book, catching errors and giving me valuable feedback. My sister Cindy Stewart, as always, was my lifeline, never too busy to take my call. My other sisters, Jo Carpenter and Nancy Robertson, and their families took plenty of calls, too.

Much love and support also came from my niece Gwendolyn Tornatore; my mother, Alice Stewart; my brother Roger Stewart and his family; and my son, Ted Harris, and his wife, Melissa Conner.

Finally, from a more distant place, I often felt good wishes and love from my sister, Sheila Harris Thacker, and my father, Ward H. Stewart.

Appendices

....

Appendix A
U.S. Coal Mining Fatalities, 1900–2011

Year	Miners	Fatalities
1900	448,581	1,489
1905	626,045	2,232
1910	725,030	2,821
1915	734,008	2,269
1920	784,621	2,272
1925	748,805	2,518
1930	644,006	2,063
1935	565,202	1,242
1940	533,267	1,388
1945	437,921	1,068
1950	483,239	643
1955	260,089	420
1960	189,679	325
1961	167,568	294
1962	161,286	289
1963	157,126	284
1964	150,761	242
1965	148,734	259
1966	145,244	233
1967	139,312	222
1968	134,467	311
1969	133,302	203

Year	Miners	Fatalities
1970	144,480	260
1971	142,108	181
1972	162,207	156
1973	151,892	132
1974	182,274	133
1975	224,412	155
1980	253,007	133
1985	197,049	68
1990	168,625	66
1995	132,111	47
2000	108,098	38
2001	114,458	42
2002	110,966	28
2003	104,824	30
2004	108,734	28
2005	116,436	23
2006	122,975	47
2007	122,936	34
2008	133,827	30
2009	133,433	18
2010	129,631*	48
Total Fatalities 1900-2011[†]		**104,722**

[†] Total includes fatalities from years not listed; *Preliminary in early 2011

Source: U.S. Department of Labor Mine Safety and Health Administration (MSHA)

http://www.msha.gov/stats/centurystats/coalstats.asp

Appendix B

Victims of the No.9 Disaster on November 13, 1954

Name	Age	Position	Status/Children
George C. Alberts	51	SF	Married
Russell W. Morris	51	MF	Widower
Harry C. Dunmire	51	MF	Married/2
Carrol Ice	51	CMO	Divorced
Charles Korsh, Jr.	34	MO	Married/1
Louis L. Beafore	29	RB	Single
Nick Koverbasich	37	SCO	Single
Charles L. Fluharty	33	RD/M	Married/2
Robert L. Sanders	36	RD	Married/3
Harry Floyd Sr.	62	P	Married
Matt Menas	43	M	Married/2
Lonnie Hartzell	49	M	Married
Clyde R. Keener	63	M	Divorced
Joe Opyoke	44	M	Married/1
Joe Gregor	47	D	Married/2
Howard Jenkins	38	L	Married/3

Key to occupations: CMO = Cutting-Machine Operator; D = Dispatcher; L = Lampman; MO = Machine Operator; MF = Maintenance Foreman; M = Mechanic; P = Pumper; RD = Rockduster; RB - Roof Bolter; SF = Section Foreman; SCO = Shuttle Car Operator

Appendix C

Locations of victims of the No.9 Disaster on November 20, 1968

Name	Occupation	Age	Date Found
Main West Haulage Road between 3North and 4North			
Lester B. Willard	MM	49	Oct. 23, 1969
Charles F. Hardman	MM	43	Oct. 24, 1969
1Right-6North			
James E. Efaw	M	46	Dec. 1, 1970
Steve Horvath	RB	42	Dec. 1, 1970
Dennis N. McDonald	UM	42	Dec. 1, 1970
George R. Kovar	SCO	31	Jan. 7, 1971
Gorman H. Trimble	SCO	55	Jan. 7, 1971
Hartzell L. Mayle	LMO	51	Jan. 11, 1971
Albert R. Deberry	CMMO	44	Jan. 12, 1971
3Right-7North			
Raymond R. Parsons	CMMO	50	June 28, 1971
Dennis L. Toler	T	25	June 28, 1971
David V. Cartwright	M	35	June 29, 1971
Jerry L. Stoneking	RD	24	June 29, 1971
Frank Tate Jr.	SCO	44	June 30, 1971

Key to occupations: CMMO = Continuous Mining Machine Operator; LMO = Loading Machine Operator; M = Mechanic; MM = Motorman; RD = Rockduster; RB = Roof Bolter; SCO = Shuttle Car Operator; T = Trackman; UM = Utility Man

Name	Occupation	Age	Date Found
David Mainella	SF	62	June 30, 1971
Goy A. Taylor	RB	47	June 30, 1971
4Right-8North			
Simon P. Hayes	SCO	43	May 11, 1972
Adron W. Morris	LMO	59	May 11, 1972
Homer E. Tichenor	CMMO	53	May 11, 1972
Wayne R. Minor	SCO	39	May 11, 1972
Thomas D. Ashcraft	RB	31	May 11, 1972
Dale E. Davis	SF	40	May 11, 1972
5Right-8North			
Henry J. Skarzinski	UM	58	Sept. 12, 1972
Russell D. Synder	RB	58	Sept. 12, 1972
John W. Toothman	M	36	Sept. 12, 1972
Walter R. Martin	T	57	Sept. 12, 1972
Forrest B. Goff	CMMO	53	Sept. 12, 1972
Albert Tackas	AMF	49	Sept. 12, 1972
James R. Kniceley	WM	43	Sept. 12, 1972
Robert L. Glover	M	40	Sept. 12, 1972
Robert J. Sigley	CM	22	Sept. 12, 1972

Key to occupations: AMF = Assistant Mine Foreman; CMMO = Continuous Mining Machine Operator; LMO = Loading Machine Operator; M = Mechanic; RB = Roof Bolter; SF = Section Foreman; SCO = Shuttle Car Operator; T = Trackman; UM = Utility Man; WM = Wireman

Name	Occupation	Age	Date Found
Llewellyn Shaft Area			
Charles E. Moody	D	46	May 3, 1973
Lloyd W. Wilson	M	46	Sept. 11, 1973
Robert D. Kerns	M	33	Sept. 20, 1973
Fred B. Rogers	M	58	Sept. 20, 1973
William T. Walker	AMF	45	Sept. 21, 1973
Harold W. Butts	SMM	42	Sept. 24, 1973
Harry L. Strait	SMM	49	Sept. 24, 1973
Joseph Muto	M	48	Sept. 25, 1973
Charles E. King	M	36	Sept. 25, 1973
John F. Gouzd	RB	32	Feb. 13, 1974
Arthur A. Anderson Jr.	MM/RD	51	Feb. 14, 1974
3Right-7South Parallel			
Roy F. Henderson	AMF	61	March 13, 1974
James H. Walter	UM	53	March 13, 1974
Thomas Boggess	UM	48	March 13, 1974
William D. Sheme	SCO	30	March 13, 1974
Lee E. Carpenter	M	37	March 13, 1974
George O. Decker	CMMO	42	March 13, 1974

Key to occupations: AMF = Assistant Mine Foreman; CM = Conveyer Man; D = Dispatcher; M = Mechanic; MM = Motorman; RD = Rockduster; RB = Roof Bolter; SCO = Shuttle Car Operator; SMM = Supply Motorman; UM = Utility Man

Name	Occupation	Age	Date Found
Paul O. Moran	LMO	60	March 13, 1974
Dewey Tarley	RB	28	March 13, 1974
Jimmy Barr	SCO	31	March 13, 1974
6Right-7South			
Jerry R. Yanero Jr.	CM/T	20	March 14, 1974
Nicholas Petro	T	28	March 14, 1974
Randall R. Parsons	T	19	March 14, 1974
Joe Feris	T	40	March 14, 1974
Hoy B. Taylor	CM	40	Sept. 26, 1977
Roscoe M. Triplett	LMO	54	Sept. 28, 1977
Elbert E. Hartzell	RB	27	Sept. 28, 1977
James Jones	SCO	42	Dec. 2, 1977

Victims Not Recovered

Name	Occupation	Age
Oswald J. Armstrong	RB	51
Orval D. Beam	SCO	52
John J. Bingamon	MM	53

Key to occupations: CMMO = Continuous Mining Machine Operator; CM = Conveyer man; LMO = Loading Machine Operator; M = Mechanic; MM = Motorman; RB = Roof Bolter; SCO = Shuttle Car Operator; T = Trackman

Name	Occupation	Age
Louis S. Boros	LMO	38
William E. Currence	MM	49
Howard A. Deel	CM	30
Virgil A. Forte	RB	45
Hilery W. Foster	RB	50
Aulda G. Freeman Jr.	MM	30
Paul F. Henderson Jr.	UM	24
Junior M. Jenkins	SCO	42
Pete J. Kaznoski Sr.	SCO	59
Frank Matish	LMO	57
Emilio D. Megna	SF	48
Jack D. Michael	M	44
John Sopuch	CMMO	42
William L. Tackas	RB	22
Edwin A. Tennant	SCO	45
Edward A. Williams	M	49

Source: "Informational Report of Investigation." U.S. Department of Labor, Mine Safety and Health Administration, 1990.

Key to occupations: CMMO = Continuous Mining Machine Operator; CM = Conveyer man; LMO = Loading Machine Operator; M = Mechanic; MM = Motorman; RB = Roof Bolter; SF = Section Foreman; SCO = Shuttle Car Operator; UM = Utility Man

Appendix D

Chronology of Federal Coal Mine Laws
and Selected Major Underground Coal Mine Disasters

This list does not include all major explosions.

1891	Congress passed the first federal mine safety statute that established minimum ventilation requirements and prohibited the employment of children under 12 years of age.
1907	Monongah Nos.6 and 8, Monongah, West Virginia, Killed: 362–500
1909	Cherry Mine, Cherry, Illinois, Killed: 259
1910	Public Law 61–179. Bureau of Mines created in the Department of the Interior. Federal safety and health role limited to research. No inspection powers given.
1913	Stag Canon No.2, Dawson, New Mexico, Killed: 263
1940	Pond Creek No.1, Bartley, West Virginia, Killed: 91
1940	Willow Grove No.10, St. Clairsville, Ohio, Killed: 72
1941	Public Law 77–49. Federal inspectors allowed to enter mines. No safety or health regulations mandated.
1947	Centralia No.5, Centralia, Illinois, Killed: 111
1947	Public Law 80–328. Congress authorized the formulation of coal mine safety standards.
1951	Orient No.2, West Frankfort, Illinois, Killed: 119
1952	Public Law 82–552. Allowed federal inspectors to conduct an annual inspection for underground coal mines, except small mines that employed fewer than 15 people. If inspectors found imminent danger, they could order miners to leave the mine. If the owners refused to obey the order they could be fined up to $2,000.
1954	Jamison No.9 Mine, Farmington, West Virginia. Killed: 16
1954	No.34 Mine, McDowell County, West Virginia. Killed: 37
1957	Marianna No.58 Mine, Marianna, Pennsylvania. Killed: 6
1957	No.31 Mine, McDowell County, West Virginia. Killed: 11
1958	Bishop No.34 Mine, McDowell County, West Virginia. Killed: 22
1958	Burton Mine, Craigsville, West Virginia. Killed: 14
1958	Lundale Mine, Lundale, West Virginia. Killed: 6
1959	River Slope Mine, Port Griffin, Pennsylvania. Killed: 12
1962	Blue Haze Coal Company, Herrin, Illinois. Killed: 11

1962   U.S. Steel Robena Mine No.3, Carmichaels, Pennsylvania. Killed: 37

1963   Clinchfield Coal Compass No.2 Mine, Dola, West Virginia. Killed: 22

1963   Carbon Fuel Company No.2 Mine, Helper, Utah. Killed: 9

1965   Clinchfield Coal Company Mars No.2 Mine, Wilsonburg, West Virginia. Killed: 7

1965   Mid-Continent Coal Dutch Creek Mine, Redstone, Colorado. Killed: 9

1966   Public Law 89-376. Extended coverage of 1952 law to small underground coal mines. Provided for orders of withdrawal in cases of repeated unwarrantable failures to comply with standards. Education and training programs expanded.

1966   The New River Company Siltix Mine, Mount Hope, West Virginia. Killed: 7

1966   Valley Camp No.3 Mine, Triadelphia, Ohio. Killed: 4

1968   Consol No.9, Farmington, West Virginia. Killed: 78

1968   Saxsewell No.8 Mine, Leivasy, West Virginia. Killed: 4

1969   Public Law 91–173. Federal Coal Mine Health and Safety Act of 1969. Enforcement powers in coal mines increased vastly. Surface mines covered. Four annual inspections required for each underground coal mine. Stricter standards for gassy mines abolished, but additional inspections required in these mines. Miners given right to request a federal inspection. Mandatory fines for all violations. Criminal penalties for knowing and willful violations. Safety standards for all coal mines strengthened, and health standards adopted. Procedures incorporated for developing new health and safety standards. Training grant program instituted. Benefits provided to miners disabled by black lung disease.

1970   Finley Coal No.15 and No.16, Hyden, Kentucky. Killed: 38

1972   Consol Coal No.1, Blacksville, West Virginia. Killed: 9

1972   Itmann Coal No.3, Itmann, West Virginia. Killed: 5

1973   Mining Enforcement and Safety Administration (MESA) created as a new Interior Department agency and assumed safety and health enforcement functions formerly carried out by the Bureau of Mines.

1976   Scotia Mine, Oven Fork, Kentucky. Killed: 26

1977   Public Law 95-164. Federal Mine Safety and Health Act of 1977. Placed coal mines, metal and nonmetal mines under a single law, with enforcement provisions similar to 1969 Act. Moved enforcement agency to Department of Labor and named it Mine Safety and Health Administration (MSHA). Required four annual inspections at all underground mines, two at all surface mines. Provisions for mandatory miner training. Mine rescue teams required for all underground mines. Increased involvement of miners and their representatives in health and safety activities.

1977–2005   Total fatalities: 1,976

2006   Sago Mine, Buckhannon, West Virginia. Killed: 12

2006   Darby Mine No.2, Middlesboro, Kentucky. Killed: 5

2006   Aracoma Alma No.1, Logan County, West Virginia. Killed: 2

2006   Public Law 109-236. Mine Improvement and New Emergency Response Act (MINER Act). Required mine-specific emergency response plans in underground coal mines; new regulations regarding mine rescue teams and sealing of abandoned areas; prompt notification of mine accidents; and enhanced civil penalties.

2007   Crandall Canyon, Huntington, Utah, Killed: 6

2010   Upper Big Branch, Montcoal, West Virginia. Killed: 29

Sources:

U.S. Department of Labor, Mine Safety & Health Administration (MSHA):

http://www.msha.gov/MSHAINFO/FactSheets/MSHAFCT7.HTM

http://www.msha.gov/mshainfo/factsheets/mshafct8.htm

http://www.msha.gov/stats/centurystats/coalstats.asp

http://www.msha.gov/MSHAINFO/MSHAINF2.HTM#

Notes

....

In cases where internet URLs fall across two lines of text, please type the address into your Web browser's address bar without hyphens introduced by line breaks.

Introduction

1. U.S. Department of Labor. Inspection Violations for Upper Big Branch Mine. January 1 through April 5, 2010. *http://www.msha.gov/drs/ASP/InspectionViolations.asp*
2. W.Va. Department of Mines. Inspection Reports 2010. Upper Big Branch Mine. *http://www.wvminesafety.org/performanceubbmc.htm*

Chapter 1: Good night, Dad

1. Joseph Megna. Interview with author. Worthington, West Virginia. May 21, 2008.
2. Ibid.
3. Barbara Smith. "Miner's Widow: Sara Kaznoski." Goldenseal. Summer 1988.
4. James Matish. Interview with author. Clarksburg, West Virginia. July 5, 2007.

Chapter 2: Dangerous History

1. Rakes, "Acceptable Casualties," 2002.
2. "A Brief History of Coal and Safety Enforcement in West Virginia." *http://www.wvminesafety.org/History.htm*
3. U.S. Department of Labor. *Historical Summary of Mine Disasters.* Vol. 1, 13.
4. "Metal/Nonmetal Fatalities for 1900 through 2009." *http://www.msha.gov/stats/centurystats/mnmstats.asp*
5. Ibid.
6. McAteer, 2007, 241.
7. U.S. *Historical Summary of Mine Disasters.* Vol. 1. 3, 22–36.
8. "Disaster Due to Coal Dust." *The New York Times.* September 4, 1910.
9. U.S. *Informational Report of Investigation, Underground Coal Mine Explosion and Fire, Consol No. 9 Mine, Mountaineer Coal Company, Division of Consolidation Coal Company, Farmington, West Virginia, November 20, 1968.* Submitted by William J.

Tattersall, assistant secretary for Mine Safety and Health. March 1990. 1. *Informational Report of Investigation.* Consol No.9 Mine. March 1990, 1.

10. Ibid.

11. Ibid.

12. Ibid. 107.

13. W.Va. Department of Mines. *Inspection Report.* April 1935.

14. W.Va. *Inspection Report.* January 1936.

15. W.Va. *Inspection Report.* September 1936.

16. W.Va. *Inspection Report.* October 1937.

17. W.Va. *Inspection Reports. Jamison Coal & Coke Company. Mine No.9.* 1930–1940.

18. U.S. Department of the Interior. *Confidential Report on the Jamison No.9.* 1943.

19. Ibid.

20. Ibid.

21. Ibid.

22. Ibid.

23. Ibid.

24. U.S. *Inspection Report.* May 1951.

25. U.S. Department of the Interior. *Press Release.* June 4, 1951.

26. U.S. *Inspection Report.* January 1952.

27. Ibid.

28. U.S. Department of the Interior. *Final Report on Major Explosion. 1954.* 4.

Chapter 3: How Such Things Happen

1. U.S. *Final Report on Major Explosion. November 1954.* 3.

2. U.S. Department of Commerce. *Meteorological Review of Farmington Disasters.* Weedfall. 1–4.

3. U.S. *Historical Summary of Mine Disasters.* Vol. 1. 249.

4. "Notes on Farmington Explosion." *The West Virginian.* November 15, 1954. A-1.

5. U.S. *Final Report on Major Explosion.* 1954.

6. "Notes on Farmington Explosion." *The West Virginian.* November 15, 1954. A-1.

7. U.S. *Final Report on Major Explosion.* 1954. 1.

8. Ibid. 17.

9. "One Man Dies at Pit Portal." *The Charleston Gazette.* November 14, 1954. A-1.

10. U.S. *Final Report on Major Explosion.* 1954. 2.

11. Ibid.

12. Krovishy, "Mrs. Duncil Remembers '54."

13. "Survivors Cling to Hope Doomed Miners Still Live." *The Charleston Gazette*. November 15, 1954.

14. U.S. *Final Report on Major Explosion*. 1954. 1.

15. Krovisky, "Mrs. Duncil Remembers '54."

16. Carroll, "More Blasts Jarring Mine."

17. Ibid.

18. Carroll, "Mine Sealed Off as Inquiry Starts."

19. W.Va. *Official Hearing*. Part I. 117–120.

20. W.Va. *Official Hearing*. Part I. 172–176.

21. W.Va. *Official Hearing*. Part II. 2–19.

22. U.S. Congress. Federal Coal Mine Safety Act of 1952.

23. W.Va. *Official Hearing. Jamison No.9 Mine Explosion*. Part 1. 38–55.

24. Ibid.

25. W.Va. *Official Hearing. Jamison No.9 Mine Explosion*. Part 1. 235–242.

26. Ibid.

27. W.Va. *Official Hearing. Jamison No.9 Mine Explosion*. Part 1. 128.

28. W.Va. *Inspection Report. No.9 Mine*, by M.B. Horton. December 21–31, 1953.

29. U.S. Department of the Interior. Bureau of Mines. *Coal Mine Inspection Report. No.9 Mine*, January 13–25, 1954.

30. W.Va. *Inspection Report. No.9 Mine*, March 15–18, 22, 24–26, 1954.

31. U.S. *Coal Mine Inspection Report. No.9 Mine*, May 20, 21, 24–28 and June 1–2, 1954.

32. U.S. *Coal Mine Inspection Report. No.9 Mine*, October 6–20, 1954.

33. U.S. Department of Labor. *Excerpts from the Report on the Conditions of the Bodies Recovered after the 1954 Explosion*.

34. William Bunner. Interview with author. March 3, 2009.

35. Ibid.

36. Ibid.

37. Ibid.

38. W.Va. Department of Mines. *Official Hearing, Coal Mine Explosion, Consol No. 9 Mine, Mountaineer Coal Company, Division of Consolidation Coal Company, Farmington, Marion County, West Virginia, November 20, 1968*. December 5–7, 1968. 282.

39. U.S. Department of Labor. *Final Report on Major Explosion.* 1954. 26-27; and *Excerpts from the Report on the Conditions of the Bodies Recovered after the 1954 Explosion.*

40. U.S. *Final Report.* 1954. 35.

41. U.S. Department of the Interior. *The Use and Misuse of Explosives in Coal Mining.*

42. W.Va. *Official Hearing. Jamison No.9 Mine Explosion.* Part 2. 156–162.

43. Ibid. 20-38.

44. W.Va. *Official Hearing. Jamison No.9 Mine Explosion.* Part 1. 144–156.

45. W.Va. *Official Hearing. Jamison No.9 Mine Explosion.* Part 1. 188.

46. Ibid.

47. Ibid.

Chapter 4: Rules of Survival

1. U.S. Department of the Interior. *Special Investigation Report, Pillar Bleeders, Jamison No.9 Mine, Consolidation Coal Company, Farmington, Marion County, West Virginia.* January 3 and 5–6, 1958.

2. U.S. *Coal Mine Inspection Report. No.9 Mine.* March 2–4, 6, 9, 11–13 and 23–25, 1964.

3. U.S. *Coal Mine Inspection Report. Consol No.9 Mine.* July 19, 21–23 and August 3–6, 9–13 and 16–20, 1965.

4. U.S. *Coal Mine Inspection Report. Consol No.9 Mine.* November 29-30 and December 1–3, 6–10, 13–16, and 20, 1965.

5. U.S. *Historical Summary of Mine Disasters in the United States. Vol.1, Coal Mines, 1959–1998.* 25–31.

6. Schrum, May 2, 1965.

7. Ibid.

8. Ibid.

Chapter 5: A Beautiful Mine

1. Bunner, March 3, 2009.

2. Ibid.

3. Ibid.

4. Ibid.

5. Ibid.

6. Ibid.

7. U.S. *Informational Report of Investigation.* 1990. 1.

8. Stanley Plachta. Interview with author. Farmington, West Virginia. July 11, 2008.

9. Ibid.

10. Pete Sehewchuk. Interview with author. Fairmont, West Virginia. July 21, 2008.

11. Ibid.

Chapter 6: Methane Madness

1. U.S. Energy Information Administration. *Coal Production in the United States—An Historical Overview.* October 2006. 1.

2. U.S. Department of Labor. *Historical Data 1931-1977 Bituminous Mines in the United States.* http://www.msha.gov/STATS/PART50/WQ/1931/wq31bi10.asp

3. U.S. *Coal Mine Inspection Report. No.9 Mine.* April 2–5, 8–12, 15–19, 22 and 24–25, 1968.

4. U.S. Department of Commerce. Census of Population 1970.

5. U.S. *Coal Mine Inspection Report. No.9 Mine.* April 2–5, 8–12, 15–19, 22 and 24–25, 1968.

6. United Mine Workers of America. *National Bituminous Coal Wage Agreement of 1968.* October 1, 1968.

7. "Police Called to Stop Chants of Protesters." *The Fairmont Times.* Oct. 14, 1969.

8. U.S. Office of the Secretary of Defense. *U.S. Military Fatal Casualties of the Vietnam War for Home-State-of-Record: West Virginia,* Part of Record Group 30. http://www.archives.gov/research/vietnam-war/casualty-lists/state-level-alpha.html

9. U.S. *Coal Mine Inspection Report. No.9 Mine.* August 1–2, 5–9, 12–16, 19–23, and 26–30, 1968. 2.

10. W.Va. *Official Hearing.* Dan Thomas. 340–343.

11. W.Va. *Official Hearing.* Joseph Duda. 361–364.

14. Wayne Fetty. Interview by author. August 8, 2008.

15. W.Va. *Official Hearing.* Lawrence H. Riggs. 43–44.

16. Ibid.

17. W.Va. *Official Hearing.* Walter Slovekosky. 61–77.

18. Ibid.

19. Ibid.

20. Ibid.

21. W.Va. *Official Hearing.* Layman Hall. 338.

22. W.Va. Department of Mines. *Check-Inspection Report. Mountaineer Coal Company. No.9 Mine.* February 16, 1968.

23. W.Va. *Official Hearing.* 304–312.

24. W.Va. *Check-Inspection Report. Mountaineer Coal Company. No.9 Mine*, by Walter Miller. February 16, 1968.

25. W.Va. *Official Hearing*. Dana E. Harris Sr. 304–312.

26. U.S. *Coal mine Inspection Report. No.9 Mine*, by Matthew I. Duncan. April 2–5, 8–12, 15–19, 22 and 24–25, 1968.

27. W.Va. *Inspection Report. Mountaineer Coal Company. No.9 Mine*. June 11–14,17,18 and July 23,25,29,30 and August 5 and 8, 1968.

28. W.Va. *Inspection Report. Mountaineer Coal Company. No.9 Mine*. October 8–11, 21–25, 28–31, 1968.

29. W.Va. *Official Hearing*. Dana E. Harris, Sr. 304–312.

30. W.Va. *Official Hearing*. Robert Bland. 90.

31. U.S. Bureau of Mines. *Report of Investigation No. 8474, Spontaneous Combustion Susceptibility of U.S. Coals*, by J. M. Kutchta, V. R. Rowe, and D. S. Burgess. 1980.

32. Glover, George. *Abandoned Book Only. Fire Boss Record Book. November 19, 1968*.

33. U.S. *Coal Mine Inspection Report. No.9 Mine*. August 1–2, 5–9, 12–16, 19–23, and 26–30, 1968.

34. U.S. Department of the Interior. *Coal Mine Inspectors' Manual*. September 1967.

35. W.Va. *Inspection Report. Mountaineer Coal Company. No.9 Mine*. October 8–11, 21–25, 28–31, 1968.

36. W.Va. *Official Hearing*. Arthur Eugene Cook. 358-360.

37. Ibid.

Chapter 7: Dry and Dusty

1. National Institute for Occupational Safety and Health. *Float Coal Dust Explosion Hazards*. No. 515. April 2006.

2. West Virginia Code. Chapter 22. Mines and Minerals. 22-1-2. March 7, 1967,

3. W.Va. *Inspection Report, No.9 Mine*. February 15, June 16 and October 27, 1967.

4. W.Va. *Inspection Report, No.9 Mine*. February 7–9, 12,13,15 and 19-23, 1968.

5. U.S. *Coal Mine Inspection Report. Consol No.9 Mine*. April 25, 1968.

6. W.Va. *Inspection Report, No.9 Mine*. June 11–14, 17, 18 and July 23,25, 29, 30 and August 5 and 8, 1968.

7. U.S. *Coal Mine Inspection Report. Consol No.9 Mine*. August 30, 1968.

8. W.Va. *Inspection Report, No.9 Mine*. October 8–11, 21–25 and 28–31, 1968.

9. W.Va. *Official Hearing*. Lewis Lake, 134–146.

10. W.Va. *Official Hearing.* Dana E. Harris. 305–311.

11. W.Va. *Official Hearing.* Ancle B. Morris. 369–376.

12. Ibid.

Chapter 8: Warning Signs

1. W.Va. *Official Hearing.* Walter Slovekosky. 61–77.

2. Ibid.

3. Ibid.

4. George Glover. *Fireboss Record Book. Fireboss Book Only. November 17, 1968.*

5. U.S. Department of Commerce. *Climate, Weather and Coal Mine Explosions with a Meteorological Review of the Farmington Disasters. Report 15.* By Robert O. Weedfall. April 16–17, 1970.

6. George Glover. *Fireboss Record Book. Fireboss Book Only. November 17, 1968.*

7. U.S. Department of Commerce. National Oceanic & Atmospheric Administration. *Surface Weather Observations and Barograms for Morgantown, West Virginia, November 13–20, 1968.* Letter and attachments from NOAA Director Daniel B. Mitchell to Ronald L. Keaton, U.S. Department of Labor, Mine Safety & Health Administration. December 3, 1979.

8. Ibid.

9. Ibid.

10. George Glover. *Fireboss Record Book. Fireboss Book Only. November 18, 1968.*

11. Paul Watson. *Fireboss Record Book. Fireboss Book Only. November 18, 1968.*

12. U.S. *Surface Weather Observations and Barograms for Morgantown, West Virginia, November 13–20, 1968.* Letter and attachments from NOAA Director Daniel B. Mitchell to Ronald L. Keaton, U.S. Department of Labor, Mine Safety & Health Administration. December 3, 1979.

13. Ibid.

14. W.Va. *Official Hearing.* George Wilson. 115-133; Gary Martin. 147–155.

15. *Sections Only. Section Foremen Fireboss Reports.* November 19, 1968.

16. W.Va. *Official Hearing.* Layman Hall. 334–339.

17. *Sections Only. Section Foremen Fireboss Reports.* November 19, 1968.

18. W.Va. *Official Hearing.* Stanley Plachta. 258–265.

19. Ibid.

20. U.S. *Surface Weather Observations and Barograms for Morgantown, West Virginia,*

November 13-20, 1968. Letter and attachments from NOAA Director Daniel B. Mitchell to Ronald L. Keaton, U.S. Department of Labor, Mine Safety & Health Administration. December 3, 1979.

21. Pete Sehewchuk. Interview with author. Fairmont, West Virginia. July 21, 2008.

22. W.Va. *Official Hearing.* Robert Cook. 312–317.

23. U.S. Department of Commerce. *Climate, Weather and Coal Mine Explosions with a Meteorological Review of the Farmington Disasters. Report 15.* By Robert O. Weedfall. April 16–17, 1970. 4–5.

24. *Sections Only. Section Foremen Fireboss Reports.* November 19, 1968.

25. George Glover. "Abandoned Book Only. Fire Boss Record Book." November 19, 1968; George Glover. *Fireboss Record Book. Fireboss Book Only. November 18, 1968.*

26. W.Va. *Official Hearing.* Paul Watson. 323–333.

27. *Sections Only. Section Foremen Fireboss Reports.* November 19, 1968.

Chapter 9: The Last Shift

1. U.S. *Surface Weather Observations and Barograms for Morgantown, West Virginia, November 13–20, 1968.* Letter and attachments from NOAA Director Daniel B. Mitchell to Ronald L. Keaton, U.S. Department of Labor, Mine Safety & Health Administration. December 3, 1979.

2. Ibid.

3. W.Va. *Official Hearing.* Walter Slovekosky. 64.

4. W.Va. *Official Hearing.* Alex M. Kovar. 45–51 and 381–383.

5. W.Va. *Official Hearing.* Samuel Stout, testimony. 78–85.

6. W.Va. *Official Hearing.* Walter Slovekosky, testimony. 61–77

7. W.Va. *Official Hearing.* Mrs. James A. Simons, testimony. 179–182.

8. W.Va. *Official Hearing.* James A. Simons, testimony. 297–304.

9. W.Va. *Official Hearing.* Alex M. Kovar. 45–51 and 381–383.

10. W.Va. *Official Hearing.* Russell Foster, testimony. 1–6.

11. W.Va. *Official Hearing.* Edgell Wilson, testimony. 7–11.

12. W.Va. *Official Hearing.* Issac (sic) R. Kuhn, testimony. 13–22.

13. Anna Belle Currence vs. Consolidation Coal Company, Civil Action No. 78-C-538 Circuit Court of Marion County, West Virginia (1978). Deposition of H. Eugene Mauck. May 11, 1981.

14. Ibid.

15. Ibid.

16. Ibid.

17. National Institute for Occupational Safety and Health. *Escape from Farmington No.9. An Oral History. An Interview with Gary Martin and Waitman "Bud" Hillberry*, by Michael J. Brnich Jr. and Charles Vaught. Department of Health and Human Services Publication No. 2009-142D. May 2009.

18. W.Va. *Official Hearing.* Lewis L. Lake. 134–146.

19. *Official Hearing.* Gary Martin. 147–155.

20. Ibid.

21. W.Va. *Official Hearing.* Alex M. Kovar. 45–51 and 381–383

22. W.Va. *Official Hearing.* Mrs. James A. Simons, testimony. 179–182.

23. W.Va. *Official Hearing.* James A. Simons, testimony. 297–304.

24. W.Va. *Official Hearing.* James "Jimmie" Herron, testimony. 92–104.

25. W.Va. *Official Hearing.* Lewis Parker, testimony. 86–88.

26. W.Va. *Official Hearing.* Lawrence H. Riggs, testimony. 28–44.

27. National Institute. *Escape from Farmington No.9.* May 2009.

28. W.Va. *Official Hearing.* Henry Conway, testimony. 23–27.

29. W.Va. *Official Hearing.* James "Jimmie" Herron, testimony. 92–104.

30. National Institute. *Escape from Farmington No.9.* May 2009.

31. W.Va. *Official Hearing.* Lewis L. Lake, testimony. 134–146.

32. National Institute. *Escape from Farmington No.9.* May 2009.

33. W.Va. *Official Hearing.* Cecil Selders, testimony. 183–197.

34. National Institute. *Escape from Farmington No.9.* May 2009.

35. Ibid.

Chapter 10: The Disaster Hits Home

1. Joseph Megna. Interview with author. Worthington, West Virginia. May 21, 2008.

2. John Brock. Interview with author. Mannington, West Virginia. May 28, 2007.

3. Tom Boone, Interview with author. Farmington, West Virginia. July 21, 2008.

4. John Veasey. "They Came . . . and They Waited in Silence." *The West Virginian.* November 20, 1968.

5. Robert Morris. Interview with author. Weston, West Virginia. August 2008.

6. Fannie Hoffman. "21 Miners are Rescued." *The West Virginian.* November 20, 1968.

7. Morris, August 2008.

8.   Matish, July 5, 2007.

9.   David Patrick Mainella. Interview with author. Fairmont, West Virginia. June 17, 2008.

10. Bunner, March 3, 2009.

11. "78 Miners Entombed in Farmington No.9 After Blasts." November 21, 1968.

12. Megna, May 21, 2008.

13. U.S. Department of the Interior. "Hand-written Explosion Logs." November 20–December 4, 1968 and November 20–November 25.

14. Ben A. Franklin. "78 Trapped in Mine by Blasts and Fire." *The New York Times*. November 21, 1968.

15. "74 Trapped, 8 Rescued In West Va. Mine Blast." *Record American* (Boston). November 21, 1968.

Chapter 11: A Paralyzed Community

1.   William Frederici. "Their Men Gone, Their Hope Too." *Daily News*. November 23, 1968. C-5.

2.   Joseph A. Loftus. "Mine Safety Law Held Inadequate." *The New York Times*. November 22, 1968.

3.   Ibid.

4.   Ibid.

5.   "Hope Dim for 78 Miners." *Knickerbocker News*. November 22, 1968.

6.   "Boyle Has Praise for Consol Safety." *The Fairmont Times*. November 22, 1968.

7.   South-East Coal Company v. Consolidation Coal Company v. United Mine Workers of America. 424 F.2d 767. U.S. Appeals Court. 1970.

8.   Ben A. Franklin. "Hopes Dim for 78 Caught in Mine Fire." *The New York Times*. November 21, 1968.

9.   "New Disturbance Dims Hope at Mine." *Times-Union* (Albany, NY). November 22, 1968.

10. U.S. Department of the Interior. "Explosion Logs Kept by Consol Employees." November 20–December 4, 1968.

11. Fannie Hoffman. "Fire Continues to Rage." *The West Virginian*. November 22, 1968. A-1.

12. Megna, May 21, 2008.

13. U.S. *Informational Report of Investigation*. 1990. 12.

14. Brock, May 28, 2007.

15. U.S. *Informational Report of Investigation*. 1990. 12–13.

16. "Ministerial Head Proclaims Sunday As Day of Prayer." *The West Virginian*. November 22, 1968.

17. James L. Weeks and Maier Fox. "Fatality Rates and Regulatory Policies in Bituminous Coal Mining, United States, 1959–1981." *American Journal of Public Health, Vol. 73, No.11*, November 1983.

18. Michael Wallace. Ohio State University. "Dying for Coal: The Struggle for Health and Safety Conditions in American Coal Mining, 1930–82." *Social Forces, Vol. 66:2*, December 1987.

19. "Mine Rescuers Find Nothing: Drill Through." *The Charleston Gazette*. November 25, 1968.

20. Niles Jackson. "Stone Blocks Dropped into Burning Mine." *The Knickerbocker News*. November 23, 1968.

21. Ben A. Franklin. "Miners' Relatives Urge Greater Efforts to Save 78. *The New York Times*. November 24, 1968.

22. "No Seal Pledge Renewed." *The Fairmont Times*. November 25, 1968.

23. U.S. "Hand-written Explosion Logs." November 20–December 4, 1968.

24. "Hole into Section Silent." *The Fairmont Times*. November 25, 1968.

25. "Air Samples Dim Hope for Miners." *The New York Times*. November 26, 1968.

26. "Many Letters Received with Ideas for Rescue." *The West Virginian*. November 27, 1968.

27. "Work Resumes at Area Mines; Walkout Ended." *The West Virginian*. November 27, 1968.

28. "Mine Laws Weak—Hechler." *The West Virginian*. November 26, 1968.

29. Peggy Edwards. "Fresh Air Said Not Circulating Inside Mine." *The West Virginian*. November 26, 1968.

30. "Governor-Elect Makes 2nd Trip to Tragedy Site." *The West Virginian*. November 29, 1968.

31. Niles Jackson. "Prayer at the Mine: I Want . . . Some Sign." *The West Virginian*. November 27, 1968.

32. Ibid.

33. Letters to Mary Matish, 1968 and 1969.

34. Matish, July 5, 2007.

35. U.S. "Hand-written Explosion Logs." November 20–December 4, 1968.

36. "Thanksgiving Marked by New Explosion." *The West Virginian.* November 29, 1968.

37. Ibid.

38. Welling, "Blast Victims Sealed in Fire-Ravaged Mine." November 30, 1968.

39. Ibid.

40. Matish, July 5, 2007.

41. Ibid.

42. Megna, May 21, 2008.

43. Robert C. Welling. "Blast Victims Sealed in Fire-Ravaged Mine." *The Knickerbocker News.* November 30, 1968.

44. Niles Jackson. "He's Worried About Us . . . That's the Kind of Man He Is." *The West Virginian.* November 27, 1968.

45. U.S. "Hand-written Explosion Logs." November 20–December 4, 1968.

46. Edwards, Peggy. "LBJ Asks Stronger Mine Safety Laws." *The West Virginian.* December 2, 1968.

47. Letters to Mary Matish, 1968 and 1969.

48. Ron Jackson. "Silent Tributes Paid to Victims." *The Associated Press.* December 2, 1968.

Chapter 12: Bungled Investigation

1. U. S. Department of the Interior. *Memorandum from Earl T. Hayes to the Secretary of the Interior.* Dec. 4, 1968.

2. W.Va. *Official Hearing, Coal Mine Explosion, Consol No.9 Mine, Mountaineer Coal Company, Division of Consolidation Coal Company, Farmington, Marion County, West Virginia, November 20, 1968. December 5–7, 1968.*

3. Sehewchuk, July 21, 2008.

4. Joseph McNece. "Receipt for Certified Mail." December 4, 1968.

5. W.Va. *Official Hearing, Coal Mine Explosion, Consol No.9 Mine, Mountaineer Coal Company, Division of Consolidation Coal Company, Farmington, Marion County, West Virginia, November 20, 1968. December 5–7, 1968.*

6. W.Va. *Official Hearing.* Robert Cook. 312–317.

7. Ibid.

8. Ibid.

9. W.Va. *Official Hearing.* Alva G. Davis. 160–166.

10. Ibid.

11. Ibid.

12. W.Va. *Official Hearing*. George K. Glover. 250–257.

13. *West Virginia Code*. Chapter 22, Mines and Minerals. Article 2. Section 2395 (7): Gassy Mines; Nongassy Mines; Examination.

14. W.Va. *Official Hearing*. George K. Glover. 250–257.

15. Ibid.

16. Ibid

17. Ibid.

18. W.Va. *Official Hearing*. Jess G. Bowers. 266–296.

19. Ibid.

20. Ibid.

21. George Glover. *Fireboss Record Book. Fireboss Book Only. November 17, 1968.*

22. W.Va. *Official Hearing*. Fay Casseday. 213–229.

23. W.Va. *Official Hearing*. Eugene Lieving. 242–249.

24. W.Va. *Official Hearing*. Fay Casseday. 213–229.

25. W.Va. *Official Hearing*. Lawrence H. Riggs. 28–44.

26. W.Va. *Official Hearing*. Fay Casseday. 213–229.

27. W.Va. *Official Hearing*. Lawrence H. Riggs. 28–44.

28. W.Va. *Official Hearing*. Cecil Selders. 183–197.

29. W.Va. *Official Hearing*. Alex M. Kovar. 45–51.

30. *West Virginia Code*. Chapter 22, Mines and Minerals. Article 2. Section 2391 (4) Fans.

31. W.Va. *Official Hearing*. "Official statement presented at the hearing by Alex M. Kovar." Appendix A.

32. Herron, July 7, 2009.

33. W.Va. *Official Hearing*. Arthur Merrifield. 365–368.

34. Kessler, David J. to Bonnie E. Stewart. Written response to Freedom of Information Requests (1–5) dated March 17, 2009 (Consolidation Coal Farmington No.9 Mine Disaster). Kessler is an administrator with W.Va. Office of Miners' Health, Safety & Training. March 31, 2009.

35. Micheal, J. D. "Memo to Rita to type the No.9 explosion report and handwritten copy of the report." November 29, 1979.

36. McAteer, J. Davitt to Wayne Veneman (MSHA). Freedom of Information Request for Federal Report on No.9 Disaster. July 3, 1986.

37. Ronald J. Schell (MSHA) to J. Davitt McAteer. Response to Freedom of Information Request for Federal Report on No.9 Disaster. July 23, 1986.

38. "Briefing Outline. (Three versions.) Consol No.9 Mine. Purpose: To obtain approval for release of the Informational Report of Investigation."

Chapter 13: Widows and Wildcat Strikes

1. Richard Nixon. The American Presidency Project. *Special Message to the Congress on Coal Mine Safety.* March 3, 1969. *http://www.presidency.ucsb.edu/ws/index. php?pid=2442&st=coal+min*

2. Diana Nelson Jones. "25 Years Ago, Their World Collapsed in a Fiery Mine Explosion." *Pittsburgh Post-Gazette.* November 21, 1993.

3. U.S. Department of Labor. Mine Safety & Health Administration. *Coal Fatalities for 1900 through 2008. http://www.msha.gov/stats/centurystats/coalstats.asp*

4. U.S. Congress. Senate. Committee on Labor and Public Welfare. Subcommittee on Labor. *Coal Mine Safety Act: Hearing on S. 355, S. 467, S.1094, S. 1178, S. 1300 and S. 1907 before the Subcommittee on Labor.* 91st Cong., 1st sess., February 27, March 7, 12, 13, 14, 18, 20, 26 and May 2, 1969. Part 1, Part 2. Mrs. Sara Lee Kaznoski, testimony.

5. Ibid.

6. Ibid.

7. Ibid.

8. Senate Subcommittee Hearing 1969, Mrs. Mary Kay Rogers, testimony.

9. Alan Derickson. "Down Solid: The Origins and Development of the Black Lung Insurgency." *Journal of Public Health Policy. Vol. 4, No. 1.* (March 1983), 25–44.

10. "New Chest Disease Found in Coal Miners." *Science News 89:197.* March 26, 1966.

11. Alan Derickson. "Black Lung: Anatomy of a Public Health Disaster." Cornell University Press. 1998.

12. Frank Reynolds and David Snell. "Black Lung/Miners' Strike." *ABC Evening News,* February 20, 1969.

13. Senate Subcommittee Hearing 1969, W. A. Boyle (UMW), testimony.

14. Betty Louise Dotson-Lewis. "Coal Mining in Appalachia: the Federal Coal Mine Health and Safety Act of 1969, Interview with Ken Hechler." June 28, 2001. *http:// www.appalachiacoal.com/ken%20hechler.htm*

15. U.S. Congress. Senate. Committee on Labor and Public Welfare. Subcommittee on Labor. *Coal Mine Safety Act: Hearing on S. 355, S. 467, S.1094, S. 1178, S. 1300 and S. 1907 before the Subcommittee on Labor.* 91st Cong., 1st sess. March 7, 1969. "Major Differences Among Proposed Senate Bills, 1952 Act, and Interior's Proposed Bill." 527–528.

16. Ibid.

17. Senate Subcommittee Hearing 1969, Elmer Yocum, testimony.

18. Ibid.

19. Ibid.

20. Senate Subcommittee Hearing 1969, Senator Robert C. Byrd (W.Va.), testimony.

21. Senate Subcommittee Hearing 1969, Elijah Wolford, testimony.

22. Ibid.

23. Ibid.

24. FTC v. Sperry & Hutchinson Co., 405 U.S. 233 (1972), *http://caselaw.lp.findlaw.com/scripts/getcase.pl?court=us&vol=405&invol=233*

25. Senate Subcommittee Hearing 1969, Elijah Wolford, testimony.

26. Senate Subcommittee Hearing 1969, Rep. Ken Hechler (W.Va.), testimony.

27. Senate Subcommittee Hearing 1969, John O'Leary, director, U.S. Bureau of Mines, testimony.

28. Senate Subcommittee Hearing 1969, Elmer Yocum, testimony.

29. U.S. Congress. The 1952 Coal Mine Federal Coal Mine Safety Act. Public Law 82–552.

30. Senate Subcommittee Hearing 1969, U.S. Surgeon General, Dr. William H. Stewart, testimony.

31. U.S. Congress. Senate. Committee on Labor and Public Welfare. Subcommittee on Labor. *Coal Mine Safety Act: Hearing on S. 355, S. 467, S.1094, S. 1178, S. 1300 and S. 1907 before the Subcommittee on Labor.* 91st Cong., 1st sess. March 7, 1969. "Major Differences Among Proposed Senate Bills, 1952 Act, and Interior's Proposed Bill." 527–528.

32. Senate Subcommittee Hearing 1969, Cloyd D. McDowell, testimony.

33. Senate Subcommittee Hearing 1969, James R. Garvey, testimony.

34. Senate Subcommittee Hearing 1969, Huda Bailey, testimony.

35. Ibid.

36. Ibid.

37. Senate Subcommittee Hearing 1969, Henry Mann, testimony.

38. Senate Subcommittee Hearing 1969, Otis Ratliff, testimony.

39. Senate Subcommittee Hearing 1969, Senator Robert C. Byrd (W.Va.), testimony.

40. Ibid.

41. Senate Subcommittee Hearing 1969, Senator Randolf Jennings (W.Va.), testimony.

42. Martha Bryson Hodel. "Hechler's Hecklers Gather for Reunion." The Associated Press State & Local Wire. September 14, 1998.

43. Richard Nixon. The American Presidency Project. *Statement on Signing the Federal Coal Mine Health and Safety Act of 1969.* December 30,1969, *http://www.presidency. ucsb.edu/ws/index.php?pid=2389&st=coal+mine&st1*

44. Jimmy Carter. The American Presidency Project. Black Lung Benefits Reform Act of 1977. Remarks on Signing H.R. 4544 Into Law. March 1, 1978, http://www.presidency. ucsb.edu/ws/index.php?pid=30433&st=black&st1=lung

Chapter 14: Body Production

1. Roger Stuart. "Where 78 Miners Died: Grief, Friction Prevail." *The Pittsburgh Press.* September 14, 1969.

2. D. H. Davis to K. K. Kincell, H. E. Mauck, L. H. Riggs, J. G. Bowers, R. M. Henderson and Norris Brooks. "Personal & Confidential Memo." March 25, 1969. Produced during discovery. Anna Belle Currence v. Consolidation Coal Company, Civil Action No. 78-C-538 Circuit Court of Marion County, West Virginia (1978).

3. "Preliminary Plans for Reopening No.9 Mine." No date.

4. D. H. Davis. "Large Diameter Boreholes for Opening No.9. Feasibility, Cost, Driller, Etc." May 15, 1969.

5. "Minutes from meeting attended by federal, state, UMW, Consol and Mountaineer Coal officials." June 16, 1969.

6. Henderson, R. M. "Status of Mine Atmosphere." August 8, 1969. Produced during discovery.

7. "Minutes from meeting attended by federal, state, UMW, Consol and Mountaineer Coal officials." June 16, 1969. Produced during discovery.

8. Ibid.

9. Ibid.

10. Ibid.

11. Ibid.

12. D. H. Davis. "Large Diameter Boreholes for Opening No.9. Feasibility, Cost, Driller, Etc." May 15, 1969. Produced during discovery.

13. "Preliminary Plans for Reopening No.9 Mine." No date. Produced during discovery.

14. Ibid.

15. Ibid.

16. Brock, John. Interview with author. Mannington, West Virginia. May 28, 2007.

17. U.S. Department of the Interior. Bureau of Mines. *Report of Surface Gas Explosion, Consol No.9 Mine*, by John Paul Phillips and Carl J. Shaffer. July 29, 1969.

18. "Minutes from meeting attended by federal, state, UMW, Consol and Mountaineer Coal officials." August 12, 1969.

19. Ibid.

20. Ibid.

21. Ibid.

22. Jeanne M. Rasmussen. "The Hot Edge of Hell." Unpublished manuscript.

23. Ibid.

24. Roger Stuart. "Volunteers Begin Risky Job of Unsealing Farmington Mine." *The Pittsburgh Press*. September 12, 1969.

25. Niles Jackson. "Service Held for Miners." *The Fairmont Times*. September 13, 1969.

26. Ibid.

27. Roger Stuart. "Volunteers Begin Risky Job of Unsealing Farmington Mine." *The Pittsburgh Press*. September 12, 1969.

28. U.S. *Informational Report of Investigation*. 1990. 19.

29. "Two Teams Begin W.Va. Mine Hunt." *The Pittsburgh Press*. September 15, 1969.

30. "Black With Soot, Park Says of Mine." *The Fairmont Times*. September 16, 1969.

31. "No.9 Mine Yields First of 78 Explosion Victims: Bad Air, Rock Fall Delay Search for Second Miner." *The Fairmont Times*. October 24, 1969.

32. W.Va. *Official Hearing, Coal Mine Explosion, Consol No.9 Mine, Mountaineer Coal Company, Division of Consolidation Coal Company, Farmington, Marion County, West Virginia, November 20, 1968. December 5–7, 1968*. Walter Slovekosky. 61–77.

33. "No.9 Mine Yields First of 78 Explosion Victims: Bad Air, Rock Fall Delay Search for Second Miner." *The Fairmont Times*. October 24, 1969.

34. Ibid.

35. Ibid.

36. John Floyd. Interview with author. May 15, 2008.

37. Ibid.

38. U.S. *Informational Report of Investigation*. 1990. 21.

39. Ibid. 21–25.

40. Ibid. 21–26.

Chapter 15: In Search of Justice

1. "Memorial Services Held for Miners." The Associated Press. November 20, 1969.
2. Ibid.
3. Ibid.
4. Barbara Smith. "Miner's Widow: Sara Kaznoski." *Goldenseal.* Summer 1988.
5. Ben A. Franklin. "Union Seeks to Avoid Paying Reward in Killings." *The New York Times.* February 1, 1987.
6. Bob Robertson. "Legacy to the UMW." *The Pittsburgh Post-Gazette.* December 30, 1994.
7. Ibid.
8. Ibid.
9. Pete Kaznoski. Interview with author. November 15, 2009.
10. Ibid.
11. Smith, Summer 1988.
12. Kaznoski, November 15, 2009.
13. Smith, Summer 1988.
14. Ibid.
15. Kaznoski, November 15, 2009.
16. Ibid.
17. "No.9 Dependents Get State Checks." *The Charleston Gazette.* December 16, 1968.
18. Megna, May 21, 2008.
19. "No.9 Widows Get $1,319 Each from Contributed Funds." *The Fairmont Times.* October 14, 1969.
20. Richard T. Cooper. "Fund Dispute Compounds Widows' Grief." *The Los Angeles Times.* April 21, 1969.
21. "Obituary: Kenneth J. Yablonski." *The Pittsburgh Post-Gazette.* September 11, 2002.
22. Rev. Everett F. Briggs to John Corcoran, president, Consolidation Coal. Letter dated December 11, 1970. From the legal files of James Matish.
23. "Agreement Between Consolidation Coal Company and Bereaved Families of the Victims of the No.9 Farmington Mine Disaster of November 20, 1968."
24. Ken Hechler to Walter J. Hickel. Letter dated November 17, 1970. From the legal files of James Matish.
25. Ben A. Franklin. "Safety Officials Assail Accord By Coal Company and Widows." *The New York Times.* November 19, 1970.

26. "Agreement Between Consolidation Coal Company and Bereaved Families of the Victims of the No.9 Farmington Mine Disaster of November 20, 1968. With two amendments." Signed by Consolidation Coal Vice President D. H. Davis. November 12, 1970.

27. Rev. Everett F. Briggs to Governor Arch Moore. Letter dated December 11, 1970.

28. Hollis M. Dole to Father Briggs. Letter dated January 11, 1971.

29. Lewis E. Evans to Father Briggs. Letter dated December 21, 1970.

30. Rev. Everett F. Briggs to Lewis E. Evans. Letter dated January 8, 1971.

31. John Corcoran to Father Everett Briggs. Letter dated December 21, 1970.

Chapters 16: Three More Men

1. Arch A. Moore Jr. to Sara L. Kaznoski. Letter dated July 21,1970. From legal files of Brent Beveridge, Beveridge Law Offices. Fairmont, West Virginia.

2. Ibid.

3. U.S. *Informational Report of Investigation, Underground Coal Mine Explosion and Fire, Consol No.9 Mine, Mountaineer Coal Company, Division of Consolidation Coal Company, Farmington, West Virginia, November 20, 1968*, submitted by William J. Tattersall, assistant secretary for Mine Safety and Health. March 1990. 27.

4. Ibid.

5. "Handwritten Notes." Copied from the U.S. Bureau of Mine's Daily Recovery Logs for the No.9 Mine. 1969–1978.

6. Ibid.

7. "Minutes of Four Agency Meeting for No.9 Recovery." September 1, 1970.

8. Ibid.

9. Ibid.

10. Ibid.

11. U.S. Department of the Interior. Bureau of Mines. "Ventilation Survey, Consol No.9 Mine." September 14–18, 1970.

12. D. H. Davis. "No.9 Ventilation." Typed notes by D. H. Davis from October 20, 1970.

13. "Opening of 6North, Mine 9, Mountaineer Coal Company." December 1, 1970. Initialed HEM (H. Eugene Mauck) with note by DHD (David H. Davis).

14. Ibid.

15. Ibid.

16. Ibid.

17. Ibid.

18. Matthew D. Sztajnkrycer, MD, Ph.D." Medical Aspects of Blast Injuries." Mayo Clinic. 2008, *www.pitt.edu/~super7/17011-18001/17971.ppt*, and Capt. Dana C. Covey. U.S. Navy. "Blast and Fragment Injuries of the Musculoskeletal System." The Journal of Bone and Joint Surgery. 84:1221-1234. (2002)

19. Anna Belle Currence v. Consolidation Coal Company, Civil Action No. 78-0044-C(H). U.S. District Court for the Northern District of West Virginia. Deposition of H. Eugene Mauck. June 10, 1980.

20. Ibid.

21. "Opening of 6North, Mine 9, Mountaineer Coal Company." December 1, 1970. Initialed HEM (H. Eugene Mauck) with note by DHD (David H. Davis).

22. "Bodies Found in Death Mine." *The Pittsburgh Press*. December 2, 1970.

23. U.S. *Informational Report of Investigation*. 1990.

Chapter 17: Hidden Evidence

1. Sarah L. Kaznoski, Administratrix of the Estate of Pete Kaznoski, Sr., Deceased, et al. V. Consolidation Coal Company et al. Civil A. Case No. 70-1322. U.S. District Court for the Western District of Pennsylvania.

2. Ibid.

3. "Continental Oil 70 Net is Expected to Exceed the $146.4 million of 1969." *The Wall Street Journal*. February 3, 1970.

4. Larry L. Layne. Interviews with author. Jasper, Alabama. January 17–18, 2009.

5. Larry L. Layne to James D Micheal. Memo. September 15, 1970.

6. James D. Micheal to W.R. Park. Memo. U.S. Department of the Interior, Bureau of Mines. September 30, 1970.

7. Ibid.

8. Larry L. Layne. Interviews with author. Jasper, Alabama. January 17–18, 2009.

9. Ibid.

10. Ibid.

11. Ibid.

12. Ibid.

13. Ibid.

14. Ibid.

15. Ibid.

16. Ibid.

17. Ibid.

18. Ibid.

19. Ibid.

20. W.Va. *Official Hearing, Coal Mine Explosion, Consol No.9 Mine, Mountaineer Coal Company, Division of Consolidation Coal Company, Farmington, Marion County, West Virginia, November 20, 1968. December 5–7, 1968.* Alex Kovar, 44–51 and Appendix A.

21. Ibid. Appendix A.

22. Ibid. Appendix A.

23. Ibid. Appendix A.

24. W.Va. *Official Hearings.* Cecil Selders. 183–197.

25. Ibid.

26. Ibid. Appendix A.

27. W.Va. *Official Hearings.* Cecil Selders. 183–197.

28. Ibid.

29. Anna Belle Currence v. Consolidation Coal Company, Civil Action No. 78-0044-C(H). U.S. District Court for the Northern District of West Virginia. Deposition of H. Eugene Mauck. June 10, 1980.

30. Ibid.

31. Ibid.

32. Ibid.

33. David J. Kessler to Bonnie E. Stewart. *Re: Freedom of Information Act (FOIA)requests (1–5) dated March 17, 2009 (Consolidation Coal Farmington No.9 Mine Disaster.* Letter. March 31, 2009.

34. "Bristol's Recording Pressure Gauge Chart; #1, 11-13-68." Oak Hill Regional Office of the W.Va. Office of Miners' Health Safety and Training. Box D33. Oak Hill, West Virginia.

35. W.Va. *Official Hearing, Coal Mine Explosion, Consol No.9 Mine, Mountaineer Coal Company, Division of Consolidation Coal Company, Farmington, Marion County, West Virginia, November 20, 1968. December 5–7, 1968.* Alex Kovar, 44–51 and Appendix A.

36. "Bristol's Recording Pressure Gauge Chart; #1, 11-20-68." Oak Hill Regional Office of the W.Va. Office of Miners' Health Safety & Training. Box D33. Oak Hill, West Virginia.

37. "Bristol's Recording Pressure Gauge Chart; #2, 11-13-68." Oak Hill Regional Office of the W.Va. Office of Miners' Health Safety and Training. Box D33. Oak Hill, West Virginia.

38. Joseph Marshalek. *Notes. No.9 Explosion.* Handwritten notes on file at the Technical Information Center and Library, National Mine Health and Safety Academy, Beaver, West Virginia.

39. "Bristol's Recording Pressure Gauge Chart; #3, 11-18-68." Oak Hill Regional Office of the W.Va. Office of Miners' Health Safety & Training. Box D33. Oak Hill, West Virginia.

40. W.Va. *Official Hearing, Coal Mine Explosion, Consol No.9 Mine, Mountaineer Coal Company, Division of Consolidation Coal Company, Farmington, Marion County, West Virginia, November 20, 1968. December 5–7, 1968.* Alex Kovar, 44–51 and Appendix A.

41. "Bristol's Recording Pressure Gauge Chart; #3, 11-18-68."

42. Ibid.

43. "List of Slides, Nos.1–56."

44. Ibid.

45. Frances to Mr. Park. Memo. Dated 11/24/70.

46. Ibid.

47. Ibid.

48. Ibid.

49. Joseph Megna. Interview with author. Worthington, West Virginia. May 21, 2008.

50. "Farmington27fanchart.jpg." Provided by Technical Information Center and Library, National Mine Health and Safety Academy, Beaver, West Virginia.

Chapter 18: Ungodly Work

1. Kaznoski, November 15, 2009.

2. "Federal Recovery Logs from No.9 Disaster." January 7, 1971.

3. Ibid.

4. "Federal Recovery Logs from No.9 Disaster." January 8, 1971.

5. "Federal Recovery Logs from No.9 Disaster." January 11, 1971.

6. Ibid.

7. "Federal Recovery Logs from No.9 Disaster." January 12, 1971.

8. D. H. Davis. "Notes of D. H. Davis. Meeting on No.9, January 30, 1971. Produced during discovery.

9. D. H. Davis. "Notes of D.H. Davis. Meeting on No.9. February 1971."

10. D. H. Davis. "No.9 Recovery. Meeting of Four Agencies. February 12, 1971." Consol internal memo.

11. Rev. Everett F. Briggs. Press release. February 12, 1971.

12. Sara Lee Kaznoski. "Meeting Minutes and Notes from Widows' Committee."

13. Sara Lee Kaznoski. "May 19, 1971 Entry in Personal Notebook."

14. Ben A. Franklin. "Mine Chief Ousts Disaster Expert." *The New York Times*. April 1, 1971.

15. Ibid.

16. Ben A. Franklin. "A Second Bureau of Mines Official Ousted; Coal Safety Record Cited." September 2, 1971.

17. Ibid.

18. U.S. Government Accounting Office. "Report to the Subcommittee on Labor and Public Welfare. U.S. Senate: Problems in Implementation of the Federal Coal Miner Health and Safety Act of 1969." May 31, 1971.

19. Ibid.

20. U.S. Government Accounting Office. "Report to the Subcommittee on Labor and Public Welfare. U.S. Senate: Problems in Implementation of the Federal Coal Miner Health and Safety Act of 1969." May 31, 1971. 50.

21. U.S. Government Accounting Office. "Report to the Subcommittee on Labor and Public Welfare. U.S. Senate: Problems in Implementation of the Federal Coal Miner Health and Safety Act of 1969." May 31, 1971. 68–70.

22. Sara Lee Kaznoski. "April 3, 1971 entry in Personal Notebook."

23. Ibid.

24. Sara Lee Kaznoski. "Entry in Personal Notebook." May 1, 1971.

25. Ben A. Franklin. "Re-check Was Overdue." *The New York Times*. January 1, 1971.

26. U.S. Department of Labor. Mine Safety and Health Administration. National Mine Health and Safety Academy. *Historical Summary of Mine Disasters in the United States. Vol. 2, Coal Mines, 1959–1998. Nos. 15 and 16 Mines, Finley Coal Company, Hyden, Kentucky. December 30, 1970.* Reprinted 2001. 57–59.

27. Ibid.

28. Ibid.

29. U.S. Department of Labor. Mine Safety and Health Administration. "Mining Statistics for 1900 through 2009." *http://www.msha.gov/stats/centurystats/coalstats.asp#*

30. "Coal Company Fined." *The New York Times*. July 9, 1975.

31. "Kentucky Disaster Lawsuit Not Revived." *The Associated Press*. November 3, 1980.

32. U.S. *Informational Report of Investigation*. 1990. 37–38.

33. Ibid.

34. Niles Lee Jackson. "Baby Due, Wife Keeps Vigil at Mine Head." *The Associated Press.* November 23, 1968.

35. Ibid.

36. "Consol No.9: A Decent Burial." *Time.* December 14, 1970.

37. Mainella, June 17, 2008.

38. Ibid.

39. U.S. *Informational Report of Investigation.* 1990. 39.

40. U.S. Department of the Interior, Bureau of Mines. "Report of Fatal Coal-Mine Haulage Accident. Consol No.9 Mine," by Michael J. Lawless. November 16, 1971.

Chapter 19: Inundated by Death

1. James Herron. Interview with author. Mannington, West Virginia. October 3, 2008.

2. "Federal Recovery Logs from No.9 Disaster." May 11, 1972.

3. Ibid.

4. Ibid.

5. U.S. *Historical Summary of Mine Disasters in the United States. Vol. 2, Coal Mines, 1959–1998.* 72–77.

6. Ibid.

7. Ibid.

8. Ibid.

9. "Law Held Violated in Fatal Mine Fire." *The New York Times.* July 30, 1972.

10. U.S. *Historical Summary of Mine Disasters in the United States. Vol. 2, Coal Mines, 1959–1998.* 72–77.

11. "Federal Recovery Logs from No.9 Disaster." September 12, 1972.

12. Ibid.

13. James D. Micheal to James Westfield. Memo and attachment. "Locations of Men in the Mine at the Time of the Explosion." August 29, 1970. U.S. Mine Health and Safety Administration.

14. "Federal Recovery Logs from No.9 Disaster." September 12, 1972.

15. Ibid.

16. Stanley Plachta. Interview with author. Farmington, West Virginia. December 6, 2008.

17. Ibid.

18. Ibid.

19. Frank Manejewicz and Tom Braden. "Death of a Coal Miner." *St. Paul Pioneer Press.* December 11, 1968.

20. "Federal Recovery Logs from No.9 Disaster." September 12, 1972. Technical Information Center and Library, National Mine Health and Safety Academy, Beaver, West Virginia.

21. Ibid.

22. John Toothman. Interview with author. September 10, 2007. Fairmont, West Virginia.

23. Ibid.

24. Ibid.

25. Ibid.

26. Ibid.

27. Ibid.

28. Ibid.

29. Ibid.

Chapter 20: Who Can Stop Us?

1. K. K. Kincell to W. N. Poundstone. "Ventilation of the East End of #9 Mine. Changes Possible to comply with Federal Health and Safety Act to operate." Inter Office Communication, "Personal and Confidential." December 14, 1972.

2. "Miller UMW Victory Certified." *The Wall Street Journal.* December 21, 1972.

3. "UMW Officers Take Salary Cuts Fulfilling Pledge From Campaign." *The Wall Street Journal.* January 5, 1973.

4. Ken Ward Jr. "Arnold Miller Helped Reform the UMW." *The Charleston Gazette.* January 24, 1999.

5. "Miller Debates Coal Executive." *The New York Times.* December 18, 1972.

6. Ibid.

7. Ibid.

8. Ibid.

9. Ibid.

10. U.S. *Historical Summary of Mine Disasters in the United States. Vol. II, Coal Mines, 1959–1998.* Itmann No. 3 Mine. Reprinted 2001. 77–79.

11. Ken Hechler, U.S. Representative, to Elmer B. Staats, U.S. comptroller general. Letter. June 26, 1972.

12. U.S. Comptroller General. "Follow-up on Implementation of the Federal Coal Mine Health and Safety Act of 1969; Bureau of Mines." July 5, 1973.

13. Ibid. 15.

14. "Mine-Safety Penalty System Is Upset." *The New York Times*. March 11, 1973.

15. Ibid.

16. Federal Daily Recovery Logs for the No.9 Mine. 1969-1978. Mine Safety and Health Administration Technical Information Center and Library, Beaver, West Virginia.

17. Anna Belle Currence v. Consolidation Coal Company, Civil Action No. 78-C-538 Circuit Court of Marion County, West Virginia (1978). Deposition of Eugene Mauck. 1-90.

18. Ibid.

19. Federal Daily Recovery Logs for the No.9 Mine. 1969–1978.

20. Federal Daily Recovery Logs for the No.9 Mine. 1969–1978. September 10–25, 1973.

21. Ibid. February 13, 1974.

22. Ibid. February 14, 1974.

23. "Offer of Consolidation Coal Company to the Bereaved Families of the Victims of the No.9 Farmington Mine Disaster of November 20, 1968. DRAFT June 1973."

24. Ibid.

25. Thomas J. Whyte. "Offer of Consolidation Coal Company to the Bereaved Families of the Victims of the No.9 Farmington Mine Disaster of November 20, 1968." January 8, 1974.

26. Sarah L. Kaznoski, Administratrix of the Estate of Pete Kaznoski, Sr., Deceased, et al. V. Consolidation Coal Company et al. Civil A. Case No. 70-1322. U.S. District Court for the Western District of Pennsylvania. Decision, January 9, 1974.

27. Federal Daily Recovery Logs for the No.9 Mine. 1969–1978.

28. Ibid.

29. Pete Sehewchuk. Interview with author. Fairmont, West Virginia. July 21, 2008.

30. Ibid.

31. Plachta, July 11, 2008.

32. Ibid.

33. Sehewchuk, July 21, 2008.

34. Ibid.

35. Sehewchuk, July 21, 2008.

36. Federal Daily Recovery Logs for the No.9 Mine. 1969–1978. Mine Safety and Health Administration Technical Information Center and Library, Beaver, West Virginia. March 13, 1974.

37. Ibid.

38. W.Va. *Official Hearing, Coal Mine Explosion, Consol No.9 Mine, Mountaineer Coal Company, Division of Consolidation Coal Company, Farmington, Marion County, West Virginia, November 20, 1968. December 5–7, 1968.* Lewis Lake, 134–146.

39. Federal Daily Recovery Logs for the No.9 Mine. 1969–1978. Mine Safety and Health Administration Technical Information Center and Library, Beaver, West Virginia. March 13, 1974.

40. Anna Belle Currence v. Consolidation Coal Company, Civil Action No. 78-0044-C(H). U.S. District Court for the Northern District of West Virginia. Deposition of John L. Rozance, February 9, 1982.

41. Ibid.

42. Herron, October 3, 2008.

43. U.S. *Informational Report of Investigation.* 1990. Appendix A. 1.

44. Herron, October 3, 2008.

45. Kenneth J. Yablonski to Sarah L. Kaznoski. Letter. August 15, 1973. From legal files of Brent Beveridge. Fairmont, West Virginia.

46. Ibid.

47. Sara L. Kaznoski. Handwritten notes from April 4, 1975. From the legal files of Brent Beveridge. Fairmont, West Virginia.

Chapter 21: Business is Business

1. U.S. Department of the Interior. Mining Enforcement and Safety Administration. "Coal Mine Spot Safety Report. Consol No.9 Mine." February 3, 1975.

2. W. J. Halvorsen to R. E. Garbesi. *Inter Office Communication. Consolidation Coal Company.* March 3, 1976.

3. W. J. Halvorsen to R. E. Garbesi. *Inter Office Communication. Consolidation Coal Company.* March 9, 1976.

4. U.S. *Historical Summary of Mine Disasters in the United States. Vol. 2, Coal Mines, 1959–1998.* 88–91.

5. Mauck, Eugene. "Minutes of the Meeting of Four Agencies, March 26, 1976."

6. Ibid.

7. Ibid.

8. Ibid.

9. Ibid.

10. Raymond L. Ash to Jack E. Tisdale (U.S. Mine Enforcement and Safety Administration). "Memorandum." November 16, 1976.

11. "Public Relations Plan—Closing of No.9 Mine. Confidential." December 6, 1976. 78-C-538 Circuit Court of Marion County, West Virginia (1978).

12. Ibid.

13. Ibid.

14. Ralph Hatch to Steve Young. Memo. "Procedures to be Followed in Announcing Discontinuation of Recovery Work at Farmington #9." December 8, 1976. Produced during discovery. Anna Belle Currence v. Consolidation Coal Company, Civil Action No. 78-C-538 Circuit Court of Marion County, West Virginia (1978).

15. Eugene Mauck (Consol). "Minutes, January 5, 1977 meeting."

16. C. W. Parisi to R. E. Samples. Inter Office Communication. "Sealing or Ventilating Old Works at #9 Mine." March 25, 1977.

17. R. E. Samples(Consol) to Mr. Ed Gilbert (UMW). Letter dated May 3, 1978.

18. U.S. Department of the Interior. Mining Enforcement and Safety Administration. Memorandum. "Recovery Operations—Consol No.9 Mine." By James D. Micheal. November 3, 1977.

19. National Institute for Occupational Safety and Health. Center for Disease Control. "Recovery of Farmington No.9: An Interview with Danny Kuhn." March 2002.

20. "SGY (Stephen G. Young) Notes." Handwritten notes from 1978.

21. James Herron. Interview with author. Mannington, West Virginia. October 3, 2008.

22. Ibid.

23. H. A. Cochran to R. E. Samples and B. R. Brown. Inter-Office Communication. "Closing of the No.9." April 14, 1978.

24. Ibid.

25. Haze Cochran to B. R. Brown. "Complete Set of Everything to be Used by No.9 Notification Group on Wednesday." April 17, 1978.

26. R. E. Samples to Ed Gilbert (UMW). Letter. May 3, 1978.

27. Associate solicitor to assistant secretary, Mine Safety & Health, U.S. Department of Labor. Memorandum. "Farmington Disaster Investigation." M.R. Tidwell. June 6, 1978.

28. "Union Fight Plan to Seal No.9 Mine." *The Clarksburg Exponent.* April 22, 1978.

Chapter 22: Widows' Last Stand

1. James Matish. Interview with author. Clarksburg, West Virginia. July 5, 2007.

2. Ibid.

3. Anna Belle Currence v. Consolidation Coal Company, Civil Action No. 78-C-538. Circuit Court of Marion County, West Virginia (1978). Case removed to federal court. Anna Belle Currence v. Consolidation Coal Company, Civil Action No. 78-0044-C(H). U.S. District Court for the Northern District of West Virginia.

4. Ibid.

5. Anna Belle Currence v. Consolidation Coal Company, Civil Action No. 78-0044-C(H). U.S. District Court for the Northern District of West Virginia. Deposition of William N. Poundstone.

6. Henderson, R. M. "Status of Mine Atmosphere." August 8, 1969.

7. U.S. Department of the Interior. Mine Enforcement and Safety Administration. "Report on Barrier Pillar Between Abandoned No.44 Mine, Bethlehem Mines Corporation, and the No.9 Mine, Consolidation Coal Company," by Paul J. Componation. October 23, 1974.

8. H. E. Mauck to Jack E. Tisdale (Federal MESA). Letter. November 26, 1974.

9. Anna Belle Currence v. Consolidation Coal Company, Civil Action No. 78-0044-C(H). U.S. District Court for the Northern District of West Virginia. Deposition of H. Eugene Mauck. June 10, 1980.

10. "Mine No.9 Explosion Recovery Operations for Period November 20, 1968 thru February 28, 1978, Operating Losses and Capital Budget Expenditures."

11. Anna Belle Currence v. Consolidation Coal Company, Civil Action No. 78-0044-C(H). U.S. District Court for the Northern District of West Virginia. "Plaintiff's Fourth Set of Interrogatories to Defendant Consolidation Coal," and "Defendant's Answers to the Fourth Set of Interrogatories."

12. Anna Belle Currence v. Consolidation Coal Company, Civil Action No. 78-0044-C(H). U.S. District Court for the Northern District of West Virginia. Deposition of H. Eugene Mauck. June 10, 1980.

13. Anna Belle Currence v. Consolidation Coal Company, Civil Action No. 78-0044-C(H). U.S. District Court for the Northern District of West Virginia. "Plaintiff's Fourth Set of Interrogatories to Defendant Consolidation Coal," and "Defendant's Answers to the Fourth Set of Interrogatories."

14. Ibid.

15. Anna Belle Currence v. Consolidation Coal Company, Civil Action No. 78-0044-C(H). U.S. District Court for the Northern District of West Virginia. "Motion to Confirm Settlement Agreement for Dismissal."

16. Matish, 2008.

17. Anna Belle Currence v. Consolidation Coal Company, Civil Action No. 78-0044-C(H). U.S. District Court for the Northern District of West Virginia. Deposition of H. Eugene Mauck. June 10, 1980.

18. Gerald M. Stern. "The Buffalo Creek Disaster." Vintage Books. 1976.

19. U.S. *Historical Summary of Mine Disasters in the United States. Vol. II, Coal Mines, 1959–1998.* Reprinted 2001. 65–72.

20. U.S. *Historical Summary of Mine Disasters in the United States. Vol. II, Coal Mines, 1959–1998.* 88–91.

21. Gerald M. Stern. "The Scotia Widows." Random House. 2008.

22. "Settlement in Coal Mine Deaths." *The Washington Post.* February 19, 1983.

23. U.S. Department of Labor. Mine Safety and Health Administration. Press Release. "Virginia Mine Operator Gets Six Months for Violating Law." September 14, 1995.

24. Ted Birdis. "Three Coal Executives Sentenced in Deadly 1989 Explosion." *The Associated Press.* June 12, 1996.

25. Ken Ward Jr. "Two more Sago lawsuits settled." *The Charleston Gazette.* January 27, 2009.

26. Ken Ward Jr. "Aracoma assessed record fine." *The Charleston Gazette.* December 24, 2009.

27. U.S. Department of Labor. Mine Safety and Health Administration. "Crandall Canyon Accident Investigation Summary and Conclusions." http://www.msha.gov/Genwal/ccSummary.asp

28. John Toothman. Telephone interview with author. August 30, 2007.

29. Herron, July 2009.

Glossary

....

Abandoned Workings: Areas where the coal has been removed and no more mining will be done.

Airway: A tunnel or passage through which air passes.

Arc: As applied to electricity, the luminous bridge formed by the passage of a current across a gap between two conductors or terminals.

Barometric pressure: The force exerted on objects by the weight of the atmosphere.

Belt or belt conveyor: A looped belt on which coal is carried away from the working section to a loading or unloading area.

Bituminous coal: Dense, black coal that usually has a high heat value.

Black damp: A deadly mix of carbon dioxide and nitrogen in an atmosphere without oxygen.

Bleeders or bleeder entries: Airways that continuously move air-methane mixtures from the gobs and/or the working face away from the active sections. The bad air is funneled into the return airways and taken out of the mine.

Bottom: The floor of the mine.

Brattice: Wooden or cloth barrier used to control ventilation in an underground mine.

Brattice cloth: Heavy cloth used in mine tunnels to confine fresh air and direct it into working sections and to the working face. Also called "line curtain."

Buggy or shuttle car: A vehicle used to carry coal from the working face to a coal conveyor belt or to coal cars on the haulageways.

Cage: An elevator car that carries workers and supplies in and out of a mine shaft.

Cap: A miner's hat.

Cap block: A piece of wood inserted between a roof support post and the roof to provide bearing support.

Cap lamps: A battery operated light that attaches to a coal miner's hat. The battery pack is worn on the miner's belt. In the early years of mining, the lights were open flames.

Cateye shift: The third shift that begins at midnight and ends at 8 a.m.

Coalbed: A bed or stratum of coal; also called a coal seam.

Coal dust: Particles of coal that can pass through a No. 20 sieve, which has openings that are 0.0331 inches.

Continuous miner: A machine that grinds coal from the working face and loads it onto another machine, eliminating the use of explosives.

Crosscut: A tunnel driven between an entry and its parallel airway for ventilation purposes. Also a tunnel driven from one seam to another, which is sometimes called a "breakthrough."

Curtains: Another name for brattice cloth.

Cutting machine: A power-driven machine used to undercut the wall of coal at the working face. Once the cut is made, a miner drills holes in the face, inserts explosives and sets off an explosion, which shatters the coal.

Dinner bucket: A lunch box, usually metal, that contains food and the miner's supply of water.

Dinner hole: A small area carved out of the mine wall where the miners may eat their food or take a break.

Explosion doors: Doors on the air shafts that open to release pressure when a coal mine explodes. This helps protect the large fans that are placed near the shafts to send air into the mine.

Explosive magazine: Storage area for explosives.

Face or Working face: The immediate area from which coal is being mined.

Fireboss: A person trained to examine the mine or sections of the mine for methane gas and other dangers.

Firebossing: Checking the mine or areas of the mine for dangerous conditions, including methane gas.

Float dust: Fine coal dust particles produced by mining machinery at the working face and other places. Often found along coal conveyor belts and along haulage roads. It can be easily carried long distances throughout the mine by the ventilating air and is usually controlled by rock dusting.

Gob: The part of the mine from which coal has been removed. In room-and-pillar mining, slate and un-mined coal may collect in the gobs. Gobs can become dangerous because they often harbor methane gas.

Jeep: An underground vehicle that carries miners along a railway through the tunnels of a coal mine. The jeeps operate like trolley cars, energized by rods attached to an electrically charged line that runs along the roof of the mine.

Lamphouse: A building near the entrance of a mine used to house the lights, called lamps, miners wear on their caps. Their metal identification check-in tags also are kept there.

Locomotive: A large vehicle used to pull and/or push coal cars through the mine. Also called a "motor."

Man shaft: A shaft that contains a cage to carry miners from the surface to the floor of the mine.

Man trip: A vehicle to carry men to and from the sections. It could have rubber tires or be a rail car.

Methane gas: A gas encountered when mining coal, which becomes explosive when it reaches concentrations of 5 percent to 15 percent in the air.

Motor: Another name for a locomotive.

Permissible: Explosives and/or equipment approved by the government.

Personnel carrier: An underground vehicle that transports coal miners.

Pillar: An area of coal left to support the roof of the mine.

Red dog: An ash-like byproduct of burning coal.

Return air: Air that has passed through and ventilated the working places in the mine.

Return airways: Tunnels that carry away the air that has passed through the working faces.

Rib: The walls of the mine's tunnels.

Rock dust: Pulverized inert material, usually limestone, used to neutralize coal dust.

Roof: The ceiling in an underground mine. Also called the "top."

Roof bolt: A long, steel rod driven into the roof to stabilize the layers of coal and slate above the tunnels and prevent the roof from collapsing. A steel plate anchors the rod.

Roof fall: A cave-in of the top of a tunnel.

Room-and-pillar coal mining: Mining machines cut tunnels, or entries, into the coal bed and connect them with crosscuts, leaving pillars of coal to support the mine roof and help control the flow of air. This creates rooms of coal that are mined out. Once all the rooms are empty, the miners knock down the pillars and abandon that section.

Self-rescuer: A small breathing device that fits into the mouth and filters out carbon monoxide and smoke. It contains fused calcium chloride that absorbs water vapor from the air. Maximum use time is 30 minutes to an hour.

Shelter holes: Small areas carved out of the tunnels where miners can protect themselves from rail traffic and other vehicles.

Shot-firer: Someone trained to use explosives underground.

Shuttle car or Jeep: A vehicle used to carry coal from the working face to a conveyor belt or a rail car.

Slope: A graded tunnel that gradually leads underground.

Splice: A connection made where a cable has broken or been damaged. Splices can be temporary or permanent, depending upon how they are made.

Stoppings: Physical barriers erected between entries to separate intake and return airways to prevent fresh air from mixing with tainted air. Temporary stoppings may be constructed of metal, jute fabric or plastic. Permanent stoppings usually are constructed with concrete blocks and must be airtight.

Stumps: A small pillar of coal.

Tipple: A facility used to load coal into rail cars or trucks.

Top: Another name for the mine's roof.

Ton or short ton: A unit of weight that equals 2,000 pounds.

Trailing cable: A flexible, portable electric cable connecting mine equipment to a power source.

Trolley wires: Uninsulated copper wire that carries direct current (D.C.) power to track equipment.

Working face: The immediate area where miners are extracting coal from the mountain.

Glossary Sources

1. Kentucky Coal Education, Glossary of Mining Terms. *http://www.coaleducation.org/glossary.htm#R*

2. National Institute for Occupational Safety and Health Bulletins. *http://www.cdc.gov/niosh/*

3. Thrush, Paul W. "A Dictionary of Mining, Mineral and Related Terms." Department of the Interior. U.S. Bureau of Mines. 1968. *http://www.msha.gov/century/rescue/rstart.asp*

4. Pennsylvania Department of Environmental Protection. Glossary: Mining Terms. *http://www.portal.state.pa.us/portal/server.pt/community/training/14001/glossary__mining_terms/589150*

5. U.S. Mine Safety and Health Administration*http://www.msha.gov*

6. W.Va. Office of Miners' Health Safety and Training. *http://www.wvminesafety.org/*

7. U.S. Energy Information Administration. *http://www.eia.doe.gov/*

Bibliography

"Agreement Between Consolidation Coal Company and Bereaved Families of the Victims of the No.9 Farmington Mine Disaster of November 20, 1968." Produced during discovery. Anna Belle Currence v. Consolidation Coal Company, Civil Action No. 78-C-538. Circuit Court of Marion County, West Virginia (1978).

"Agreement Between Consolidation Coal Company and Bereaved Families of the Victims of the No.9 Farmington Mine Disaster of November 20, 1968.With two amendments." Signed by Consolidation Coal Vice President D. H. Davis. November 12, 1970.

Anna Belle Currence. Consolidation Coal Company, Civil Action No. 78-0044-C(H). U.S. District Court for the Northern District of West Virginia. Deposition of H. Eugene Mauck. June 10, 1980.

———, Civil Action No. 78-0044-C(H). U.S. District Court for the Northern District of West Virginia. Deposition of H. Eugene Mauck. June 10, 1980. Deposition of John L. Rozance, February 9, 1982.

———, Civil Action No. 78-0044-C(H). U.S. District Court for the Northern District of West Virginia. "Motion to Confirm Settlement Agreement for Dismissal."

———, Civil Action No. 78-0044-C(H). U.S. District Court for the Northern District of West Virginia. "Plaintiff's Fourth Set of Interrogatories to Defendant Consolidation Coal," and "Defendant's Answers to the Fourth Set of Interrogatories."

———, Civil Action No. 78-C-538. Circuit Court of Marion County, West Virginia (1978). Case removed to federal court. Anna Belle Currence v. Consolidation Coal Company, Civil Action No. 78-0044-C(H). U.S. District Court for the Northern District of West Virginia.

Ash, Raymond L. to Jack E. Tisdale (U.S. Mine Enforcement and Safety Administration). "Memorandum." November 16, 1976.

Associate Solicitor to Assistant Secretary, Mine Safety & Health, U.S. Department of Labor. Memorandum. "Farmington Disaster Investigation." M. R. Tidwell. June 6, 1978.

Baldwin, W. D. U.S. Department of the Interior. Bureau of Mines. *Coal Mine Inspection Report. No.9 Mine.* January 13-25, 1954.

———. U.S. Department of the Interior. Bureau of Mines. *Coal Mine Inspection Report. No.9 Mine.* May 20, 21, 24-28 and June 1-2, 1954.

———. U.S. Department of the Interior. Bureau of Mines. *Coal Mine Inspection Report. No.9 Mine.* October 6-20, 1954.

Birdis, Ted. "Three Coal Executives Sentenced in Deadly 1989 Explosion." *The Associated Press.* June 12, 1996.

"Black With Soot, Park Says of Mine." *The Fairmont Times.* September 16, 1969.

"Bodies Found in Death Mine." *The Pittsburgh Press.* December 2, 1970.

Boone, Tom. Interview with author. Farmington, West Virginia. July 21, 2008.

"Boyle Has Praise for Consol Safety." *The Fairmont Times.* November 22, 1968.

"Briefing Outline. (Three versions.) Consol No.9 Mine. Purpose: To obtain approval for release of the Informational Report of Investigation." On file at the Mine Safety and Health Administration Technical Information Center and Library, Beaver, West Virginia.

Briggs, Everett F. "Press Release" February 12, 1971. From legal files of James Matish.

Briggs, Everett F. to Arch Moore. Letter dated December 11, 1970. From the legal files of James Matish.

Briggs, Everett F. to John Corcoran, Consolidation Coal. Letter dated December 11, 1970. From the legal files of James Matish.

Briggs, Everett F. to Lewis E. Evans. Letter dated January 8, 1971. From the legal files of James Matish.

"Bristol's Recording Pressure Gauge Chart; #1, 11-13-68." Oak Hill Regional Office of the W.Va. Office of Miners' Health Safety & Training. Box D33. Oak Hill, West Virginia.

———; #1, 11-20-68." Oak Hill Regional Office of the W.Va. Office of Miners' Health Safety & Training. Box D33. Oak Hill, West Virginia.

———; #2, 11-13-68." Oak Hill Regional Office of the W.Va. Office of Miners' Health Safety & Training. Box D33. Oak Hill, West Virginia.

———; #3, 11-18-68." Oak Hill Regional Office of the W.Va. Office of Miners' Health Safety & Training. Box D33. Oak Hill, West Virginia.

Brnich, Michael J. Jr. and Charles Vaught. National Institute for Occupational Safety and Health. *Escape from Farmington No.9. An Oral History. An Interview with Gary Martin and Waitman "Bud" Hillberry* Department of Health and Human Services Publication No. 2009-142D. May 2009.

Brock, John. Interview with author. Mannington, West Virginia. May 28, 2007.

Bunner, Bill. Interview with author. Fairmont, West Virginia. March 3, 2009.

Carroll, Logan. "Mine Sealed Off as Inquiry Starts." *The West Virginian.* November 16, 1954. A-1.

———. "More Blasts Jarring Mine." *The West Virginian.* November 15, 1954. A-1.

Carter, Jimmy. The American Presidency Project. Black Lung Benefits Reform Act of 1977. Remarks on Signing H.R. 4544 into Law. March 1, 1978. *http://www.presidency.ucsb. edu/ws/index.php?pid=30433&st=black&st1=lung*

Chase, Frank, Christopher Mark and Keith A. Heasley. National Institute for Occupational Safety and Health. *Deep Cover Pillar Extraction in the U.S. Coalfields.* 2002. *http://www. cdc.gov/niosh/mining/pubs/pubreference/outputid162.htm*

"Coal Company Fined." *The New York Times.* July 9, 1975.

Cochran, Haze to B. R. Brown. "Complete Set of Everything to be Used by No.9 Notification Group on Wednesday." April 17, 1978. Produced during discovery. Anna Belle Currence v. Consolidation Coal Company, Civil Action No. 78-C-538. Circuit Court of Marion County, West Virginia (1978).

Componation, Paul J. U.S. Department of the Interior. Mine Enforcement and Safety Administration. "Report on Barrier Pillar Between Abandoned No.44 Mine, Bethlehem Mines Corporation, and the No.9 Mine, Consolidation Coal Company." October 23, 1974.

"Continental Oil '70 Net Is Expected to Exceed the $146.4 Million of 1969." *The Wall Street Journal.* February 3, 1970.

Cooper, Richard T. "Fund Dispute Compounds Widows' Grief." *The Los Angeles Times.* April 21, 1969.

Corcoran, John to Father Everett Briggs. Letter dated December 21, 1970. From the legal files of James Matish.

Covey, Dana C. "Blast and Fragment Injuries of the Musculoskeletal System." *The Journal of Bone and Joint Surgery.* 84 (2002):1221-1234.

Crago, George A. "21 Men Saved; Mine Is Inferno." *The Dominion-News.* November 21, 1968.

Davis, D. H. "Large Diameter Boreholes for Opening No.9. Feasibility, Cost, Driller, Etc." May 15, 1969. Produced during discovery. Anna Belle Currence vs. Consolidation Coal Company, Civil Action No. 78-C-538. Circuit Court of Marion County, West Virginia (1978).

———. "Meeting No.9, January 30, 1971. Produced during discovery. Anna Belle Currence vs. Consolidation Coal Company, Civil Action No. 78-C-538 Circuit Court of Marion County, West Virginia (1978).

———. "No.9 Recovery. Meeting of Four Agencies. February 12, 1971." Consol internal memo. Produced during discovery. Anna Belle Currence vs. Consolidation Coal Company, Civil Action No. 78-C-538 Circuit Court of Marion County, West Virginia (1978).

———. "No.9 Ventilation." Typed notes by D. H. Davis from October 20, 1970. Produced during discovery. Anna Belle Currence v. Consolidation Coal Company, Civil Action No. 78-C-538. Circuit Court of Marion County, West Virginia (1978).

———. "Notes of D. H. Davis. Meeting on No.9. February 1971." Produced during discovery. Anna Belle Currence v. Consolidation Coal Company, Civil Action No. 78-C-538. Circuit Court of Marion County, West Virginia (1978).

——— to K. K. Kincell, H. E. Mauck, L. H. Riggs, J. G. Bowers, R. M. Henderson and Norris Brooks. "Personal & Confidential Memo." March 25, 1969. Produced during discovery. Anna Belle Currence v. Consolidation Coal Company, Civil Action No. 78-C-538. Circuit Court of Marion County, West Virginia (1978).

Derickson, Alan. "Black Lung: Anatomy of a Public Health Disaster." Cornell University Press: Ithaca, NY. 1998.

———. "Down Solid: The Origins and Development of the Black Lung Insurgency." *Journal of Public Health Policy* 4, no. 1(March 1983): 25-44.

"Disaster Due to Coal Dust." *The New York Times.* September 4, 1910.

Dole, Hollis M. to Everett Briggs. Letter dated January 11, 1971. From the legal files of James Matish.

Dorazio, Mike. U.S. Department of the Interior. Bureau of Mines. *Coal Mine Inspection Report. Consol No.9 Mine.* November 29-30 and December 1-3, 6-10, 13-16, and 20, 1965.

Dotson-Lewis, Betty Louise. "Coal Mining in Appalachia: the Federal Coal Mine Health and Safety Act of 1969, Interview with Ken Hechler." June 28, 2001. *http://www.appalachia-coal.com/ken%20hechler.htm*

Duncan, Matthew I. U.S. Department of the Interior. Bureau of Mines. *Coal Mine Inspection Report. Consol No.9 Mine.* March 2-4, 6, 9, 11-13 and 23-25, 1964.

———. U.S. Department of the Interior. Bureau of Mines. *Coal Mine Inspection Report. Consol No.9 Mine.* April 25, 1968.

Edwards, Peggy. "Eight Miners Await Rescue for 4 Hours." *The West Virginian.* November 20, 1968.

Estep, Roy C. and Matthew I. Duncan. U.S. Department of the Interior. Bureau of Mines. *Special Investigation Report, Pillar Bleeders, Jamison No.9 Mine, Consolidation Coal Company, Farmington, Marion County, West* Virginia. January 3 and 5-6, 1958.

Evans, Lewis E. to Everett Briggs. Letter dated December 21, 1970. From the legal files of James Matish.

"Farmington27fanchart.jpg." Provided by Technical Information Center and Library, National Mine Health and Safety Academy, Beaver, West Virginia.

Federal Coal Mine Safety Act of 1952. Public Law 82-522, U.S. Congress.

Federal Daily Recovery Logs for the No.9 Disaster. March 13, 1974.

"Federal Recovery Logs from No.9 Disaster." On file at the Technical Information Center and Library, National Mine Health and Safety Academy, Beaver, West Virginia. [Chronology]:January 7, 1971; January 8, 1971; January 11, 1971; January 12, 1971; June 28, 1971; June 29, 1971; June 30, 1971.

Fetty, Edwin Wayne. Interview with author. Fairmont, West Virginia. August 8, 2008.

Floyd, John. Interview with author. May 15, 2008.

Frances to Mr. Park. Memo. Dated 11/24/70. On file at the Technical Information Center and Library, National Mine Health and Safety Academy, Beaver, West Virginia.

Franklin, Ben A. "78 Trapped in Mine by Blasts and Fire." *The New York Times.* November 21, 1968.

———. "Mine Chief Ousts Disaster Expert." *The New York Times.* April 1, 1971.

———. "Miners' Relatives Urge Greater Efforts to Save 78. *The New York Times.* November 24, 1968.

———. "Re-check Was Overdue." *The New York Times.* January 1, 1971.

———. "Safety Officials Assail Accord by Coal Company and Widows." *The New York Times.* November 19, 1970.

———. "A Second Bureau of Mines Official Ousted; Coal Safety Record Cited." September 2, 1971.

———. "Union Seeks to Avoid Paying Reward in Killings." *The New York Times.* February 1, 1987.

———. "U.S. Begins Counting Mine Union Votes." *The New York Times.* December 13, 1972.

Frederici, William. "Their Men Gone, Their Hope Too." *Daily News.* November 23, 1968. C-5.

FTC v. Sperry & Hutchinson Co., 405 U.S. 233 (1972). *http://caselaw.lp.findlaw.com/scripts/getcase.pl?court=us&vol=405&invol=233*

Glover, George. *Abandoned Book Only. Fire Boss Record Book. November 19, 1968.* Oak Hill
  Regional Office of the W.Va. Office of Miners' Health Safety & Training. Box D33. Oak
  Hill, West Virginia.

———. *Fireboss Record Book. Fireboss Book Only. November 17, 1968.* Oak Hill Regional
  Office of the W.Va. Office of Miners' Health Safety & Training. Box D33. Oak Hill,
  West Virginia.

———. *Fireboss Record Book. Fireboss Book Only. November 18, 1968.* Oak Hill Regional
  Office of the W.Va. Office of Miners' Health Safety & Training. Box D33. Oak Hill,
  West Virginia.

———. *Fireboss Record Book. Fireboss Book Only. November 19, 1968.* Oak Hill Regional
  Office of the W.Va. Office of Miners' Health Safety & Training. Box D33. Oak Hill,
  West Virginia.

Halvorsen, W. J. to R. E. Garbesi. *Inter Office Communication. Consolidation Coal Com-*
  pany. March 3, 1976. Document produced during discovery. Anna Belle Currence v.
  Consolidation Coal Company, Civil Action No. 78-C-538. Circuit Court of Marion
  County, West Virginia (1978).

———. March 9, 1976. Document produced during discovery. Anna Belle Currence v.
  Consolidation Coal Company, Civil Action No. 78-C-538 Circuit Court of Marion
  County, West Virginia (1978).

"Handwritten Notes." Copied from the U.S. Bureau of Mine's Daily Recovery Logs for the
  No.9 Mine. 1969-1978. From the legal files of Brent Beveridge.

Hatch, Ralph to Steve Young. "Procedures to Be Followed in Announcing Discontinuation
  of Recovery Work at Farmington #9." Memo. December 8, 1976. Document produced
  during discovery. Anna Belle Currence v. Consolidation Coal Company, Civil Action
  No. 78-C-538. Circuit Court of Marion County, West Virginia (1978).

Hayes, Earl T. to the Secretary of the Interior, Bureau of Mines. Memorandum. Dec. 4, 1968.

Hechler, Ken to Elmer B. Staats. Letter dated June 26, 1972.

Hechler, Ken to Walter J. Hickel. Letter dated November 17, 1970. From the legal files of
  James Matish.

Henderson, R. M. "Status of Mine Atmosphere." August 8, 1969. Produced during discovery. Anna Belle Currence vs. Consolidation Coal Company, Civil Action No. 78-C-538
  Circuit Court of Marion County, West Virginia (1978).

Herron, James. Interviews with author. Mannington, West Virginia. October 3, 2008 and
  telephone interview on July 7, 2009.

Hodel, Martha Bryson. "Hechler's Hecklers gather for reunion." The Associated Press State & Local Wire. September 14, 1998.

Hoffman, Fannie. "21 Miners are Rescued." *The West Virginian.* November 20, 1968.

———. "Fire Continues to Rage." *The West Virginian.* November 22, 1968.

"Hope Dim for 78 Miners." *Knickerbocker News.* November 22, 1968.

Jackson, Niles. "Service Held for Miners." *The Fairmont Times.* September 13, 1969.

Jackson, Niles. "Service Held for Miners." *The Fairmont Times.* September 13, 1969.

———. "Stone Blocks Dropped Into Burning Mine." *The Knickerbocker News.* November 23, 1968.

Jackson, Niles Lee. "Baby Due, Wife Keeps Vigil at Mine Head." *The Associated Press.* November 23, 1968.

Jones, Diana Nelson. "25 Years Ago, Their World Collapsed in a Fiery Mine Explosion." *Pittsburgh Post-Gazette.* November 21, 1993.

Kaznoski, Pete Jr. Interview with author. Fairmont, West Virginia. November 15, 2009.

Kaznoski, Sara Lee. "April 3, 1971 entry in Personal Notebook." From legal files of Brent Beveridge, Fairmont, West Virginia.

———. "Entry in Personal Notebook." From legal files of Brent Beveridge, Fairmont, West Virginia. May 1, 1971.

———. Handwritten notes from April 4, 1975. From the legal files of Brent Beveridge. Fairmont, West Virginia.

———. "May 19, 1971 entry in Personal Notebook." From legal files of Brent Beveridge, Fairmont, West Virginia.

———. "Meeting Minutes and Notes from Widows Committee." Notebook from legal files of Brent Beveridge, Fairmont, West Virginia.

Kessler, David J. to Bonnie E. Stewart. Written response to Freedom of Information Requests (1-5) dated March 17, 2009 (Consolidation Coal Farmington No.9 Mine Disaster). March 31, 2009.

Kincell, K. K. to W. N. Poundstone. "Ventilation of the East End of #9 Mine. Changes Possible to Comply with Federal Health and Safety Act to Operate." Inter-Office Communication, "Personal and Confidential." December 14, 1972. Produced during discovery. Anna Belle Currence v. Consolidation Coal Company, Civil Action No. 78-C-538. Circuit Court of Marion County, West Virginia (1978).

Krovisky, Joe. "Mrs. Duncil Remembers '54." *The Associated Press.* November 24, 1968.

Kutchta, J. M., V. R. Rowe, and D. S. Burgess. U.S. Bureau of Mines. *Report of Investigation No. 8474, Spontaneous Combustion Susceptibility of U.S. Coals,* by 1980.

Lawless, Michael J. U.S. Department of the Interior, Bureau of Mines. "Report of Fatal Coal-Mine Haulage Accident. Consol No.9 Mine." November 16, 1971.

Layne, Larry L. Interviews with author. Jasper, Alabama. January 17-18, 2009.

——— to James D. Micheal. Memo. September 15, 1970.

"List of Slides, Nos. 1-56." Oak Hill Regional Office of the West Virginia Office of Miners' Health Safety & Training. Box D33. Oak Hill, West Virginia.

Loftus, Joseph A. "Mine Safety Law Held Inadequate." *The New York Times.* November 22, 1968. 50.

Mainella, David Patrick. Interview with author. Fairmont, West Virginia. June 17, 2008.

Man, C. K. and K. A. Teacoach. National Institute for Occupational Safety and Health. *How Does Limestone Rock Dust Prevent Coal Dust Explosions in Coal Mines?* September 2009. *www.cdc.gov/niosh/mining/pubs/pdfs/hdlrdp.pdf*

Marshalek, Joseph. Notes. No.9 Explosion. Handwritten notes on file at the Technical Information Center and Library, National Mine Health and Safety Academy, Beaver, West Virginia.

———. U.S. Department of the Interior. Bureau of Mines. *Coal Mine Inspection Report. Consol No.9 Mine.* July 19, 21-23 and August 3-6, 9-13 and 16-20, 1965.

Matish, James. Interview with author. Clarksburg, West Virginia. July 5, 2007.

Mauck, Eugene (Consol). "Minutes, January 5, 1977 Meeting." Produced during discovery. Anna Belle Currence v. Consolidation Coal Company, Civil Action No. 78-C-538. Circuit Court of Marion County, West Virginia (1978).

———. "Minutes of the Meeting of Four Agencies, March 26, 1976." Document produced during discovery. Anna Belle Currence v. Consolidation Coal Company, Civil Action No. 78-C-538. Circuit Court of Marion County, West Virginia (1978).

Mauck, H. E. to Jack E. Tisdale (Federal MESA). Letter. November 26, 1974.

McAteer, Davitt. "Monongah." West Virginia University Press: Morgantown, WV. 2007.

McAteer, Davitt to Wayne Veneman (MSHA). Freedom of Information Request for Federal Report on No.9 Disaster. July 3, 1986.

McNece, Joseph. "Receipt for Certified Mail." December 4, 1968. Oak Hill Regional Office of the W.Va. Office of Miners' Health Safety & Training. Box D33. Oak Hill, West Virginia.

Megna, Joseph. Interview with author. Worthington, West Virginia. May 21, 2008.

"Memorandum: No.9 Recovery Work." Dated July 23, 1970. Carried the initials of Consolidation Coal's Kenny K. Kincell. Produced during discovery. Anna Belle Currence v. Consolidation Coal Company, Civil Action No. 78-C-538. Circuit Court of Marion County, West Virginia (1978).

"Memorial Services Held for Miners." *The Associated Press*. November 20, 1969.

Micheal, J. D. "Memo to Rita to Type the No.9 Explosion Report and Handwritten Copy of the Report." November 29, 1979. On file at the National Mine Health and Safety Academy's Technical Information Center and Library. Beaver, West Virginia.

———. U.S. Department of the Interior. Mining Enforcement and Safety Administration. Memorandum. "Recovery Operations—Consol No.9 Mine." November 3, 1977.

Micheal, J. D. to W. R. Park. Memo. U.S. Department of the Interior, Bureau of Mines. September 30, 1970.

"Miller Debates Coal Executive." *The New York Times*. December 18, 1972.

"Miller UMW Victory Certified." *The Wall Street Journal*. December 21, 1972.

"Mine No.9 Explosion Recovery Operations for Period November 20, 1968 thru February 28, 1978, Operating Losses and Capital Budget Expenditures." Produced during discovery. Anna Belle Currence v. Consolidation Coal Company, Civil Action No. 78-C-538. Circuit Court of Marion County, West Virginia (1978).

"Mine Rescuers Find Nothing: Drill Through." *The Charleston Gazette*. November 25, 1968.

"Mining Agency Said to Lag on Safety." *The New York Times*. August 6, 1972.

"Mine-Safety Penalty System is Upset." *The New York Times*. March 11, 1973.

"Ministerial Head Proclaims Sunday as Day of Prayer." *The West Virginian*. November 22, 1968.

"Minutes from Meeting Attended by Federal, State, UMW, Consol and Mountaineer Coal Officials." June 16, 1969. Produced during discovery. Anna Belle Currence v. Consolidation Coal Company, Civil Action No. 78-C-538. Circuit Court of Marion County, West Virginia (1978).

"Minutes of Four Agency Meeting for No.9 Recovery." September 1, 1970.

Mitchell, Daniel B., NOAA Director, to Ronald L. Keaton, U.S. Department of Labor, Mine Safety & Health Administration. Letters and attachments. U.S. Department of Commerce. National Oceanic & Atmospheric Administration. *Surface Weather Observations and Barograms for Morgantown, West Virginia, November 13-20, 1968*. December 3, 1979.

Moore, Arch A. Jr. to Sara L. Kaznoski. Letter dated July 21, 1970. From legal files of Brent Beveridge, Beveridge Law Offices. Fairmont, West Virginia.

Morris, Robert. Interview with author. Weston, West Virginia. August 2008. *www.msha. gov/S&HINFO/TECHRPT/P&T/COALDUST.pdf*

National Institute for Occupational Safety and Health. *Float Coal Dust Explosion Hazards.* No. 515. April 2006.

"New Chest Disease Found in Coal Miners." *Science News* 89 (March 26, 1966): 197.

"New Disturbance Dims Hope at Mine." *Times-Union* (Albany, NY). November 22, 1968.

Nixon, Richard. The American Presidency Project. *Special Message to the Congress on Coal Mine Safety.* March 3, 1969. *http://www.presidency.ucsb.edu/ws/index. php?pid=2442&st=coal+min*

———. The American Presidency Project. *Statement on Signing the Federal Coal Mine Health and Safety Act of 1969.* December 30, 1969. *http://www.presidency.ucsb.edu/ws/ index.php?pid=2389&st=coal+mine&st1*

"No.9 Dependents Get State Checks." *The Charleston Gazette.* December 16, 1968.

"No.9 Mine Yields First of 78 Explosion Victims: Bad Air, Rock Fall Delay Search for Second Miner." *The Fairmont Times.* October 24, 1969.

"No.9 Recovery. Minutes of the Four Agency Meeting." Feb. 12, 1970. Produced during discovery. Anna Belle Currence v. Consolidation Coal Company, Civil Action No. 78-C-538. Circuit Court of Marion County, West Virginia (1978).

"No.9 Widows Get $1,319 Each from Contributed Funds." *The Fairmont Times.* October 14, 1969.

"Notes on Farmington Explosion." *The West Virginian.* November 15, 1954. A-1.

"Obituary: Kenneth J. Yablonski." *The Pittsburgh Post-Gazette.* September 11, 2002.

"Offer of Consolidation Coal Company to the Bereaved Families of the Victims of the No.9 Farmington Mine Disaster of November 20, 1968. DRAFT June 1973." Document produced during discovery. Anna Belle Currence v. Consolidation Coal Company, Civil Action No. 78-C-538. Circuit Court of Marion County, West Virginia (1978).

"One Man Dies at Pit Portal in Marion Co." *The Charleston Gazette.* November 14, 1954. A-1.

"Opening of 6North, Mine 9, Mountaineer Coal Company." December 1, 1970. Initialed HEM (H. Eugene Mauck) with note by DHD (David H. Davis). Produced during discovery. Anna Belle Currence v. Consolidation Coal Company, Civil Action No. 78-C-538. Circuit Court of Marion County, West Virginia (1978).

Parisi, C. W. to R. E. Samples. Inter-Office Communication. "Sealing or Ventilating Old Works at #9 Mine." March 25, 1977. Produced during discovery. Anna Belle Currence

v. Consolidation Coal Company, Civil Action No. 78-C-538. Circuit Court of Marion County, West Virginia (1978).

Phillips, John Paul and Carl J. Shaffer. U.S. Department of the Interior. Bureau of Mines. *Report of Surface Gas Explosion, Consol No.9 Mine.* July 29, 1969.

Plachta, Stanley. Interview with author. Farmington, West Virginia. July 11, 2008.

"Police Called to Stop Chants of Protesters." *The Fairmont Times.* Oct. 14, 1969.

"Public Relations Plan—Closing of No.9 Mine. Confidential." December 6, 1976. Document produced during discovery. Anna Belle Currence v. Consolidation Coal Company, Civil Action No. 78-C-538. Circuit Court of Marion County, West Virginia (1978).

Rakes, Paul H. "Acceptable Casualties: Power, Culture, and History in the West Virginia Coalfields, 1990-1945." Dissertation. West Virginia University. 2002.

Rasmussen, Jeanne M. "The Hot Edge of Hell." Unpublished manuscript. Box 1, Folder 19. Jeanne M. Rasmussen Collection. Archives of Appalachia, East Tennessee State University. Johnson City, Tennessee.

Reynolds, Frank and David Snell. "Black Lung/Miners' Strike." *ABC Evening News.* February 20, 1969.

Robertson, Bob. "Legacy to the UMW." *The Pittsburgh Post-Gazette.* December 30, 1994.

Rutledge, J. J. "The Use and Misuse of Explosives in Coal Mining." U.S. Department of the Interior. Bureau of Mines. 1916.

Samples, R. E. (Consol) to Mr. Ed Gilbert (UMW). Letter dated May 3, 1978.

Sarah L. Kaznoski, Administratrix of the Estate of Pete Kaznoski Sr., Deceased, et al. v. Consolidation Coal Company et al. Civil A. Case No. 70-1322. U.S. District Court for the Western District of Pennsylvania.

Schell, Ronald J. (MSHA) to J. Davitt McAteer. Response to Freedom of Information Request for Federal Report on No.9 Disaster. July 23, 1986.

Schrum, Warren. "Ignition of Methane Gas Said Cause of County Mine Tragedy." *Times-West Virginian.* May 2, 1965.

Sections Only. Section Foremen Fireboss Reports. November 19, 1968. Oak Hill Regional Office of the W.Va. Office of Miners' Health Safety & Training. Box D33. Oak Hill, West Virginia.

Sehewchuk, Pete. Interview with author. Fairmont, West Virginia. July 21, 2008.

"Settlement in Coal Mine Deaths." *The Washington Post.* February 19, 1983.

"SGY (Stephen G. Young) Notes." Handwritten notes from 1978. Produced during discovery. Anna Belle Currence v. Consolidation Coal Company, Civil Action No. 78-C-538. Circuit Court of Marion County, West Virginia (1978).

Smith, Barbara. "Miner's Widow: Sara Kaznoski, Fighter and Survivor." *Goldenseal*. Summer 1988.

South-East Coal Company v. Consolidation Coal Company v. United Mine Workers of America. 424 F.2d 767. U.S. Appeals Court. 1970.

Stephan, Clete R. U.S. Department of Labor. Mine Safety and Health Administration. Stephan, *Coal Dust Explosion Hazards*. March 2009.

Stern, Gerald M. "The Buffalo Creek Disaster." Vintage Books. 1976.

———. "The Scotia Widows." Random House. New York, N.Y. 2008.

Stevenson, J. W. and D. S. Kingery. U.S. Department of the Interior. Bureau of Mines. "Effects of Bleeder Entries During Atmospheric Pressure Changes." *Report of Investigations No. 6786*, by Washington D.C. 1966.

Stuart, Roger. "Volunteers Begin Risky Job of Unsealing Farmington Mine." *The Pittsburgh Press*. September 12, 1969.

———. "Where 78 Miners Died: Grief, Friction Prevail." *The Pittsburgh Press*. September 14, 1969.

"Support State Workman's Compensation Bill." *The Shinnston (W.Va.) News*. March 11, 1976.

"Survivors Cling to Hope Doomed Miners Still Live." *The Charleston Gazette*. November 15, 1954. A-1.

Sztajnkrycer, Matthew D., M.D. "Medical Aspects of Blast Injuries." Mayo Clinic. 2008. *www.pitt.edu/~super7/17011-18001/17971.ppt*

Tattersall, William J., submitted by Assistant Secretary for Mine Safety and Health. U.S. Department of Labor. Mine Safety and Health Administration. Division of Safety. *Informational Report of Investigation, Underground Coal Mine Explosion and Fire, Consol No.9 Mine, Mountaineer Coal Company, Division of Consolidation Coal Company, Farmington, West Virginia, November 20, 1968*. March 1990.

Toothman, John. Telephone interview with author. August 30, 2007.

"Two Teams Begin W.Va. Mine Hunt." *The Pittsburgh Press*. September 15, 1969.

"UMW Officers Take Salary Cuts Fulfilling Pledge from Campaign." *The Wall Street Journal*. January 5, 1973.

"Union Fights Plan to Seal No.9 Mine." *The Clarksburg Exponent*. April 22, 1978.

U.S. Comptroller General. "Follow-up on Implementation of the Federal Coal Mine Health and Safety Act of 1969; Bureau of Mines." July 5, 1973.

U.S. Congress. Senate. Committee on Labor and Public Welfare. Subcommittee on Labor.

Coal Mine Safety Act: Hearing on S. 355, S. 467, S.1094, S. 1178, S. 1300 and S. 1907 before the Subcommittee on Labor. 91ˢᵗ Cong., 1ˢᵗ sess., February 27, March 7, 12, 13, 14, 18, 20, 26 and May 2, 1969. Part 1, Part 2.

U.S. Congress. Senate. Committee on Labor and Public Welfare. Subcommittee on Labor. *Coal Mine Safety Act: Hearing on S. 355, S. 467, S.1094, S. 1178, S. 1300 and S. 1907 before the Subcommittee on Labor.* 91ˢᵗ Cong., 1ˢᵗ sess. March 7, 1969. "Major Differences Among Proposed Senate Bills, 1952 Act, and Interior's Proposed Bill." 527-528.

U.S. Congress. Senate Subcommittee Hearing 1969. [Testimonies]:

Boyle, W. A.

Byrd, Sen. Robert C. (W.Va.).

Garvey, James R.

Hechler, Rep. Ken (W.Va.).

Kaznoski, Sara Lee.

McDowell, Cloyd D.

O'Leary, John. Director, U.S. Bureau of Mines.

Ratliff, Otis.

Rogers, Mary Kay.

Stewart, William H., M.D. U.S. Surgeon General.

Wolford, Elizah.

Yocum, Elmer.

U.S. Congress. The 1952 Coal Mine Federal Coal Mine Safety Act. Public Law 82-552.

U.S. Department of Commerce. Social and Economic Statistics Administration. Bureau of the Census. Census of Population 1970. Marion County, West Virginia.

U.S. Department of the Interior. Bureau of Mines. *Coal Mine Inspection Report, No.9 Mine, Jamison Coal and Coke Company. Farmington, Marion County, West Virginia.* May 15-18 and 21-23, 1951.

———. Bureau of Mines. *Coal Mine Inspection Report, No.9 Mine, Jamison Coal and Coke Company. Farmington, Marion County, West Virginia.* January 17-18 and 21-25, 1952.

———. Bureau of Mines. *Coal Mine Inspectors' Manual.* September 1967.

———. Bureau of Mines. District C. *Final Report on Major Explosion and Fire Disaster, No.9 Mine, Jamison Coal and Coke Company, Farmington, West Virginia,* November 13, 1954.

———. Bureau of Mines. "Explosion Logs Kept by Consol Employees." November 20–December 4, 1968. On file at the MSHA Technical Information Center and Library. Beaver, West Virginia.

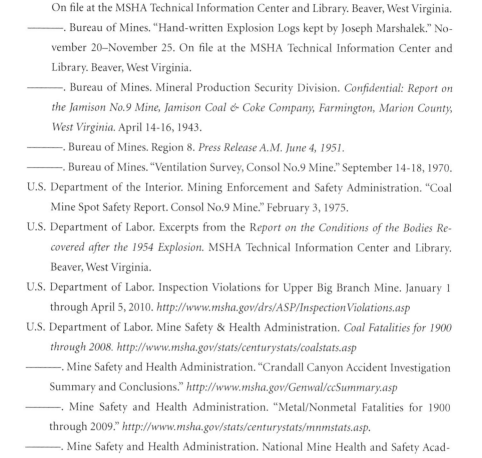

———. Bureau of Mines. "Hand-written Explosion Logs." November 20–December 4, 1968. On file at the MSHA Technical Information Center and Library. Beaver, West Virginia.

———. Bureau of Mines. "Hand-written Explosion Logs kept by Joseph Marshalek." November 20–November 25. On file at the MSHA Technical Information Center and Library. Beaver, West Virginia.

———. Bureau of Mines. Mineral Production Security Division. *Confidential: Report on the Jamison No.9 Mine, Jamison Coal & Coke Company, Farmington, Marion County, West Virginia.* April 14-16, 1943.

———. Bureau of Mines. Region 8. *Press Release A.M. June 4, 1951.*

———. Bureau of Mines. "Ventilation Survey, Consol No.9 Mine." September 14-18, 1970.

U.S. Department of the Interior. Mining Enforcement and Safety Administration. "Coal Mine Spot Safety Report. Consol No.9 Mine." February 3, 1975.

U.S. Department of Labor. Excerpts from the *Report on the Conditions of the Bodies Recovered after the 1954 Explosion.* MSHA Technical Information Center and Library. Beaver, West Virginia.

U.S. Department of Labor. Inspection Violations for Upper Big Branch Mine. January 1 through April 5, 2010. *http://www.msha.gov/drs/ASP/InspectionViolations.asp*

U.S. Department of Labor. Mine Safety & Health Administration. *Coal Fatalities for 1900 through 2008. http://www.msha.gov/stats/centurystats/coalstats.asp*

———. Mine Safety and Health Administration. "Crandall Canyon Accident Investigation Summary and Conclusions." *http://www.msha.gov/Genwal/ccSummary.asp*

———. Mine Safety and Health Administration. "Metal/Nonmetal Fatalities for 1900 through 2009." *http://www.msha.gov/stats/centurystats/mnmstats.asp.*

———. Mine Safety and Health Administration. National Mine Health and Safety Academy. *Historical Summary of Mine Disasters in the United States. Vol. 1, Coal Mines, 1810-1958.* 1998.

———. Mine Safety and Health Administration. National Mine Health and Safety Academy. *Historical Summary of Mine Disasters in the United States. Vol. 1, Coal Mines, 1959-1998.* 1998. Reprinted 2001.

———. Mine Safety and Health Administration. National Mine Health and Safety Academy. *Historical Summary of Mine Disasters in the United States. Vol. 2, Coal Mines, 1959-1998.* Itmann No. 3 Mine. Reprinted 2001. 77-79.

———. Mine Safety and Health Administration. Press Release. "Virginia Mine Operator Gets Six Months for Violating Law." September 14, 1995.

U.S. Government Accounting Office. "Report to the Conservation and Natural Resources Committee on Government Operations. House of Representatives. Improvements Needed in the Assessment and Collection of Penalties—Federal Coal Mine Health and Safety Act of 1969." July 5, 1972.

————. "Report to the Subcommittee on Labor and Public Welfare. United States Senate: Problems in Implementation of the Federal Coal Miner Health and Safety Act of 1969." May 31, 1971.

"Vealey, Gunman in Yablonski Shooting, Dies at 55." *The Associated Press*. February 4, 1999.

Veasey, John. "They Came . . . and They Waited in Silence." *The West Virginian*. November 20, 1968.

Wallace, Michael. Ohio State University. "Dying for Coal: The Struggle for Health and Safety Conditions in American Coal Mining, 1930-82." *Social Forces* 66 (December 1987): 2.

Ward, Ken Jr. "Aracoma Assessed Record Fine." *The Charleston Gazette*. December 24, 2009.

————. "Arnold Miller Helped Reform the UMW." *The Charleston Gazette*. January 24, 1999.

————. "Two more Sago lawsuits settled." *The Charleston Gazette*. January 27, 2009.

Watson, Paul. *Fireboss Record Book. Fireboss Book Only. November 18, 1968*. Oak Hill Regional Office of the W.Va. Office of Miners' Health Safety & Training. Box D33. Oak Hill, West Virginia.

Weedfall, Robert O. U.S. Department of Commerce. National Oceanic & Atmospheric Administration. *Climate, Weather and Coal Mine Explosions with a Meteorological Review of the Farmington Disasters. Report 15*. April 16-17, 1970.

Weeks, James L. and Maier Fox. "Fatality Rates and Regulatory Policies in Bituminous Coal Mining, United States, 1959-1981." *American Journal of Public Health* 73, no. 11 (November 1983).

West Virginia Code. Chapter 22, Mines and Minerals. 22-1-2. March 7, 1967.

————. Chapter 22, Mines and Minerals. Article 2. Section 2391 (4) Fans.

————. Chapter 22, Mines and Minerals. Article 2. Section 2395 (7): Gassy Mines; Nongassy Mines; Examination.

W.Va. *Inspection Report. Jamison Coal & Coke Company. Mine No.9.* [Chronology] 1930–1940: April, 1935; January, 1936; September, 1936.; ctober, 1937; 1938-1950.

W.Va. *Inspection Report. No.9 Mine.* [Chronology with inspector's name] December 21-31, 1953. (M. B. Horton)

March 15-18, 22, 24-26, 1954. (M. B. Horton)

February 7-9, 12, 13, 15 and 19-23, 1968. (Joseph Marshall Jr. and Leslie Ryan)

June 11-14, 17, 18 and July 23, 25, 29, 30 and August 5 and 8, 1968. (Joseph Marshall Jr. and Leslie Ryan)

October 8-11, 21-25 and 28-31, 1968. (Joseph Marshall Jr. and Leslie Ryan)

W.Va. Inspection Reports 2010. Upper Big Branch Mine. http://www.wvminesafety.org/performanceubbmc.htm

W.Va. *Official Hearing. Jamison No.9 Mine Explosion.* Conducted by Julius C. Olzer. February 7-8, 1956. Part 1. 1-267.

———. *Official Hearing. Jamison No.9 Mine Explosion.* Conducted by Julius C. Olzer. February 7-9, 1956. Part 2. 1-162.

W.Va. *Official Hearing, Coal Mine Explosion, Consol No.9 Mine, Mountaineer Coal Company, Division of Consolidation Coal Company, Farmington, Marion County, West Virginia, November 20, 1968. December 5-7, 1968.*

Official Hearings:

Bland, Robert. 89-92.

Bowers, Jess G. 266-296.

Casseday, Fay. 213-229.

Conway, Henry, testimony. 23-27.

Cook, Arthur Eugene. 358-360.

Cook, Robert. 312-317.

Davis, Alva G. 160-166.

Duda, Joseph. 361-364.

Foster, Russell, testimony. 1-6.

Garcia, Joseph S., testimony. 12-17.

Hall, Layman. 334-339.

Harris, Dana E., Sr. 304-312.

Herron, James (Jimmie), testimony. 92-104.

Kovar, Alex M., testimony and written statement. 45-51 and 381-383.

Kuhn, Issac [*sic*] R., testimony. 13-22.

Lake, Lewis. 134-146.

Lieving, Eugene. 242-249.

Martin, Gary. 147-155.

Merrifield, Arthur. 365-368.

Morris, Ancle B. 369-376.

Official Hearings *continued:*

    Parker, Lewis, testimony. 86-88.

    Plachta, Stanley. 258-265.

    Riggs, Lawrence H. 43.

    Selders, Cecil. 197.

    Simons, James A., testimony. 297-304.

    Simons, Mrs. James A., testimony. 179-182.

    Slovekosky, Walter. 61-77.

    Starkey, Ralph L., testimony. 167-173.

    Stout, Samuel, testimony. 78-85.

    Thomas, Dan. 340-343.

    Watson, Paul. 323-333.

    Wilson, Edgell, testimony. 7-11.

    Wilson, George. 115-133.

W.Va. Office of Miners' Health Safety and Training. "A Brief History of Coal and Safety Enforcement in West Virginia." *http://www.wvminesafety.org/History.htm.*

Whyte, Thomas J. "Offer of Consolidation Coal Company to the Bereaved Families of the Victims of the No.9 Farmington Mine Disaster of November 20, 1968." January 8, 1974.

Williams, William G. *The Coal King's Slaves: A Coal Miner's Story.* Burd Street Press: Shippensburg, PA. November 2002.

"74 Trapped, 8 Rescued In West Va. Mine Blast." *Record American* (Boston). November 21, 1968.

"78 Miners Entombed in Farmington No 9 After Blasts." *The Fairmont Times.* November 21, 1968.

Index

....

Bonnie E. Stewart is an investigative journalist for Oregon Public Broadcasting's Local Journalism Center in Portland, where she covers environmental issues in the Pacific Northwest. She researched and wrote *No.9* during her six years as a faculty member of the P.I. Reed School of Journalism at West Virginia University, where she earned tenure and the rank of associate professor. A former newspaper reporter in Indiana and California, Stewart has won numerous journalism awards, including Long Island University's George Polk Award and the national Society of Professional Journalists' Sigma Delta Chi Award for Public Service. Her work has been published by National Public Radio, *The Indianapolis Star, The Indianapolis News, The Press-Enterprise, The Pittsburgh Post-Gazette, Poynter Online,* and *Quill.* She holds a Master's Degree in English from California State University, Sacramento. Photo by Nancy Robertson.